An Introduction to Quality Assurance for the Retailers

Pradip V. Mehta, P.E.

NEW AGE INTERNATIONAL PUBLISHERS

Information contained in this book has been obtained from sources believed to be reliable and based on author's work experience and education. However, the author does not guarantee the accuracy or completeness of any information published here in, and the author shall not be responsible for any errors, omissions, or damages arising out of the use of this information. This book is published with the understanding that its author is supplying information, but is not attempting to render technical/engineering or other professional services. If such services are required, the assistance of an appropriate professional should be sought.

First Indian Sub-Continent Edition : 2008
by New Age International (P) Ltd., Publishers

This special low-priced edition is for sale in India, Bangladesh, Bhutan, Mayanmar (Burma), Sri Lanka, Pakistan and Nepal only.

Originally Published in the *United States of America.*

Printed in India at Sanjeev Offset Printers, Delhi.
1 2 3 4 5 6 7 8 9 10
C-07-12-2148

ISBN (13): 978-81-224-2266-5
ISBN (10): 81-224-2266-7
Original Edition Price: $ 26.95
Indian Edition Price: Rs. 295.00

PUBLISHING FOR ONE WORLD
NEW AGE INTERNATIONAL (P) LIMITED, PUBLISHERS
4835/24, Ansari Road, Daryaganj, New Delhi - 110002
Visit us at www.newagepublishers.com

An Introduction to Quality Assurance for the Retailers

To All those hundreds of thousands of workers in the consumer products manufacturing factories, small and large, throughout the world without whose toil we would not be able to enjoy the standard of living we take for granted.

—Pradip V. Mehta

Contents

Acknowledgement

I am very thankful to the following individuals who took time to review my manuscript either in its entirety or some parts and offered valuable suggestions for making it better. While this book is certainly better because of the review process it went through, I take full responsibility as the author for any shortcomings this book may have.

Thomas F. Bennett, Director, Quality Assurance, J. C. Penney Co.
Dick Koch, Manager, Merchandise Test Center (Retd.), J. C. Penney Co.
Jerry Oleskiw, Director of Quality Assurance, Research & Education (Retd.), J. C. Penney Co.
Robert W. Peach, Manager, Quality Assurance (Retd.), Sears, Roebuck & Co., and Management Consultant
Joseph Williams, Navy Exchange, U.S.A.
Ken Wilson, Director, Quality Assurance (Retd.), Army & Air Force Exchange Service, U.S.A.
George Zelazny, Manager, Product Safety Group, Sears, Roebuck & Co.
Dr. Steven Spivak, Professor Emeritus, Fire Protection Engineering, University of Maryland and an international expert on standards and standardization
Ram Ramaswamy, Global Manager, Source Verification and Inspection, Underwriters Laboratories, Inc.
Jack Howlett, Director, Product Quality (Soft lines), Sears, Roebuck & Co.

I am thankful to the following individuals and their respective organizations for permission to reproduce certain materials.

Judy Colbert, G.G., Manager of Visual Resources, Gemological Institute of America (GIA)
John Drengenberg, Manager Consumer Affairs and Gary Hansen, Manager, Label Operations, Underwriters Laboratories, Inc.
Jennifer Szwalek, Vice President of Communications, Juvenile Products Manufacturers Association (JPMA)
Debbie Gustafson, Associate Director, The Art & Creative Materials Institute, Inc.
Eli Szamosi, Manager, New Business Development, CSA International

Donald L. Mays, Vice President, Retail and Consumer Product Services, Intertek Testing Services and formerly Technical Director, Good Housekeeping Institute

My special thanks to my employer, **Army & Air Force Exchange Service** (AAFES) for their permission to let me publish this book.

Finally, last but not the least, I am very grateful to my wife **Jayshree** for her support and patience while I spent countless hours working on this book.

Preface

A lot has been written about quality, however, searching Amazon and Barnes & Noble web sites www.amazon.com and www.barnesandnoble.com, respectively for any book(s) on quality of consumer products or quality control, quality assurance, or quality management for retail, out of 2,358 and 1,974 titles, respectively on quality, not a single title came up on the subject. Browsing through bookstores on the National Retail Federation's website www.nrf.com and the Retail Industry Leaders Association's web site www.retail-leaders.org produced similar results, i.e. not a single book on quality! Also, in my 30 years of working in quality assurance of consumer products, I have not seen a single book that contains all relevant information for addressing quality of consumer products at the retail level by mass merchandisers. Therefore, this book is an attempt to fill this void. The purpose of this book is to present a body of knowledge (BOK) in the area of quality management for the students pursuing a career in retail industry as well as provide a quick reference manual to those practicing quality management in the retail industry, or thinking about starting a quality management program for a retailer. The BOK (body of knowledge) and principles presented here are applicable to any segment of mass merchandising industry, i.e., broad line mass retailers, super center and hypermarket chains, wholesale clubs, mid-tier chains, off-price apparel department stores chains, variety/close-out chains, and specialty stores.

Retailers sell a variety of consumer products and rely on their suppliers to provide them quality products. However, retailers must have some way of verifying that they are receiving products at quality levels they planned or specified. Retailers also should be able to specify quality levels, if necessary. This book will outline various approaches available to retailers to assure product quality.

Product safety is an integral part of product quality. Therefore, wherever applicable, product safety is also addressed in this book. Other topics covered by this book are product testing, end item inspection, product recalls, product liability, standards and specifications, supplier quality system evaluation, supplier rating, supplier partnership, customer returns and customer satisfaction. The chapter on customer returns and customer satisfaction is deliberately kept short as there is considerable information available on these subjects so there is no sense in reinventing the wheel.

Since most retailers ask their QA organizations to monitor working conditions in factories of their suppliers, a chapter on social audits and corporate social responsibility is also added.

In addition to such information, I have provided job descriptions for various positions in quality assurance, training plans for those positions, standard operating procedures, standard inspection procedures, defect characteristics guides for various products, quality terms and conditions, and guidelines to quality in order to help one manage quality function.

Quality management is using standards, specifications, quality assurance procedures and practices as well as customer feedback to manage quality of products and services to gain competitive advantage just as effectively managing marketing, logistics, or manufacturing functions to gain competitive advantage.

While various standards and regulations mentioned in this book are for the most part American and some European as well as international, this book is relevant worldwide. Reference to an American, European, or international standard or regulation should trigger a thought or raise a flag in a retailer's mind in India or in Brazil or anywhere else to see if a similar standard or regulation exists in the respective country, and if not, whether he or she should adopt an American or European or international standard or regulation.

This book does not claim to have all the answers because that is not why it is written. Also, this book does not claim to present best practices because "the best practice" is a relative term. What may be the best practice for one retailer may not be the best for another retailer. The goal of this book is to present, in as simple manner as possible, various approaches and sound principles to address the quality of consumer products and current body of knowledge required to manage quality function in mass retailing and get the managers and executives to think about issues such as product quality, product safety, product liability, etc. in as much a broad sense as possible. What is presented here is based on this author's 30 years of working in a variety of quality management positions with a multi-billion dollar, multi-national retail and service organization and information gathered through personal contacts with quality management executives of other multi-billion dollar retailers and suppliers as well as participating in various quality and consumer committees.

From consumers' point of view, quality in retailing has two aspects, i.e., quality of products or merchandise and quality of customer service. This book primarily addresses quality of products or merchandise, however, quality of customer service is addressed briefly in the Appendix VI.

Principles outlined in this book are applicable worldwide because the fundamentals of quality are universal and human nature is basically the same worldwide, i.e., it is innate human desire to want the highest quality of products and services one can get. To a large extent, our quality of life depends on the quality of products we use in our everyday lives. Therefore, quality assurance of consumer products is a discipline that improves quality of life of people worldwide through product quality and safety. Therefore, while on the surface this book is about the quality of products, competitiveness and bottom line, it is really about making peoples' lives better by providing them safe and quality products.

I welcome any comment(s), question(s), or criticism of this book from anyone via e-mail or regular mail.

Pradip V. Mehta, P.E.
709 Lyndsie Drive
Coppeu, Tx 75019
U.S.A.
Mehtaconsulting@gmail.com

1

Introduction

In order to manage quality effectively, it must be understood clearly. Quality is unusually slippery and difficult to come to grips with and therefore, someone has said, "quality is something I know when I see it." To some, quality defined is like 'love' explained. Once the concept of quality is understood fundamentally, it stops being slippery and becomes something which you can hold by the tail and manage it to your advantage.

1-1 What is Quality?

The simplest way to answer the question "what is quality?" is to look it up in a dictionary. According to Webster's II New Revised University Dictionary, quality is essential character: nature, an ingredient or distinguishing attribute: property, a character trait, superiority of kind, degree of grade or excellence.

From a consumers' viewpoint, quality in retailing has two aspects. They are quality of products and quality of customer service. This book is primarily about product quality as considerable literature exists on service quality. However, service quality as it relates to retailers is addressed briefly in the Appendix VI.

1-1-1 Product Quality

Quality means different things to different people. If we asked several people, "What is quality?" We may get answers like:

The best money can buy
Meeting a specification or conformance to specifications
Craftsmanship

The degree of excellence that an item possesses
No more than 1 % defective lot (the absence of defects and undesirable characteristics in a product)
Anything Japanese or German

These responses, of course, depend on peoples' perception of the value of a product or service under consideration and their expectation of performance, durability, reliability, etc. of that product or service.

According to Lamprect (2000) quality, whatever its definition, is relative to experience, culture, habits and so on. He goes to give an example that Americans are the only people in the world who think their coffee tastes good. The rest of the world considers "American coffee" as slightly inferior in taste to cod lever oil. Why? Relativity.

Quality can also mean the absence of variation in its broadest sense. For example, consider the case of Ford vs. Mazda explained by Taguchi and Clausing (1990).

> Ford owns about 25% of Mazda and asked the Japanese company to build transmissions for a car it was selling in the U.S. Both Ford and Mazda were supposed to build to identical specifications. Ford adopted zero defects as its standard. Yet, after the cars had been on the road for a while, it became clear that Ford's transmissions were generating far higher warranty costs and customer complaints about the noise. To its credit, Ford disassembled and carefully measured samples of transmissions made by both companies. At first, Ford engineers thought their gauges were malfunctioning. Ford parts were all in spec., but Mazda gear boxes betrayed no variability at all from target. Could that be why Mazda incurred lower production, scrap, rework, and warranty costs? That was precisely the reason.

An automobile battery is another example cited by the Quality Alert Institute (1990-91).

> An automobile battery is charged with an alternator. The alternator has a regulator that controls the charge to the battery. The alternator voltage regulator assembly must let out a charge of 13.2 volts to keep the battery's charge at 12 volts. If the alternator produces a charge of less than 13.2 volts, the electrolyte (acid) in the battery will gradually turn into water, resulting in failure of the battery. The lower the alternator output, the more quickly this will happen. If the alternator output is more than 13.2 volts, excessive heat will build up in battery. As the alternator output increases, this effect will occur more quickly.

Quality can also mean meeting or exceeding customer expectations, both in product quality and quality of customer service—all the time. The key here is to know accurately customer expectations on a continuing basis because unless you know customer expectations how can you meet or exceed them? The expectations of quality and the ability to distinguish various quality characteristics also vary from one group of customers to another. Generally, the more educated and sophisticated the customer, the more specific are the expectations of quality and more precise the ability of the customers to explore those expectations. What this means is that educated and sophisticated customers have a certain level of expectations of merchandise from a store and if you do not meet or exceed them they will try another store.

John Rabbitt of The Foxboro Company (1994) defines quality as

> the ability to exceed a customer's expectations while maintaining a cost competitive market position.

Garvin (1988) proposed that a definition of quality can be product based, user based, manufacturing based or value based.

A product based definition of quality views quality as a precise and measurable variable. Differences in quality reflect differences in the quantity of some ingredient or attribute possessed by a product. For example, we tend to associate finer rugs with a higher number of knots per square inch—therefore higher, better quality.

A user based definition of quality simply means that quality is whatever the customer says or wants—which goes back to meeting or exceeding customers' requirements and expectations.

A manufacturing based definition of quality means meeting specifications and conformance to requirements. Any deviation from meeting requirements means poor quality.

A value based definition of quality takes into consideration cost or price of a product or service. The question from customers' view point is, what is the value of this product or service to us? Or how valuable is a given product or service?

Garvin goes on to say that companies may want to take a multiple approach to defining quality, that is, start out with a product based approach which identifies quality characteristics or characteristics/properties through market research that connote quality. Then use a user based approach to translate those characteristics into manufacturing base approach as products are being manufactured and finally use a value based approach to offer the customer better value than your competitors. When defining quality this way, everyone in the company has a role in "quality."

Garvin also proposed that there are eight dimensions of quality. They are performance, features, reliability, conformance, durability, serviceability, aesthetics, and perceived quality. Performance is based on primary operating characteristics of a product. Features of a product are those secondary characteristics that supplement a product's basic functioning. Reliability refers to the probability of a product's malfunctioning or failing within a specified period of time. Conformance refers to the degree or extent to which a product's design and operating characteristics meet pre-established standards. Durability means length of time a product will last or product life. Serviceability refers to the speed, courtesy, competence, and ease of repair of a product. Aesthetics refers to how a product looks, feels, sounds, tastes, or smells. Perceived quality refers to what customers perceive to be the quality of a product based on image, advertising, and brand name reputation.

By influencing or varying any one or more of these eight dimensions of quality, a company can position itself in the market place, so quality is then a strategic variable.

Dr. Genichi Taguchi says that quality can be defined in terms of loss to a person or a company or society caused by a product after it is shipped. This approach is known as "Taguchi Loss Function." For example, a person buying a "durable press" shirt expects it not to require ironing, however, if it requires ironing after laundering, then the loss to that person is a one time additional price that person paid for durable press characteristics vs. non-durable press shirt plus cost in time to iron that shirt and electricity used in ironing each time after laundering for the life of that shirt. This loss can be quantified and quality can be defined in this term. Dr. Taguchi proposes that the goal of any process should be to produce a product or service as close to "target" as possible rather than "within specification" because loss to the customer increases as the performance characteristic deviates from the target value.

Why do we buy a product? We buy a product primarily because we want to use that product. Now, if the product we bought has some deficiency what happens? We can't use it, so, in that case, can we say that the product we could not use is defective? Sure, we can. Therefore, quality can be defined in terms of "fitness for use." Dr. Joseph M. Juran (1988) came up with this concept sometime in the late

50's or early 60's. Companies should judge fitness for use of a product from a customer's viewpoint and not from a manufacturer's or seller's viewpoint.

For example, the "fitness for use" concept when applied to garments means that they must:

- Be free from defects such as stains, material (fabric) defects, open seams, loose hanging (untrimmed) threads, misaligned buttons and buttonholes, defective zippers, etc.
- Fit properly for the labeled size.
- Perform satisfactorily in normal use, meaning that a garment must be able to withstand normal laundering/dry-cleaning/pressing cycles without color loss or shrinkage, seams must not come apart, fabric must not tear, etc.
- Be of prevailing fashion.

The concept of "fitness for use" when applied to an appliance such as a toaster means that the toaster should toast the bread slices uniformly in a reasonable period of time, time and again, without posing any shock or fire hazard.

Quality is also a reflection of customers' opinion on the value they see in your product compared to that of your competitor's. In other words, quality is whatever the customer says it is. The bottom line is that the customer is the final judge of quality.

We have tried to define quality from several viewpoints, now let us see how ISO (International Organization for Standardization) defines quality.

Quality is defined by ISO (2000) as "degree to which a set of inherent characteristics fulfils requirements." The term "quality" can be used with adjectives such as poor, good or excellent. "Inherent" as opposed to "assigned", means existing in some thing, especially as a permanent characteristic.

It is interesting to note that the ISO definition of quality reflects some of the concepts discussed earlier. For example, "…fulfils requirements" refers to fitness for use. Fulfilling requirements also refers to durability, reliability, and serviceability, three of the eight dimensions of quality discussed by Garvin (1988) and performance and features—two of the eight dimensions discussed by Garvin (1988) also.

Quality should not be confused with grade, even though grade is a feature or an aspect of quality. The American Society for Quality (1993) defines grade as a category or rank indicator of the totality of features and characteristics of a product or service intended for the same functional use or purpose, oriented at a specified cost related consumer/user market. Grade reflects that additional features and characteristics may be desirable, usually for added cost, and that a different version of the product or service is thus defined. For example, both, Chevrolet and Cadillac cars can be of good quality but they are certainly not in the same grade. Cadillac is targeted for an upscale, luxury automobile market while Chevrolet is targeted for an average consumer or middle class market. Similarly, Holiday Inn and Hyatt Regency hotels are of different grades but both are good quality hotels.

Having some idea of what quality is, let us look at some of the factors that influence consumers' perception of quality. These factors are:

1. *Price.* Consumers tend to associate grade (or quality) with higher price. According to Gardner (1970) there is some evidence that price is used by shoppers in grade (or quality) estimates and that for some products consumers' estimates of grade (or quality) are affected by price.
2. *Technology.* This indicates factors such as fabric and seam strength, colorfastness, shrinkage of clothing item or size of a home entertainment system and other properties or attributes that are affected by the state of technology in the industry.
3. *Psychology.* A consumer product can be reasonably priced and the best that technology can offer, but if it is not attractive in appearance, if it is not fashionable, it does not meet the aesthetic requirements of the customers, then it is not a quality product.
4. *Time Orientation.* This includes durability. Of course, the importance of durability varies with the product.
5. *Contractual.* This refers to a product guarantee, the refund policy of a store, etc.
6. *Ethical.* This refers to honesty of advertising, courtesy of sales personnel, etc.

If you can positively influence any one or more of the preceding factors, then you will be able to increase the quality (and therefore the value) of your product in a customer's mind and he or she will most likely come back to buy from you again.

Putnam and Davidson (1986) provide several examples of how retailers can use quality of products and services as a compelling competitive advantage based on their customer base and core product categories they offer.

In order to address product quality effectively, there must be company wide understanding of just what is quality, or there should be a corporate or official definition of quality. For example, in the company where the author worked, quality is defined in terms of "fitness for use." Anything that adversely affects serviceability, salability, or appearance of an item is considered a defect. Having such an understanding at all levels of the company will enable you to address quality as a business function.

1-2 Why is Quality Important?

Quality is important simply because poor quality costs. According to Juran and Gryna (1988) the annual cost of poor quality in the service sector is similar to that of manufacturing, averaging about 30% of operating expenses. Other authors (Burst and Gryna 2002) indicate the cost of poor quality such as scrap and rework, runs in the range of 5 to 35 % of sales revenue for manufacturing organizations and 25 to 40 % of operating expenses for service organizations.

While common sense would tell us that better product and service quality result in higher profits, there is overwhelming evidence to support such feeling. Better quality results in higher profits through reduced rejects, scrap, repair work, higher productivity, and better/higher customer satisfaction.

Schoeffler, Buzzell, and Henry (1974) reported results of a research study about profit impact of marketing strategies (PIMS) conducted by the Marketing Science Institute, a nonprofit research organization associated with the Harvard Business School. The basic idea behind PIMS was to provide corporate top management, divisional management, marketing executives, and corporate planners with insight and information on expected profit performance of different kinds of business under different competitive conditions. Among the 37 factors investigated and analyzed were market share, total marketing expenditures, product quality, R & D expenditures, investment intensity, etc. These factors account for more than 80% of the variation in profit in the more than 600 business units analyzed. The research results showed that product quality is related to return on investment (ROI) as shown in the following table.

	Product Quality		
Market Share	Inferior	Average	Superior
Under 12 %	4.5 % ROI	10.4 % ROI	17.4 % ROI
12 to 26 %	11.0 % ROI	18.1 % ROI	18.1 % ROI
Over 26 %	19.5 % ROI	21.9 % ROI	28.3 % ROI

Table 1-1 Relationship of Market Share, Quality and Return on Investment (ROI)

It is clear from these data that the higher the product quality, the better or higher the ROI. ROI is higher with better quality even with low market share.

Carr (1982) showed that, in general, higher or better product quality results in higher return on investment anywhere in the world as shown in the Table 1-2.

For example, with low market share and low quality, the ROI in the U. S. is 13 %, but with the same low market share, if the quality improved to be high, the ROI will increase to 18 %. The best of both worlds is to have higher market share and higher quality. If this were the case, as can be seen in the above table, that in the U. S. the ROI would be 34 %!

	Market Share									
	Low					High				
Quality	U.S.	Canada	U.K.	Europe	S. America	U.S.	Canada	U.K.	Europe	S. America
	ROI (%)					ROI (%)				
Low	13	11	17	6	8	24	24	31	20	24
High	18	24	25	20	27	34	31	30	29	28

Table 1-2 Relationship of Market Share, Quality, Return on Investment (ROI) and geography

Now, what happens in a recessionary time? How does quality affect profitability in recession? Schoeffler (1980) reported that during recession ROI is reduced by about 15 % in those companies with average and high product quality, but about 33 % in those companies with low quality. This means that during recessionary times, average to high product quality companies did twice as good as those companies with low product quality.

Another evidence of the positive impact of quality on profitability came from a Conference Board report (1989). In this study, Conference Board membership was asked, have you noticed any change in your profitability due to your quality program? Of those who responded, 95.8 % reported that their profits have noticeably increased, 2.6 % said their profits remained unchanged, and 1.6 % said their profits actually declined.

According to Goodman (2002), revenue implications of better quality and service are 10 to 20 times the cost implications.

Deming (1982) suggested that long-range improvement of market position, higher productivity, and better profits are realized by improving quality through improvement of the process. According to Deming, management can increase productivity by increasing quality. Leonard and Sasser (1982) suggested that an increase in quality always results in increased productivity or vice versa.

H. James Harrington (1989) cites a number of examples of companies such as Ford Motor Co., General Motors, Avon Products, Corning Glass Works, General Dynamics, AT & T, Hewlett-Packard Co., IBM, Motorola, 3M, North American Tool and Die Co. who have found that quality and profitability are indeed connected and concluded that:

> Extensive research has proven that improved perceived product quality is the most effective way to increase profits and the most important factor in the long-term profitability of a company.

A study by Hendricks and Singhal (1997, 1999) found that effective implementation of TQM (Total Quality Management) principles impacts bottom line business results in a positive way. The 5 year study of more than 600 quality award winners showed that as a whole, they experienced significant improvement in the value of their common stock, operating income, sales, return on sales, employment and asset growth. The winning of quality awards was used as a proxy for the effective implementation of TQM. Hendricks and Singhal compared the financial performance of nearly 600 quality award winning firms against a control sample of firms similar in size and operating in the same industries. Both groups were tracked over a five year period starting one year before to four years after the award winners won their first award. The award winners averaged significantly larger increases in several measures of financial performance than the control group. Award winners experienced a 44% higher stock price return, a 48% higher growth in operating income and 37% higher growth in sales compared to the control group. Award winners also outperformed the controls on return on sales, growth in employees, and growth in assets.

According to a Conference Board report (1994), in 1990 the Whirlpool Corporation decided to transform itself into a company that would consistently be recognized as in the top 25 percent of all companies in the world in total return to shareholders. Whirlpool wanted to know what they should focus on in order to create their regular high returns, so they benchmarked the world's best high-return companies across many industries. Whirlpool discovered that all those companies single-mindedly drove their high-performance business with measurable objectives in four simple areas—customer satisfaction, quality and productivity, growth and innovation, and high commitment and involvement of their people.

Even the U.S. Congress has recognized national importance of quality in a House Republican Research Committee report (1988), "Quality as a Means to Improve Our Nation's Competitiveness," which opens with a statement,

> It is important we recognize a significant portion of our trade deficit is due to the ability of foreign competitors to deliver higher quality products that are either novel, less costly to produce, promise better service or some combination of the above.

and concludes that

> in so many cases the answer to foreign success, and ours too is an abiding focus on quality.

While profit can be the motivating force behind quality, customers demand for quality can also be a very powerful driving force behind quality (Koshy 1995).

Baldwin (1990) reported that a New York based company called Grey Advertising conducted a survey called the "American Household of 1990s" and presented its findings to the annual convention of National Retail Merchants Association (now National Retail Federation) in January 1990. Two of their findings directly related to quality were the following:

1. Eighty-seven percent of consumers always look for top quality, meaning that the quality is always the number 1 criterion.

2. Eighty-four percent of consumers will pay more for top quality, suggesting that today, value has a different meaning. It is the best quality available for a given price.

In an ASQC/Gallup poll survey (1988) consumers said they were willing to pay a premium for higher quality products:

> When given a hypothetical baseline price for one of five "average quality" products (a car, dishwasher, television set, pair of shoes, or a sofa) and and then asked how much more than this price they would pay to get a product that met their own expectations for quality, respondents said they would pay on average 21% more for the car, 42% more for the dishwasher, 67% more for the TV or the shoes, and 72% more for the sofa.

This shows that there are consumers who are willing to pay more in order to get better than average quality in various consumer products.

Business Week (1982); Schoeffler, Buzzell, and Henry (1974); and Buzzell and Wiersema (1981) have indicated the following six benefits of quality:

Greater market share	Higher growth rate
Higher earnings	Premium price
Loyal customers	Highly motivated employees

Higher or better product quality can also be used as a product differentiation strategy in the marketplace. Actually, the easiest or the best way to make money (perhaps too obvious to notice) is to stop losing it through poor quality and customers who never return. In other words, the best way to be profitable is to have repeat customers. In order to have repeat customers, one of the most important business factors is product quality. It has been said that it is more expensive to bring in new customers than it is to retain the existing customers. Some of the companies are even calculating how much a customer is worth over his/her lifetime. For example, one retailer has estimated on an average, a customer is worth $ 80,000 over his/her life time. This means that if this retailer can keep a customer for his or her life time, that customer will purchase $ 80,000 worth merchandise over his or her life time! The logic is, if you can retain a customer over his/her entire lifetime, then you made that much money! As a matter of fact, several books have been written about customers for life (Sewell 1998, Leboeuf 2000). It is hoped that managing and improving product quality will help you retain your customers and be more profitable.

In a PriceWaterhouseCoopers (2002) survey of top executives of multinational companies, 89% cited product and service quality as a contributor to long-term shareholder return.

Based on the above information, it is clear that those retailers who are willing to meet ever changing quality expectations of their customers will be able to maintain a competitive advantage over those who are either not willing to or prepared to meet this challenge.

Key Points

- Quality can be defined in many ways.
- Having a Corporate definition of quality that is understood company-wide facilitates effective management of quality.
- Cost of poor quality varies from 25% to 40% of the operating expenses for service organizations. This means that quality improvement offers significant opportunity for better profits.
- There is a direct correlation between quality and profitability.
- The best way to make money is to stop losing it through poor quality.

References

American Society for Quality Control. 1993. *Glossary & Tables for Statistical Quality Control.* Milwaukee, WI.

ASQC/Gallup Survey. 1988. Consumers See Little Change in Product Quality. *Quality Progress.* December. Milwaukee, WI.

Baldwin, Pat. 1990. Ad Firm Charts Trends in What Shoppers Want in 1990s. *The Dallas Morning News,* Jan. 20. Dallas, TX.

Burst, Peter J. and Gryna, Frank M. 2002. Quality and Economics: Five Key Issues. *Quality Progress.* October. Pp. 64-69. American Society for Quality, Milwaukee, WI.

Business Week. 1982.Quality: The U.S. drives to catch up. November 1.Special Report.

Buzzell, Robert D. and Wiersema, Frederick D. 1981. Successful Share Building Strategies. *Harvard Business Review,* Jan.-Feb.

Carr, M. R. 1982. Evaluating Your Foreign Business: Finally Some Facts. *Planning Review,* November.

Conference Board. 1994. Linking Quality to Business Results. *Report No. 1084-94-CH*, New York, NY.

Conference Board. 1989. Current Practices in Measuring Quality. *Research Bulletin No. 234*, New York, NY.

Deming, W. E. 1982. *Quality, Productivity and Competitive Position*. Boston: MIT Center for Advanced Engineering Study.

Gardner, David M. 1970. An Experimental Investigation of the Price/Quality Relationship. *Journal of Retailing*, Vol. 46, No. 3.

Garvin, David A.1988. *Managing Quality: The Strategic & Competitive Edge*. The Free Press, New York.

Goodman, John. 2002. Quantifying the Payoff of Being easier to Do Business With. Keynote address to the annual conference of the Customer-Supplier Division of the American Society for Quality. 30 September. Louisville, KY.

Harrington, James H. 1989. *The QUALITY/PROFIT Connection*. American Society for For Quality, Milwaukee, WI.

Hendricks, K. B. and Singhal, V. R. 1997. Does Implementing an Effective TQM Program Actually Improve Performance: An Empirical Evidence From Firms that Have Won Quality Awards. *Management Science*, Vol. 44, No. 9, pp. 1258-1274.

Hendricks, K. B. and Singhal, V. R. 1999. Don't Count TQM Out. *Quality Progress*, April. Pp. 35-42. American Society for Quality, Milwaukee, WI.

House Republican Research Committee. 1988. *Quality as a Means to Improving Our Nation's Competitiveness*. A Report Prepared by the Task Force on High Technology. Washington, D.C., July 12.

ISO 9000-2000. *Quality management system-Fundamentals and vocabulary*. International Organization for Standardization, Geneva, Switzerland.

Juran, J. M. and Gryna, Frank M. 1988. *Quality Control Handbook*. McGraw-Hill Book Co. New York.

Koshy, Darlie O. 1995. *Effective Export Marketing of Apparel*. Global Business Press, New Delhi.

Leboeuf, Michael. 2000. *How to Win Customers and Keep Them for Life: Revised and Updated for Digital Age*. Berkley Pub. Group. ISBN 0425175014.

Lamprecht, James. 2000. *Quality & Power in the Supply Chain. What Industry Does for the Sake of Quality*. Butterworth-Heinemann, Woburn, Massachusetts.

Leonard, F. S. and Sasser, W. E. 1982. The Incline of Quality. *Harvard Business Review*, September-October.

PriceWaterhouseCoopers. 2002. Non-Financial Measures are Highest-rated Determinants of Total Shareholder Value. *Management Barometer*. April 22. www.barometersurveys.com

Putnam, Mandy and Davidson, William R. 1986. Quality: As a Compelling Competitive Advantage. *Management Horizons Report.* Management Horizons, A Division of Price Waterhouse. June.

Quality Alert Institute. 1990-91.*Course Brochure.*

Rabitt, John. The Foxboro Company. 1994. Linking Quality to Business Results. *A Conference Report, Report Number 1084-94-CH.* The Conference Board, New York.

Schoeffler, Sidney, Buzzell, Robert D. and Heany, Donald F. 1974. Impact of Strategic Planning on Profit Performance. *Harvard Business Review*, March-April.

Schoeffler, Sidney. 1980. Recession: Who Gets Hurt? *Planning Review*, November.

Sewell, Carl, et al. 1998. *Customers for Life: How to Turn That One-Time Buyer into a Lifetime Customer*. Pocket Books. ISBN 067102101X.

Taguchi, Genichi and Clausing, Don. 1990. Robust Quality. *Harvard Business Review*, Jan.-Feb.

Bibliography

Merrill, Peter. 1989. Quality is a Serious Business. *Textile Horizons*. February. The Textile Institute, Manchester, England.

Pratt, Herbert T. 1987. Some Thoughts on the Term "Quality." *ASTM Standardization News*, pp. 20. October. ASTM International, West Conshohocken, PA.

Straker, David. 2001. What Is Quality, Part 1. *Quality World*. April. Institute of Quality Assurance, London, England.

Straker, David. 2001. What Is Quality, Part 2. *Quality World*. May. Institute of Quality Assurance, London, England.

Groocock, John. 2001. Define Quality. *Quality World*. October. Institute of Quality Assurance, London, England.

2

Organizing for Quality

2-1 Organization

When the QA efforts in retail were started in 1911 by Sears, Roebuck & Co. and in 1929 by J C. Penney & Co. the model was to have a product testing facility of varying size and scope and a group of inspectors who inspect incoming shipments at their respective distribution centers and at the suppliers facilities. Then, in the late 70s and early 80s number of independent testing laboratories came up to support demand in product testing by retailers. As these testing organizations realized that the retailers also needed end item inspection of their shipments, they started to offer inspection services to retailers and instead of just being testing laboratories became testing and inspection companies. Some of these organizations are listed in the Chapter 10, resources. As more and more retailers started their QA efforts in the 70s and 80s, some of them chose to contract out their testing and inspection to one or more of these organizations. Thus, another model for retailers' QA efforts came in to existence known as outsourcing of QA. Today, there are three models of QA organization for retailers as follows:

a. In-house QA organization. In this model all QA activities are conducted by the employees of the retailer.
b. Outsourcing of all QA activities. In this model, the retailer has a core QA staff which coordinates all QA activities performed by another organization under contract with the retailer.
c. Combination of the above two. In this model, some QA activities are conducted in-house and some are outsourced. For example, all end item inspections in the United States may be done by the employees of

the retailer, however, all end item inspections overseas may be done by an inspection organization under contract with the retailer.

How a retailer's QA function is organized depends on the retailer. A retailer which sells a lot of brand names will most likely have a smaller QA department because the brand name companies can be relied upon to consistently produce and deliver quality merchandise as their reputation is on line. On the other hand, if a retailer sells a greater proportion of its own private label and non branded merchandise, then the QA organization will be relatively larger as the retailer has his own reputation for quality to worry about. Therefore, there is no one "best practice" or "best model" for quality organization in the retail industry, however, there is a best approach to quality management as outlined in the next chapter, Approaches to Quality, Chapter 3.

Here are two models for quality organization for retailers. Figure 2-1 shows an organization with in-house testing and inspection. Figure 2-2 shows an organization where testing and in-plant inspections are out sourced. Regardless of which model is followed, effective organization of quality function is very important to the overall quality assurance efforts of a retailer. An example of a functional statement of quality assurance is at Appendix I.

The title of Vice President, Quality Assurance, in these organization charts refers to the highest position in quality assurance in an organization. Various retailers use various titles for the head of their quality organization, such as, Vice President, Director, Chief, Manager, etc.

The VP (Vice President) of quality helps formulate the quality policy of a retailer and puts the quality management system in place, runs it and provides leadership in quality areas to purchasing/sourcing and store management. A sample job description with required qualifications for a VP of quality is in the Appendix I.

Typically, the VP of Quality derives his/her authority through expertise, professionalism and internal commitment to excellence. While, in theory, the VP of quality should be a technical person in his/her knowledge of statistics, standards and regulations, science or engineering, etc. and at the same time, be a generalist who can relate to business, in practice, the VP is often a "business" person with no technical background, and the first level of highly technical person reporting to this VP is the "director" level. Dr. Juran (1999) describes a variety of roles for the quality manager, and according to him, depending on the situation, a quality manager plays one or more roles of an inspector, an analyst, a consumer advocate, a consultant, a planner and coordinator, an assuror, the right hand man of the

CEO in any quality related matter, and the company liaison with quality professionals in government, industry, and professional societies.

The director of testing oversees product testing, specification development, product safety and regulatory compliance, store support in terms of handling quality related customer complaints, etc. The director of testing also recruits and trains QA specialists and laboratory technicians and develops them for leadership positions within QA in the future. In case, where testing is outsourced, the director of testing selects the laboratory to whom the testing is outsourced, administers the contract with the testing laboratory, monitors its performance, coordinates test results with the buying/procurement staff and suppliers, etc. Duties and qualifications required of the Director of Testing are in a sample job description in the Appendix I.

The director of inspection oversees day to day operation of inspection activities which includes inspections at suppliers' facilities, called in-plant inspections, and inspections at the retailer's distribution centers (DCs). The director of inspection also recruits and trains inspectors and develops them for leadership positions in the future. In case, where inspection is outsourced, the director of inspection selects the company to whom the inspection is outsourced, administers the contract with the inspection company, monitors its performance, coordinates inspection results with the buying/procurement staff and suppliers, etc. Duties and qualifications required of the Director of Inspection are in a sample job description in the Appendix I.

Each QA specialist manages quality of a group of products and serves a group of buyers. For example, there can be a QA specialist each for soft lines, electrical hard lines, non-electrical hard lines, shoes, luggage, etc. Soft lines can be further divided, if necessary, in to children's wear, ladies' wear, men's wear, etc. per each specialist. Typically, QA specialist develops the standard inspection procedures, writes and/or helps buyers develop specifications, when necessary and supports store management in any quality related matter, such as customer complaints, product recalls, etc. While a detailed job description for the QA specialist's position is in the Appendix I, one multi-national retailer in England had a job advertisement for a specialist several years ago in a London daily news paper which read "Working closely with both suppliers and buyers the specialist has two main objectives, to support the suppliers to deliver high quality merchandise by devising specifications and standards and to play a key role in new product development, advising buyers of new processes, materials and sources. Inevitably the role demands a high level of technical expertise; candidates must be able to demonstrate their practical ability to make commercial judgment and influence decisions and opinions within a fast moving environment." Also, the company was looking for drive, enthusiasm and self-confidence.

Both, the inspection and testing functions should work in close cooperation with each other.

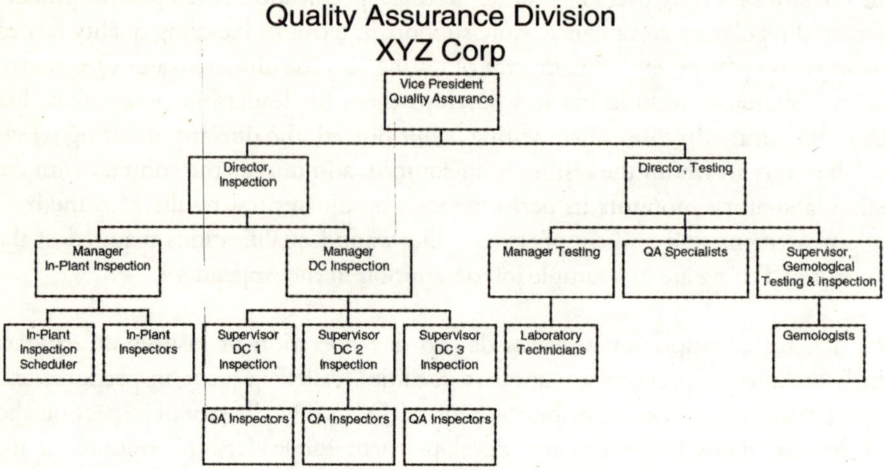

Figure 2-1 Quality Organization with In-house Testing and Inspection

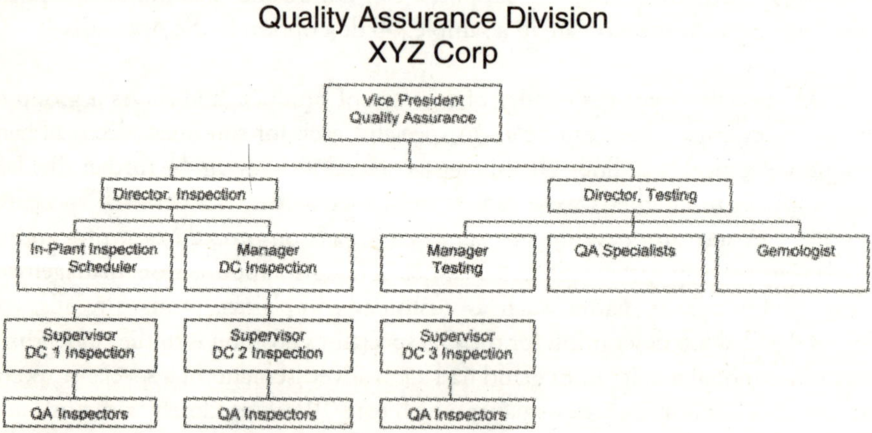

Figure 2-2 Quality Organization with Testing and In-Plant Inspection Outsourced

Examples of job descriptions of all the positions shown in the above two figures are in the Appendix I, Job Descriptions and Training Plans. Each job description outlines duties and responsibilities as well as qualification requirements for the job.

Please bear in mind that these job descriptions are not absolute. They are just some examples. Each retailer may want to customize job descriptions to suit its needs.

The salary range for each position within QA will depend on the scope of the position (job description), and the qualification desired by the retailer. The American Society for Quality (ASQ) conducts an annual salary survey in the quality profession in the United States and Canada, covering a variety of industries by job titles, education, experience, geographical location, etc. Some 20 variables are covered. Results of this survey are published each year in the December issue of the Quality Progress, a monthly published by ASQ. More detailed results of this survey are posted on the ASQ web site www.asq.org. This is an excellent source of information about compensation levels in the quality profession. A retailer's Human Resources (HR) professionals can also help in setting salary levels for positions within QA.

2-2 In-house Testing and Inspection

Factors to consider for having your own or in-house testing and inspection are:

a. Initial investment in testing facility to include laboratory space and test equipment.
b. Recruitment and retention of qualified staff for testing and inspection.
c. Ongoing investment in training of the inspection and laboratory staff and calibration, maintenance as well as updating of test equipment to make sure you are keeping up with your suppliers and new developments. Personnel issues such as yearly performance reviews and pay raises, personality conflicts, etc. associated with having your own employees.
d. Assuring that the test and inspection results are accurate.
e. Location of the in-plant inspectors and their periodic transfers (every three years or so).
f. Traveling expenses for in-plant inspectors.

Advantages of having your own inspection and testing are flexibility and quick response, consistency of performing testing and inspections as well as confidence in your own results.

2-3 Outsourcing Testing and Inspection

Factors to consider in outsourcing inspection and testing are:

a. Capability and reputation of the inspection and test agency.
b. Accuracy and reliability of the test and inspection results.
c. Their ability to respond quickly and flexibility.
d. Overall cost of their services.

There are two options for outsourcing of testing:

a. Send or have suppliers send samples to one or more testing laboratories.
b. For large enough volume, a testing laboratory will set up a testing facility on your premises manned by their employees.

Advantages of outsourcing are available expertise of the inspection and test agency, not having to deal with personnel issues, and independent (third party) results of inspection and testing. Large testing houses have laboratories in many parts of the world, making it easier to have testing done at the laboratory closest to a retailer's supplier(s), thus saving valuable time and money in shipping samples to a retailer's laboratory. Large inspection houses have multi-national locations and local nationals working as QA inspectors. Therefore, they can offer much better flexibility in scheduling inspections in a variety of countries rather fast with no language barrier or travel problems. Some inspection and test companies will work with your suppliers, for a fee, to help them improve quality of merchandise they supply to you. Some of these testing and inspection houses are capable of setting up a web page for a retailer on their web site so a retailer can check or follow-up status of inspection or testing of its merchandise or look up inspection or test results. Outsourcing of testing will also result in considerable reduction or savings in clerical efforts needed in receiving and accounting for the samples received for testing and their disposal etc.

Chapter 10, Resources, contains names of some well known inspection and test organizations with international offices. This list is by no means an exhaustive list nor is it an endorsement of the organization listed. It is only an example.

2-4 Cost of In-house Vs Outsourcing

There is no clear cost advantage in the favor of one option against the other. Various retailers who use either one of the three models mentioned earlier do so based on not only cost factor but also on other factors already mentioned in the items 2-2 and 2-3. This author knows at least two multi-billion dollar retailers who have extensive QA organization to conduct all QA activities in-house because that is what they prefer. At the same time, this author knows at least two other multi-billion dollar retailers who have outsourced most of their quality assurance activities and have a core QA staff to manage and coordinate outsourced QA activities. Again, these two retailers prefer it this way.

2-5 Quality Assurance Budget

Depending on the size and scope of the QA efforts, various retailers spend varying amounts of money for such efforts. Some retailers measure this amount as a % of sales, while some retailers measure this amount as % of cost of goods sold. For example, one multi-billion dollar retailer in the U.S. with predominantly soft lines merchandise and about 70 % of that private label merchandise, spends about 0.01 to 0.015% of sales per year on quality assurance efforts. Another multi-billion dollar retailer who has a good mix of soft lines as well as hard lines merchandise but does not have as much private label merchandise spends about 0.25 % of the cost of goods sold per year on its quality assurance efforts. Another multi-billion dollar, multi-national retail organization with about a 50-50 mix of soft lines and hard lines merchandise and about less than 10 % private label clothing currently spends about 0.04 % of sales per year on its quality assurance efforts. One multi-billion dollar, multi-national sourcing organization for retailers spends 0.5 to 0.7 % of cost of goods sold per year for its quality assurance efforts. Thus, there is no "optimum" amount of QA budget for a retailer. A retailer must decide how much money can be spent or what amount of money is appropriate to suit its own purpose.

2-6 Value of QA Function

The quality organization should strive to be a resource for the purchasing/sourcing staff and be their partner in satisfying ultimate customers. The quality organization should also play a role of consumer advocate when necessary on behalf of the customers. According to the American National Standards Institute (CIF 2002), consumers are defined as those individuals who use goods or services to satisfy their individual needs and desires, rather than to resell them or to produce other goods or services with them. The quality organization can make itself more valuable to the company by being a consultant, a teacher, and a facilitator to the purchasing/sourcing staff, rather than being a policeman. The VP of quality should never loose sight of the fact that quality function in mass merchandising is a support function, it is not the primary function such as merchandising, operations, purchasing or sourcing, etc. As such, the VP of QA does not decide the level of quality to be offered by a retailer. That's a merchandising decision. Unless it is a safety related issue, whether to accept certain shipment or add certain item to stock assortment is for the respective buyer and the merchandise manager to decide.

Quality organization should always be flexible and change as fast as buying patterns change. For example, a retailer's private label children's clothing program was domestic program with the emphasis on "Made in America" label. QA invested considerable time and efforts in evaluating quality systems of about ten suppliers and found them effective, and for about two years this program did fine. However, as soon as the merchandise manager who had put this program together retired, the whole program went to South East Asia. All of a sudden, QA's work load in the U. S. dropped some and increased some in the Far East. A good QA organization should be able to respond real fast to such changes in purchasing or sourcing. Therefore, it is very important for the VP of QA to be in constant touch with the senior management of buying in order to anticipate changes and developments and be prepared to respond. Also, QA specialists should develop good rapport with the buyers they serve so they can keep up with various developments at their levels.

It helps to hold periodic briefings for buyers and purchasing staff where they are given an overview of what QA does and can do for them, such as, help them with development of specifications, test and inspect products, help answering quality related customer and/or store complaints, help suppliers understand quality requirements and find information on regulations and laws pertaining to their products. Also, during this briefing the buyers can be reminded of quality policy of the company and be informed about laws and regulations governing consumer products, some procedures such as how to request testing and inspection, how many samples are needed for testing, who pays for the samples, where to send samples for testing, etc. If the retailer has its own testing laboratory, then a laboratory tour can be arranged for the buyers and purchasing staff where they can see some actual testing taking place and appreciate behind the scene activities to assure quality and safety of products they buy and how QA can be of help to them.

Since QA is a support function, it is up to QA management to constantly keep selling itself to the purchasing and store operations.

2-7 Selection of QA Staff

While the qualification requirements for various positions within QA are outlined in respective job descriptions in the Appendix I, careful selection of QA staff is very important because the ability of the QA staff to realistically and consistently appraise quality against product standards, or develop product standards when necessary, is vital to effective quality management of consumer products and in turn to a retail organization. This is true regardless of in-house or out sourced QA efforts. Personal traits such as helpful and cooperative attitude, courage and tact, self-confidence and poise, thoroughness and organized approach to work, good communication and persuasive ability, an interest in not only what can be failed but what can be passed, ability to learn and instruct, ability to maintain records and reports, and ability to analyze faults and real reasons thereof are very important. The QA staff should have pride and interest in their work, a strong desire to improve themselves, and above all, common sense. Their physical appearance should indicate that they have pride in themselves. It is important to have competent QA staff. Competence is the ability to apply education, training, skills and experience in varying degree depending on the situation on a consistent basis, day in and day out.

Training plans for several jobs are outlined in the Appendix I.

2-8 Standard Operating Procedures (SOPs)

In order for smooth functioning of QA activities, whether in-house or outsourced, and effective interface of QA and Purchasing or Sourcing staff, standard operating procedures (SOPs) and standard policies (SPs) should be written and be available for reference to all concerned when necessary. Some examples of SOPs and SPs are shown in different chapters in this book. Some possible SOPs are:

a. How to Report Inspection Results
b. How to Use Statistical Sampling Plans

c. Assessing Rejection/Screening/Futile Visit Costs and Charging Them Back to a Supplier
d. Conducting In-stock Inspection at DCs
e. Completing Travel Expense Voucher
f. Scheduling In-plant Inspections
g. Completing and Submitting Weekly Activity Report
h. SOP for the Testing Laboratory
i. SOP for the Gemological Laboratory
j. Reporting Customer Complaints and Store Level Defects
k. Conducting Use Test of Products by Consumer Panel
l. Packaging Evaluation for Mail Order Items
m. Conducting a Product Recall

2-9 Logistics and QA

The latest development in retail logistics is direct shipment from a supplier's facility to the stores in small quantities based on either orders from stores or sales data transmitted electronically from stores on a daily basis, and cross-docking. In cross-docking, merchandise is shipped to a retailer's DCs already pre-packed and marked for individual stores. The shipment is received at a retailer's DC on one side of the dock, immediately sorted by stores and placed in respective trucks on the other side of the dock and shipped to those stores. This is done in a matter of hours. In such cases, QA inspections at DCs are not possible because any inspection at DCs will result in delays in shipping merchandise to stores. The idea behind cross-docking is to not have such delays. In-plant inspections are not economical due to small size of shipments. The best and perhaps, the only way to handle such cases would be to audit the quality system of such suppliers and "certify" their quality systems. By certifying a supplier's quality system a retailer is exhibiting confidence in that supplier's ability to ship quality merchandise on a consistent basis. For more on supplier certification, see Chapter 3, Approaches to Quality. It may be worthwhile for a retailer to make a policy that no supplier will be placed on "direct shipment" or "cross-dock" unless it is cleared by QA. This way, suppliers whose quality levels have not been verified or certified are prevented from shipping merchandise to the stores without QA inspections.

Key Points

- Quality assurance efforts can be in-house, outsourced, or the combination of the two.
- The level of QA efforts vary from retailer to retailer depending on the merchandise mix and procurement approach. As a result, QA budget varies considerably from a retailer to retailer.
- Quality function of a retailer should be a resource for purchasing and store operations staff, i.e. QA staff should be consultants, teachers, and facilitators to the purchasing staff as well as suppliers in order to satisfy, and preferably, delight the ultimate customer.
- Well written Standard Operating Procedures (SOPs) and Standard Inspection Procedures (SIPs) as well as Standard Policies (SPs) are vital to effective quality assurance activities.
- The way merchandise is shipped to the stores has an impact on how end item inspection is conducted.

References

CIF (Consumer Interest Forum). 6 November 2002. Operating Guidelines. American National Standards Institute (ANSI), New York, NY.

Juran, Joseph A. 1999. Editor-in-Chief. Juran's Quality Handbook, 5th edition. Quality Press, Milwaukee, WI.

3

Approaches to Quality

Before we discuss various approaches to quality management, let us review some definitions. These definitions have been taken from ISO 9000 (2000) and ASQ (1996). These definitions will make it easier to follow the rest of the text.

Defect—A departure of a quality characteristic from its intended level or state that occurs with a severity sufficient to cause an associated product or service not to satisfy intended normal, or reasonably foreseeable, usage requirements. Defects are generally classified as:

Class 1 Serious (Critical)—Any defect leading to injury, fatal injury, or catastrophic economic loss. A lasting tack in a pair of shoes, an exposed or cut wire that may pose an electrical shock hazard, etc. are some of the examples of critical defect.

Class 2 Major—Anything adversely affecting the function of an item.

Class 3 Minor—Anything adversely affecting the appearance but not the function of an item.

Inspection—Inspection is defined as the process of measuring, examining, testing, gauging or otherwise comparing the unit with the applicable requirements (ASQ 1996). The term "requirements" sometimes is used broadly to include standards of good workmanship. Inspection also means conformity evaluation by observation and judgment accompanied as appropriate by measurement, testing, or gauging (ISO 9000-2000).

Quality Management System—Management system to direct and control an organization with regard to quality.

Quality Management—Coordinated activities to direct and control an organization with regard to quality. Direction and control with regard to quality generally includes establishment of quality policy and quality objectives, quality planning, quality control, quality assurance and quality improvement.

Quality Planning—Part of quality management focused on setting quality objectives and specifying necessary operational processes and related resources to fulfill the quality objectives.

Quality Policy—Overall intentions and direction of an organization related to quality as formally expressed by top management.
Note: Generally the quality policy is consistent with the overall policy of the organization and provides a framework for the setting of quality objectives.

Quality Objective—Something sought, or aimed for, related to quality. Quality objectives are generally based on the organization's quality policy, and are generally specified for relevant functions and levels in the organization.

Quality Control—Part of quality management focused on fulfilling quality requirements. This includes operational techniques and activities which sustain a quality of product or service that will satisfy given needs.

Quality Assurance—Part of quality management focused on providing confidence that quality requirements will be fulfilled. Quality assurance, generally, has a broader connotation than quality control.

Quality Improvement—Part of quality management focused on increasing the ability to fulfill quality requirements. This includes a continuing evaluation of adequacy and effectiveness with a view to having timely corrective measures and feedback initiated when necessary. For a specific product or service, quality assurance involves the necessary plans and actions to provide confidence through verifications, audits, and the evaluation of quality factors that affect the adequacy of the design for intended applications, specification, production, installation, inspection and use of the product or service.

Testing—Testing is defined as a means of determining the capability of an item to meet specified requirements by subjecting the item to a set of physical, chemical, environmental, or operating actions and conditions (ASQ 1996). Testing also means determination of one or more characteristics according to a procedure (ISO 9000-2000).

Top Management—Person or group of people who directs and controls an organization at the highest level.

Throughout this book, the term quality assurance (QA) is used to discuss quality management efforts of retailers.

The terms "supplier" and "vendor" generally mean the same, however, the term "vendor" has a connotation of arms length relationship and a relationship where the purchasing decision is strictly driven by the price. The term "supplier" has a connotation of long term relationship, a relationship where there is exchange of information and price is not the only factor driving purchasing decisions. Throughout this book the term "supplier" is used. The term supplier also means either a manufacturer who is supplying directly to the retailer or an agent, distributor, importer, or any company supplying to the retailer.

The best way to make sure you receive quality merchandise from your suppliers is to

a. Communicate your quality expectations to your suppliers. An example of such communication is shown in the Appendix IV, Guidelines to Quality, and

b. Insist that the suppliers must have a quality system in place and they must control quality of items they receive from their suppliers, sub-contractors, etc. Make this a part of requirements for doing business with you. An example of this is shown in the Appendix V, Quality Terms and Conditions.

Some retailers post this information on their web site. For an excellent example of this, visit the web site of the Army & Air Force Exchange Service at www.aafes.com. Once on this web site, click on "About AAFES." Then, click on "General Information for Vendors" and "Quality Assurance Program."

When it comes to quality, a retailer can take one or more approaches as follows:

a. *No quality assurance efforts.* Under this approach, the retailer strictly relies upon suppliers to make sure that only quality products are shipped to the retailer and the retailer does not do anything to verify the quality of merchandise sold in the stores. This approach will work if the suppliers are well-known and reputable companies and if the retailer has a long trusting relationship with the suppliers.

b. *Testing.* This involves testing of consumer products from consumers' viewpoint. Testing and product analysis are conducted to check performance and various features of a product to assist buying decisions, to verify what the retailer received is what was bought, and to verify or validate customer complaints/returns. Testing is also done to develop product performance specifications and to find out how competitors' products perform.

c. *End-item inspection.* End-item inspection is visual examination of a finished product from consumers' viewpoint. This is basically to evaluate appearance, shape, size, finish (free of sharp edges, sharp points, scratches, etc.). The purpose of inspection is to make a sound judgment on acceptability of a product or a shipment. There are some consumer products that lend themselves for inspection and some do not. Consumer products such as cosmetics, tobacco, health and beauty products, detergents & shampoos, over-the-counter drugs and vitamins, etc. do not lend themselves to inspection except for packaging integrity and expiry date. Consumer products such as clothing, shoes, jewelry, sporting goods, RTA (ready to assemble) or KD (knocked down) furniture, luggage, linen & domestic (bed sheets, bedspreads, towels, curtains, drapes, carpets, etc.), home electronics (radios, stereos, TV sets, telephones, etc.), small appliances (irons, blenders, mixers, toasters, grills, can openers, toaster/ovens, microwave ovens, etc.), personal care appliances (hair dryers, curling irons, electric shavers, hair trimmers, etc.), toys, baby items (infant seats, bath seats, etc.), juvenile furniture, etc. lend themselves to inspection.

d. *Supplier quality system audit.* This involves reviewing or auditing a supplier's quality procedures and practices to see if they are adequate and effective. This approach will work only if your suppliers have quality control/assurance system in place. Also, if you have hundreds of suppliers, you may not be able to audit all of them. In that case some criteria will be needed to decide which suppliers to audit.

e. *Supplier certification.* Certifying a supplier's quality system indicates a retailer's confidence in that supplier to consistently provide good quality merchandise on time. Supplier certification is generally the end result of a supplier having passed a quality system audit. Because shipments from a certified supplier do not require constant inspection and testing, the retailer can redirect it's QA resources as where they may be needed more.

f. *Supplier survey*. Supplier surveys are generally done on prospective suppliers to learn what sort of quality procedures and practices are in place. This information helps in deciding whether to do business with those companies or not.

g. *Factory evaluation*. This involves evaluating suppliers' quality procedures and practices along with manufacturing practices and technology as they affect quality. This is usually done for new suppliers.

While there is no one best practice or best practices, those retailers who have matured in their management of quality, use a combination of items "b" through "g" in managing quality of merchandise they buy and sell. These approaches are discussed in detail in the rest of this chapter.

For example, for national or international brand merchandise such as Polo Ralph Lauren, Nautica, Van Heusen, Jockey, Fruit of the loom, Hanes, Jones of New York, Proctor-Silex, GE, Kenmore, Craftsman, Toastmaster, Black & Decker, Hamilton Beach, etc. there is no need for routine testing and inspection. In such cases, supplier certification with occasional random testing and inspection would be sufficient to monitor quality of national and international brand merchandise.

In case of supplier fashion labels and supplier house brands it may be necessary to do routine testing and inspection and then, based on the results adjust the frequency of inspection and testing and use supplier quality system audits, factory evaluations, and supplier certification on a case by case basis.

In case of retailers' private label merchandise, all approaches, i.e., supplier surveys, factory evaluations, supplier quality system audits, and routine testing and inspection would be necessary. Then, based on the quality performance of suppliers, testing and inspection frequency can be adjusted and supplier certification can be considered on a case-by-case basis.

3-1 Testing

3-1-1 Testing for Product Quality and Safety

Testing of consumer products is a vast field. An attempt is made here to provide a general overview and some examples.

Testing of products is done for a variety of reasons, however, it is very important to keep in mind that the testing should be always from consumers' view point because consumers are the ones who will buy items or products from the retailers for use. When testing is done to help the buyer make a purchasing decision, then it is called pre-purchase testing. *Pre-purchase* testing can be testing of a product by itself to see if it meets requirements or it can be for comparing several products with a view to choose which one meets or exceeds requirements and is the best. Once a product is bought and is in the system, it should be periodically tested to make sure that it is the same and performs the same as when pre-purchase tested. Such testing is called *post-award* testing because the buying is already done and the product is already in the stores. Sometimes a shipment is held at a supplier's facility or at a retailer's distribution center pending test results for the samples taken from that shipment. The shipment in question is accepted if the test results are favorable and the shipment is rejected if the test results are not favorable. Such testing is called *acceptance testing*. QA inspectors should be trained to detect anything in products while inspecting them that may cause problems later on or in use. In such cases, they should take representative samples and send them for testing, while the shipment is on hold. For example, colors from clothing with dark colors might run or fade during washing. Another reason testing is done is to verify customer complaints. Based on the nature of a customer complaint, it may be necessary to obtain a customer returned item and new samples of the same item for testing to find out actually what is the problem, if any.

The intensity and detail of testing or the scope of testing will depend on a retailer's approach to buying. Just as there is not much inspection necessary for national and international brand merchandise, there is not much testing necessary for the same because manufacturers of such merchandise are more concerned about their brand image and reputation than the retailers, and therefore, these manufacturers will take every necessary step to assure that only quality merchandise is shipped. For those products that are bought "off-the-shelf," there is no need to test for quality of design because the retailer did not specify the design. For "off-the-shelf" merchandise, performance and safety testing is necessary. While testing for the private label merchandise is necessary, the details of testing depends on whether the retailer develops and designs its own private label merchandise. Where a retailer develops and designs its own private label merchandise, detailed testing is necessary to make sure the quality of design and raw materials conform to requirements in addition to the end-item performance. Where a retailer simply puts its own label on merchandise without designing it, only performance testing is necessary.

Some retailers require the latest test results from a reputable or accredited laboratory for items under consideration for buying. This way, a retailer has an option of accepting those test results without performing any testing on its own or performing some additional testing to verify independent test results. An accredited laboratory means that the laboratory is given a formal recognition by a third party that the laboratory is capable of performing specific test methods and test procedures correctly. For example, SATRA (Shoes and Allied Trade Research Association) www.satra.co.uk offers laboratory accreditation in the area of footwear testing. Accreditation generally covers certain areas such as textiles, leather goods, electrical products, etc., and certain test methods. Accreditation is usually good for a specific time, such as three years from the date accreditation was granted. Therefore, when checking accreditation of any laboratory, always ask what is the scope of the accreditation and if the accreditation is current. It should be noted that not being accredited does not necessarily imply that the laboratory is not technically competent since not all laboratories seek or require accreditation, and accreditation programs may not exist in the laboratory's field of operation.

Competency of testing laboratories is addressed by the International Organization for Standardization (ISO) in a standard ISO/IEC 17025 General Requirements for the competence of testing & calibration laboratories.

Some retailers accept test results from their suppliers' laboratories only after reviewing their operations and verifying skills and proficiency of the laboratory technicians, i.e. "accrediting" those laboratories themselves.

There are standard test methods available for some products and for some products there are no standard test methods. A list of standard test methods of interest to retailers is in the Chapter 4, Standards and Specifications. Where there are no standard test methods available, retailers, commercial test laboratories, or manufacturers may have developed their own proprietary test methods. To see test methods used by a retailer visit the web site www.aafes.com/qa/docs/qa-testmethods.htm.

For example, there is no standard test method available for testing fit properties of women's pantyhose, however, the Merchandise Testing Laboratories (now MTL-ACTS), Canton, Massachusetts, U.S.A. has developed a test method for testing fit properties of women's pantyhose, and many well-known manufacturers of women's pantyhose use Merchandise Testing Laboratories for getting their pantyhose tested. There are no standard test methods for testing diapers and feminine hygiene products, however, manufacturers of such products have their own test methods for these products. Where there are no standard test methods, some retailers share their own test methods with their suppliers and/or and some manufacturers share their own test methods with some retailers. Whether there are standard test methods or not, considerable common sense should be used in planning and organizing for testing and actual testing. Wherever appropriate, products should be tested for safety aspects as well as to see how they will perform or hold up under actual use.

It is also very important to verify any claim made by a product manufacturer. It is unlawful to make false or unsubstantiated claims under the Federal Trade Commission (FTC) regulations. Testing products to make sure that the claims they make are justified and valid should be an integral part of the testing protocol. For example, one retailer has private label building blocks for children similar to the well known brand Lego. These private label building blocks claim to fit other brands. The testing with other brands revealed that while these private label building blocks fit other brands, they do not fit Lego as good as other brands. Therefore, their QA recommended that the statement claiming that these private label building blocks fit other brands be taken off all sets or they be improved so they fit Lego as good as they fit other brands. When a product makes a claim, it is an implied promise and raises consumer expectations.

Various test methods are listed in Chapter 4, Standards and Specifications. It is very important to use the latest test method(s) when testing a product.

All testing is not necessarily laboratory testing. Some times use test of a product is also necessary, particularly, in case of products such as detergents, creams and lotions, small appliances, personal grooming appliances, razor blades, etc. For a use test, normally, a panel of at least 35 consumers is put together and these individuals are given samples of the product to be tested as well as a form or a questionnaire to record appropriate information. In case of a comparative test, products are placed in unmarked containers and simply marked sample "A," "B," etc. so the test panel members do not know the brand and the brand name would not influence their evaluation.

For clothing products and shoes, typically, three samples are tested and an average of 3 to 5 readings are taken for each property tested. For items other than clothing, typically, one sample is tested and results reported. This is because clothing and textiles, and shoes tend to exhibit more variation in their properties than other consumer products. Since almost all consumer product testing is destructive, sometimes it is an economic decision as to how many samples to test. It is a matter of common sense and economics, unless dictated by test method(s) or an agreement between the buyer and the seller.

The interpretation of test results must be done with care and that's where "expertise," that is technical knowledge and experience comes in to play. For example, color will rub off from classic denim cotton fabric dyed with indigo because of the nature of the dyeing process in which a certain amount of dye is oxidized on the surface of the fabric. Most denims would therefore fail both wet and dry rubbing (crocking) tests before washing. Therefore, is such a failure grounds for rejecting denim jeans? Of course, not, because to do so would be to ask for impossible. After the first wash, the excess dye will wash off and in most cases there will be no color transfer in rubbing.

Here are some examples of what to test for what products.

3-1-1-1 Clothing, Linens and Domestics

Clothing may be tested for fabric weight, construction, fiber content, fabric and/or seam strength, shrinkage in laundering and/or dry cleaning, colorfastness to laundering and/or dry cleaning, sunlight, fumes, bleach, pool water, rubbing (wet and dry), durable press (wrinkle free) performance, abrasion resistance, water repellency, etc. Clothing should also be tested to verify or determine adequacy of care instructions. Some manufacturers tend to "hide behind the care label," i.e., they would label their products "Dry Clean Only," while in fact those items can be washed in cold water on delicate cycle without any adverse effect. Children's sleepwear must be tested for flammability. Some examples of clothing specifications are shown in Chapter 4, Standards and Specifications. Mehta (1992) and Mehta and Bhardwaj (1998) provide excellent discussion of testing clothing items. Kadolph (1998) also provides extensive discussion on testing of clothing and textiles. ASTM (2002) and AATCC (2002) provide standard test methods for testing fabrics and clothing. These test methods are listed in Chapter 4, Standards and Specifications.

Typically, ASTM and AATCC test methods indicate test instrument/equipment and any aids to be used with a given test method. Here is a list of various instruments/equipment and aids used for testing and evaluating fabrics and garments.

AATCC Crockmeter—Used to test fabrics for color transfer from the surface of colored textile materials to other surfaces by rubbing.

AATCC Chromatic Transference Scale—Used in evaluating the degree of color transfer in colorfastness tests.

AATCC Crease Retention Replicas—Used for evaluating crease sharpness in garments after repeated home laundering.

AATCC Gray Scale for Color Change—Used for evaluating changes in color of textiles resulting from colorfastness tests.

AATCC Perspiration Tester—Used to test fabrics for color transfer in perspiration.

AATCC Photographic Seam Smoothness Replicas—Used for evaluating seam appearance after repeated home laundering of garments.

AATCC Rain Tester—Used for measuring the resistance to the penetration of water by impact, and thus can be used to predict the probable rain penetration resistance of fabrics.

AATCC Smoothness Appearance Replicas—Used to evaluate durable press characteristics of fabrics.

AATCC Spray Tester—Used to test resistance of fabrics to wetting by water. It is especially suitable for measuring the water repellent efficacy of finishes applied to fabrics, particularly plain woven fabrics.

AATCC Spray Tester Rating Scale—Used to evaluate the degree of resistance to wetting by water or water repellency of fabrics.

AATCC Stain Release Replica—Used to evaluate the degree of stain release characteristics of fabrics.

AATCC Wrinkle Recovery Replicas—Used to evaluate wrinkle recovery property of fabrics.

Accellerator—Used for measuring abrasion resistance of fabrics.

Air Flow Tester—Used for testing air permeability of textiles.

Bean Bag Snag Tester—Used for testing snag resistance of fabrics.

Cantilever Stiffness Tester—Used for measuring fabric stiffness.

Diaphragm Bursting Strength Tester—Used for testing bursting strength of knitted fabrics.

Elmendorf Tear Tester—Used for testing tear strength of fabrics.

Fabric to Metal Cling Plate—Used to evaluate the relative clinging tendency of fabrics due to electrostatic charge generation.

Fabric Shift Tester—Used for testing resistance to yarn shift in fabrics.

Impact Penetration Tester—Used for measuring the resistance to the penetration of water by impact, and thus can be used to predict the probable rain penetration resistance of fabrics. It is especially suitable for measuring the penetration of garment fabrics.

Launderometer—Used to test colorfastness to laundering of textiles which are expected to withstand frequent laundering. The fabric color loss and surface changes resulting from detergent solution and abrasive action of five typical hand, home or commercial launderings, with or without chlorine, are roughly approximated by 45 minute test.

Macbeth Light Cabinet/Booth—Used to evaluate color change or color match in textiles using standard light sources.

Mace Tester—Used to test snag resistance of fabrics.

Martindale Abrasion Tester—Used to test abrasion resistance of fabrics and textile materials.

Photographic Standards for Snag Testing—Used to evaluate severity of snagged fabric and grade it accordingly in comparison to the standards.

Random Tumble Pilling Tester—Used to test pilling resistance of fabrics. Pilling refers to some fabric's tendency to develop small balls of fibers at cuffs, collars, and other places where there is considerable abrasion during wear, making that area unsightly.

Rating Scale for Pilling—Used to evaluate severity of pilling and grade fabrics compared to the Standard.

Schiefer Abrasion Machine—Used to test abrasion resistance of fabrics and other textile materials.

Sears Yarn Defect Scales for Knots and Slubs—Used to evaluate size of the knot or slub in a fabric and grade it compared to the standard.

Taber Abraser—Used to test abrasion resistance of fabrics and other textile materials.

Tensile Testing Machine—Used for testing tensile strength of fabrics and seam strength of garments.

The Dynamic Absorption Tester—Used for measuring the resistance of fabrics to wetting by water. It is particularly suitable for measuring the water-repellent efficacy of finishes applied to fabrics, because it subjects the treated fabrics to dynamic conditions similar to those encountered during actual use.

The Uniform Reference Scale—Used in Assessing Barré.

Thickness Guage—Used to measure thickness of textile materials.

Twist Tester—Used for testing number and direction of twists in yarns and sewing threads.

Vertical Flammability Tester—Used for testing flammability of children's sleepwear.

Washer and Dryer—Used for testing adequacy of care labels on clothing, shrinkage in laundering, any change in appearance in repeated laundering, colorfastness in laundering.

Water Flow Tester—Used to test raincoat and umbrella fabrics.

Weatherometer—Used for measuring colorfastness of textiles to sunlight and weathering.

Wrinkle Recovery Tester—Used for measuring wrinkle recovery of fabrics.

45° Angle Flammability Tester—Used to test flammability of fabrics for general clothing.

Most textile fibers are hygroscopic, that is, they have the ability to absorb or give up moisture. This moisture is picked up or absorbed by hygroscopic material from the atmosphere if the relative amount of moisture in the air is greater than that in the material. Conversely, the moisture will be given up by the material if the relative amount of moisture in the air is less than that in the material.

Under natural conditions, the amount of moisture in the air is continually changing. This results in varying the amount of moisture contained by a hygroscopic material exposed to the atmosphere, which will result in a change in the physical properties of this material. For example, cotton absorbs moisture rapidly when exposed to high humidity, and as a result, the weight of the material as well as its strength increase and other properties change. Cellulose-base manmade fibers generally show reductions in strength with corresponding increases in elongation as their moisture contents are increased. Wool fibers show a slight decrease in strength with an increase in moisture content. Practically speaking, all textile materials show increased pliability and reduced influence of static electricity with an increase in moisture content.

Therefore, in order that reliable comparisons be made among different textile materials and products, and among different laboratories, it is necessary to standardize the humidity and temperature conditions to which the textile material or product is subjected prior to and during testing. Such conditions are 65 ± 2% relative humidity and 21 ± 1°C (70 ± 2°F).

The test samples (fabrics or garments) should be left in a conditioning room with the above atmospheric condition for at least 4 hours to reach equilibrium with the standard relative humidity (RH) and temperature. Then, they should be tested under the same atmospheric conditions. If the testing is not done at standard atmospheric conditions, then this should be clearly stated in the test report, and the relative humidity and temperature at which the testing was done should be mentioned. There is a standard practice for conditioning textile materials for testing (ASTM, D-1776).

3-1-1-2 Electrical Products

Safety of electrical products is of utmost importance. Therefore, all electrical products should be tested for electrical safety, however, testing electrical safety is highly specialized and an expensive area. Therefore, most retailers have a policy that unless an electrical product is certified by a reputable third party such as

Underwriters Laboratories (UL) Inc., CSA International, ETL-Semko, etc., it will not be considered for buying. See Chapter 5, Product Safety for more on electrical product safety. Electrical products should also be tested for performance from consumers' view point, i.e., actually use test them according to the user instructions provided by the manufacturers. They should work satisfactorily for each of the functions or features mentioned in the user instructions or manual. A five speed blender, for example, should operate on five different speeds and chop and blend a variety of products. Sometimes a product functions well but may be unacceptable for aesthetic reasons. For example, we tested a white colored blender that did everything well as it claimed but as we made carrot juice in it, it's white surface developed light orange stains that could not be removed no matter how hard we tried. Thus, a perfectly working blender was not acceptable!

Instruments used for testing electrical products are:

Digital Multimeter—Used to test voltage and ampere.

Hi-Pot Tester—Used for testing leakage of electrical current or the electrical insulation.

Generator that can produce 110-240volts at 50 or 60 cycles—Used to test performance of dual voltage appliances.

According to a survey done by Discount Merchandising, when deciding to buy a certain small appliance, home electronics product, or power tool, 86 percent of respondents from U. S. and Canada rated performance as the most important quality; 80 percent of the same audience rated safety as the second most important factor (DM 1995).

3-1-1-3 Cigarette and Other Lighters

Cigarette lighters should be tested for initial and maximum flame heights, flaring, flame extinction, child resistant mechanism and structural integrity. Cigarette and other lighters should meet the requirements of ASTM F400-97 Consumer Safety Specification for Lighters.

3-1-1-4 Toys

Toys should be tested for small parts, sharp edges or corners, pinching hazard, structural integrity, age and caution labeling. ASTM has a comprehensive standard on toys (ASTM 963). Intertek Testing Services (2001) has an excellent publication on toy testing and international toy standards. Here are some of the instruments and fixtures used for toy testing. The numbers in parenthesis refer to appropriate standards.

Sharp Edge Tester # 8200—Used to determine if a product poses an unreasonable risk of injury by laceration due to sharp edges. Primarily used to test products for children under 8 years of age. (ASTM F 963, EN 71, and 16 CFR 1500.49)

Sharp Point Tester # 8210—Used to determine if a product poses a risk of injury by puncture or laceration due to sharp points. Primarily used to test products for children under 8 years of age. (ASTM F 963, EN 71, and 16 CFR 1500.48)

Small Parts Cylinder # 8215—Used to identify items that present chocking, aspiration, or ingestion hazard because of small parts. (ASTM 963, EN 71, and 16 CFR 1501)

Bite Test Clamp # 8225 (with compression discs # 8226-01 and # 8226-02)—Used to identify hazards associated with a product or a component, that has certain accessible dimensions or design configuration that would permit a child to insert a portion in mouth and break off that portion resulting in chocking hazard. (ASTM F 963, EN 71, and 16 CFR 1500.51,52, and 53)

Tension Clamp # 8220—Used to determine if projections from the main body of a product can be removed and thereby uncover an otherwise hidden hazard such as a small part, sharp point, sharp edge, etc. (ASTM F 963, EN 71, and 16 CFR 1500.51,52,53)

Pacifier Test Fixture # 8235—Used to identify pacifiers that may cause chocking or suffocation because their design permits them to enter an infant's mouth and become lodged in the throat. (ASTM F 963, EN 71, and 16 CFR 1511)

Baby Rattle Test Fixture # 8230—Used to determine if rattles may cause chocking or suffocation because their design permits them to enter an infant's mouth and become lodged in the throat. (ASTM F 963, EN 71, and 16 CFR 1510)

Supplemental Test Fixture # 8231—Used to identify non-round items that could pose a chocking or suffocation hazard. (ASTM F 963, EN 71, and 16 CFR 1500)

3-1-1-5 Dinnerware

Dinnerware should be tested for heavy metal leaching, washability in dishwasher, safe use in microwave and/or convection ovens, etc. Heavy metal leaching refers to traces of metals such as lead and cadmium leaching from subsistence carrying vessels due to improper finish or glaze and/or use of unsafe materials in manufacturing of subsistence carrying vessels. See Chapter 5, Product Safety, for more on heavy metal leaching (HML).

3-1-1-6 Ready to Assemble (RTA) or Knock Down (KD) Furniture

Such furniture should be actually assembled and the assembled piece should be evaluated for any sharp points, sharp edges, etc. and over all appearance. Also, it is important to check to see if all parts including hardware are present, because one or more missing part or hardware piece will result in incomplete assembly. It is also important to evaluate assembly instructions. Assembly instructions should also list all parts, hardwarc, and tools required to assemble the piece. Assembly instructions should be easy to understand and follow logical steps to facilitate assembly. There have been many instances where items are coming out of China or Mexico with assembly instructions translated in English from Chinese or Spanish, respectively, resulting in difficult to understand instructions in poorly written English.

3-1-1-7 Health & Beauty Care Items

These items can be tested for characteristics such as pH, viscosity, solid contents, overall appearance, etc. In addition to these characteristics, such items should be use tested by a panel of consumers. Instruments need for such testing are pH meter and viscometer.

3-1-1-8 Jewelry

Jewelry items consist of items such as chains, necklaces, rings, earrings, bracelets, etc. made out of precious metals and with or without incorporating diamonds, colored stones or pearls.

Diamonds are evaluated for color, clarity, cut and carat weight. Color of most diamonds ranges from completely colorless (most expensive) to light yellow. The completely colorless diamond is rare. If the diamond has a strong yellow fluorescence it may sell for less since this will make the diamond appear yellower in some lights than another diamond with the same color grade. The presence of blue fluorescence may make the diamond appear whiter in some lights. Some diamonds with very strong fluorescence may have "oily" or "murkey" appearance in daylight or fluorescent light. Such diamonds will sell for less than comparable diamonds without the murkey cast. If a diamond fluoresces, its true body color can be misgraded. A diamond should always be tested to see if it fluoresces or not, and to what degree, in order to color grade accurately (Matlins and Bonanno, 1995). Clarity is the degree to which a diamond is free of internal blemishes. Most diamonds contain natural inclusions. The fewer inclusions or blemishes a diamond has, the more valuable and costly it will be. Small inclusions do not affect the beauty or the appearance of a diamond. Cut is how the diamond is faceted so that it will reflect and refract light to produce the highest degree of brilliance and fire. There are five main shapes of diamonds: round, oval, emerald, pear and marquise. Carat is the weight measurement of a diamond. A carat is divided into 100 points. Therefore, a 25 point diamond weighs ¼ carat. Diamonds of the same weight can have different prices. The reason for this is quality, or the combination of color, clarity, and cut. A small diamond of the finest quality can easily be more valuable than a large diamond of lesser quality.

The key issue in inspecting low priced jewelry is not the quality of stones but whether the stones meet legal definition of a diamond or not. For a stone to be called a "diamond," it must meet Federal Trade Commission (FTC) requirement (2001).

The Gemological Institute of America (GIA) has developed a clarity and color grading scale (Figure 3-1) for diamonds that has become industry standard and is used worldwide.

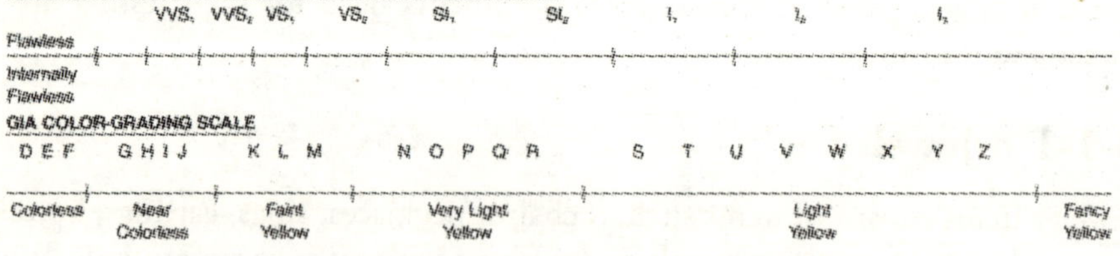

Figure 3-1 GIA Diamond Clarity and Color Grading Scale
(Reproduced with the permission of GIA)

For the quality of colored stones, color, clarity, cut and carat are important, however, the color is the most important determinant of quality in colored stones. While clarity is important and the cleaner the stone the better, flawlessness in colored stones does not usually carry the premium that it does with diamonds.

Light, pastel colored stones will require better clarity because the flaws are more readily visible in these stones. In darker toned stones the flaws may not be as important a variable because they are masked by the depth of color. Cut and proportion in colored stones are important because they affect the depth of the color and the liveliness projected by the stone. As with diamonds, weight of colored stones is measured in carats.

Pearls are evaluated for their luster, color, shape, blemishes, and size. Obviously, the higher the luster the better because the brilliance of pearls depends on luster. Generally speaking, pink color in pearls is most desirable, however, there is no 'superior' or 'inferior' pearl so far as color is concerned. It all depends on what the wearer prefers. The closest shape to the round is most desirable, but pear-shaped pearls as well as pearls of unusual form are acceptable too. Less blemish a pearl has the better, however, it is natural for pearls to have some small blemishes. The only pearls that are 100 % perfect are artificial pearls. While the size of a pearl has effect on its value, it has no effect on its quality.

Precious metal such as gold should be checked for karat content such as 14 karat, 18 karat, porosity, etc.

Some examples of jewelry specifications are shown in the Chapter 4, Standards and Specifications.

Some retailers keep "master samples" of the jewelry items in their stock assortment. A "master sample" is an item that is considered acceptable for quality and can be used as a reference standard to make "accept/reject" decisions. For example, when a shipment of a jewelry item is inspected, the samples are compared with the respective master sample and unless the samples being inspected are as good as the master sample, the shipment is not accepted. While master samples facilitate jewelry inspection, they tie down money in terms of inventory of master samples.

Here is a listing of instruments used in inspection/testing of jewelry.

<u>Following instruments and aids are used for both, diamonds and colored gemstones.</u>

Binocular Microscope with stereo magnification and adjustable zoom and lighting features—Used to inspect diamonds and colored gemstones under magnification.

Calibrated Balance/Scale—Used to weigh diamonds, gem stones, and jewelry items in grams, carats, troy ounces, and pennyweights.

Diamondlite—Diffused cool light viewing box, with translucent trays that minimize reflection. Used for color grading stones.

Fiberlite—Warm light source that is used in conjunction with a dichroscope, hand held spectroscope, refrectometer, and Chelsea filter. Also used in illuminating gemstones to view inclusions.

Leveridge Gauge—Measures stones and other items within a tenth of a millimeter.

Master Comparison Stones—GIA certified color range master stones used in determining the color of a selected diamond.

Polariscope—Used to quickly determine if a stone is singly or doubly refractive, treated or not, coated with film or not, and to spot pleochroism and diamond strain.

Presidium Multi Tester—Thermally separates diamonds, moissanite and other stimulants.

Proportionscope—Determines table percentage, pavilion depth, crown angle and height, girdle thickness and total depth.

Spectroscope—Used to measure light absorption of stones which is displayed on the visible color spectrum, and therefore, identify gemstones, whether a gemstone is treated, whether it is a synthetic, etc.

Table Gauge—It is a small clear microfilm ruler that is used to measure table percentages in tenths of a millimeter.

Ultraviolet Lamp—This is a light source that aids in the separation of natural stones from synthetics and stimulants using long and short wave length. Also used in the identification of fluorescence.

<u>Following instruments and aids are used in inspection/testing of colored gemstones.</u>

Chelsea Filter—Helps identify certain green, red, and blue stones. Also detects dyed stones.

Dichroscope—Separates colors in doubly refractive stones.

Immersion Cell—Detects enhancements, assembled stones, color zoning and inclusions.

Polaroid Filter—Hand held tool that can determine singly or doubly refractive stones. Also detects dyes in stones.

Refractometer—Indicates the specific refractive index of faceted stones.

Specific Gravity Liquids—Used to separate stones based on their buoyancy.

A listing of gem instruments suppliers is in the Chapter 10, Resources.

3-1-2 Testing for Packaging Quality

Some retailers sell merchandise through their mail order catalog and/or internet site. In such cases, quality of packaging takes on an added importance because packaging must protect the merchandise against the stress and strain of transportation and shipping. If an item does not reach a customer without breaking, then it does not matter how good the quality of that item was.

Several test methods related to packaging are listed in Chapter 4 on Standards and Specifications.

The International Safe Transit Association (ISTA) has developed test specifications for performance testing of packaged products and administers a program called "Transit Tested." Under this program testing is done according to one of several ISTA procedures in ISTA certified laboratories. For more information on packaging testing visit ISTA's web site www.ista.org

Some retailers perform drop and crush tests on their mail order and internet merchandise as follows in order to ascertain quality of packaging.

3-1-2-1 Drop Test

The packaged item is dropped on top, sides, bottom and corners from a height of 4 ½ feet onto a hard surface. If any damage results to the item, the packaging is not adequate and should be recorded as a failure. Discontinue the drop test when damage occurs, do not break more than one sample. Judgment and good common sense must be exercised when selecting an item for drop test, e.g., microwave oven, clocks, television sets, etc. should not be selected.

3-1-2-2 Crush Test

Place the package with the weakest side up. Place a weight of at least 150 pounds on the center surface of the package and leave for 10 seconds. The carton should not collapse or give enough to cause damage to the contents or allow direct pressure on the contents.

Here is a sampling plan for drop and crush tests.

Lot Size	Sample Size	Accept	Reject
2-90	3	0	1
91-500	13	1	2
501-1200	20	2	3
1201-10000	32	3	4
10001-35000	50	5	6
35001- Over 35001	80	7	8

Note: Since drop and crush tests are destructive, stop the test when you reach the rejection number.

Table 3-1 Drop and crush test sampling plan

One way to ascertain quality of packaging of mail order and internet merchandise is for the QA specialist to order some items just like an ordinary customer and see if the merchandise ordered arrives safely.

3-1-3 Reporting Test Statistics

For example, laboratory workload can be reported on a weekly basis in a tabulated form as follows.

Monday, September 09, XXXX

Lab Tests Completed Last Week

Date Received	Test Number	Supplier	Item Description	Test Started	Test Completed

Lab Tests in Progress

Date Received	Test Number	Supplier	Item Description	Test Started

Lab Tests Pending

Date Received	Test Number	Supplier	Item Description

Table 3-2 Laboratory Weekly Activity Report

The first table "Lab Tests Completed Last Week" gives a quick summary of what was accomplished during the previous week. Second table "Lab Tests in Progress" gives an idea of what is being tested and the last table "Lab Tests Pending" gives an idea of what work or test requests came in and how much back log there is.

Management reporting of testing efforts can be accomplished by reporting any one or more of the following:

Number of test projects completed for a given period of time
Number of items tested and number of items failed for a period of time, such as weekly, monthly, yearly, etc.
Average cost of testing a sample
Dollar amount tested for a period of time
Dollar amount of defective products prevented from reaching stores for a period of time

3-1-4 Sample Accountability

It is very important to establish accountability procedure for the samples. Each sample that comes in to the laboratory or is sent out for testing should be accounted for. Typically, suppliers pay for the samples for pre-purchase testing. The money for samples for post-award and customer complaint testing, typically, come from the QA budget. The sample accountability procedure should be an integral part of the laboratory operating procedure. The sample accountability procedures should also include how tested samples are disposed of. For example, some samples that fail testing may be sent back to the supplier so the supplier can see the reason for failure and be able to take corrective actions. Some samples that do not go back to the supplier but are destroyed in testing should be written-off. Those samples that were not destroyed or otherwise damaged in testing can be donated to charity.

A standard operating procedure (SOP) for laboratory operation or for outside testing should be developed and put in practice.

Some of the well known test laboratories or testing houses as they are sometimes called, are listed in the Chapter 10, Resources.

Following sites contain good information on a variety of consumer products.

www.consumerreports.org This is the site for Consumer Reports Magazine. It provides test results and product rating for a variety of consumer products.

www.consumerreview.com This site provides written consumer product reviews on a variety of consumer products.

www.consumerguide.com This site provides product reviews and buying guides for a variety of consumer products.

3-2 End-Item Inspection

Inspection here refers to visual examination of an item from a consumer's viewpoint to determine if there is anything an item has that may adversely affect its serviceability or salability. The objective of end-item inspection is to identify and prevent defective merchandise from reaching stores. The principle involved in inspection is the early detection of defects, feedback of this information to appropriate people, determination of the causes of defects, and ultimately correcting the problems and preventing those problems from happening again in the future.

A retailer has following options when it comes to end-item inspection.

3-2-1 No Inspection

If no inspection is done, little or nothing is known about a shipment. No inspection also means that next to nothing may be known about a product, and no one will be aware of any defects until that product is in the hands of the customer. Then the customer may return a defective product for a refund or may decide never to buy that product again or never to return to that store or chain. Either way, cost is increased and a loss of goodwill created, and in the long run, goodwill is invaluable. Loss of goodwill will result in the loss of repeat business. If the defective product was detected before it reached a customer, such a loss could have been avoided. Needless, to say, this alternative is not practical.

3-2-2 100% Inspection

This is the other extreme of no inspection. 100% Inspection is the inspection of every unit in a shipment. The *accept/reject* decision is not made for the entire lot or shipment, but for each unit individually, based on the results of inspecting a unit for the quality characteristic concerned. The obvious advantage of 100% inspection is that it gives a better idea of quality of a shipment than any other inspection alternative. However, generally, 100% inspection does not guarantee detection of all defects, especially when the inspection is done by human inspectors: 100% inspection is usually not 100% effective (Juran, 2003). The direct cost of 100% inspection will generally be much higher than that of any other inspection alternative. In fact, it is almost always cost prohibitive to do an effective 100 % inspection of any product. Therefore, this is also not a practical alternative.

3-2-3 Spot Checking

This represents an attempt at a compromise between no inspection at all and 100% inspection and consists of inspecting random shipments. This procedure, of course, stops some defective products from reaching customers, but it is only partially effective since many shipments are accepted without inspection. Therefore, this is also not a practical alternative.

3-2-4 Arbitrary Sampling

Under this alternative, a certain percent of a shipment is inspected and an accept/reject or pass/fail decision regarding that shipment is made, based on the inspection results of that certain percent of the shipment that was inspected. The most popular or widely used plan under this alternative is called 10% sampling. This means that regardless of the size of a shipment, 10% of that shipment is inspected and the results are used as the basis for a decision regarding the entire shipment. Although this alternative is better than the previous three alternatives, it still has some drawbacks. For some shipments or lots, 10% is too small a sample to be representative, whereas for other shipments or lots, it may be too large. Also, as with any sampling, certain risks (chances) of making a wrong decision exist. Too often, the users of arbitrary sampling have little idea of the risks inherent in their procedure, but at least, they will have some idea about product quality. However, there is a better way to gather such information, and that is statistical sampling.

3-2-5 Statistical Sampling

This inspection alternative also provides a compromise between 100% inspection and no inspection at all. Still it has certain distinct advantages. Under this method a portion of a shipment is inspected and *accept/reject* decision for the shipment is based on the inspection results of the portion of the shipment inspected. However, this method differs from arbitrary sampling in that the selection of a portion of a shipment has a statistical basis. Therefore, large shipments or lots are not over inspected; small shipments or lots are not under inspected, and most important, the risks of making a wrong decision (such as accepting a defective lot or rejecting a good lot) are known and controllable. This is usually the most practical and economical means for determining product quality. Statistical sampling has the advantage of flexibility with regard to the amount of inspection to be performed at any given time, depending on the importance of the product and apparent product quality.

Although statistical sampling is generally superior to the previous four alternatives, whenever a portion of a shipment or lot submitted for inspection is defective, some defective pieces are likely to be accepted or passed by a statistical sampling plan. Under a statistical sampling procedure, there are several sampling plans available. The risks associated with those sampling plans (probabilities of acceptance or rejection) are known or can be calculated, and then it is possible to choose a sampling plan that provides the desired degree of protection (probability of rejection) with due consideration for the various costs involved.

Statistical sampling is equally applicable to incoming inspections of shipments of raw materials or partially finished products, products at various stages of manufacture, and finished products as well as outgoing shipments.

Before we discuss statistical sampling any further, let us look at a few terms used in conjunction with statistical sampling. The definitions of these terms are taken from the Sampling Procedures and Tables for Inspection by Attributes, ANSI/ASQC Z1.4(1993). This standard was formerly known as MIL-STD-105E. The international designation of this standard is ISO 2859-1 (1999).

Sample. A sample consists of one or more units of a product drawn from a lot or batch, the units of the sample being selected at random without regard to their quality. The number of units of a product in the sample is the sample size.

Lot or Batch. The term lot or batch shall mean "inspection lot" or "inspection batch," that is, a collection of units of a product from which a sample is to be drawn and inspected to determine conformance with the acceptability criteria, and may differ from a collection of units designated as a lot or batch for other purposes (e.g., production, shipment, etc.).

Note: A shipment or a purchase order may be grouped into more than one lot for inspection purpose. Typically, a lot for inspection purpose consists of like items. If a purchase order or a shipment has three styles or models of toys, then, for inspection purpose that shipment should be divided into three lots. Similarly, if a shipment has four styles of ladies' dresses with noticeable difference in the construction, type of fabric, and price, then, for inspection purpose each style should be considered a "lot." If the merchandise for a purchase order is produced over a period of time and shipped out at two different times, each shipment would be considered a "lot."

Lot or Batch Size. The lot or batch size is the number of units of a product in a lot or batch

$$\textit{Percent defective} = \frac{\text{number of defective samples found}}{\text{number of samples inspected}} \times 100$$

Note: A defective sample can have more than one defect.

Process Average. The process average is the average percent defective of a product submitted by the supplier for original inspection. Original inspection is the first inspection of a particular quantity of a product, as distinguished from the inspection of a product that has been resubmitted after prior rejection.

AQL (Acceptable Quality Level). The AQL is the maximum percent defective that, for the purpose of sampling inspection, can be considered satisfactory as a process average while using ANSI/ASQC Z 1.4 or ISO 2859-1 sampling plans. When a retailer designates some specific value of AQL for a certain group of merchandise, he indicates to the supplier that his acceptance sampling plan will accept the great majority of the lots or batches that the supplier submits, provided the percent defective in these lots or batches is no greater than the designated value of AQL. Thus, the AQL is a designated value of percent defective that the retailer indicates will be accepted most of the time by the retailer that uses ANSI/ASQC Z 1.4 or ISO 2859-1 sampling plans.

The AQL is generally expressed in percent (%). The AQLs most widely used in the retail industry are 2.5, 4.0, and 6.5 depending on the price and product. For example, for low price products an AQL of 6.5 may be quite appropriate, however, for higher price products AQLs of 2.5 and 4.0 may be appropriate. Generally, AQLs of 4.0 and 6.5 are used for soft line, soft side luggage, jewelry, furniture with cut and sew pieces, etc. while an AQL of 2.5 is used for hard line merchandise.

3-2-5-1 Selecting a Sampling Plan

To select a sampling plan, you must know the lot size and have decided on the average percent defective you are willing to accept over the long run in the shipments, i.e. an AQL or the average quality level. Over the long run generally means at least 10 shipments or 300 samples of the same product from the same supplier. Knowing the lot size and an AQL, we can decide how many samples to inspect from that lot by using Tables 3-3 and 3-4 as explained in the following examples.

Table 3-3 gives various lot or batch sizes and sample size code letters. Table 3-4 shows how many samples to select for inspection based on the code letter chosen from Table 3-3, which in turn depends on the lot or batch size. Table 3-4 also indicates when to accept or reject a lot or batch based on the number of samples found defective and the AQL selected.

Lot or Batch Size		Sample Size Code Letter
2 to	8	A
9 to	15	B
16 to	25	C
26 to	50	D
51 to	90	E
91 to	150	F
151 to	280	G
281 to	500	H
501 to	1200	J
1201 to	3200	K
3201 to	10000	L
10001 to	35000	M

From MIL-STD-105E. The Sampling Procedures and Tables for Inspection by Attributes or ANSI/ASQ Z 1.4 The Sampling Procedures and Tables for Inspection by Attributes

Table 3-3 Sample Size Code Letters

Sample Size Code Letter	Sample Size	Acceptable Quality Level					
		2.5		4.0		6.5	
		Ac	Re	Ac	Re	Ac	Re
A	2	0	1	0	1	0	1
B	3	0	1	0	1	0	1
C	5	0	1	0	1	0	1
D	8	0	1	1	2	1	2
E	13	1	2	1	2	2	3
F	20	1	2	2	3	3	4
G	32	2	3	3	4	5	6
H	50	3	4	5	6	7	8
J	80	5	6	7	8	10	11
K	125	7	8	10	11	14	15
L	200	10	11	14	15	21	22
M	315	14	15	21	22	21	22

From MIL-STD-105E. The Sampling Procedures and Tables for Inspection by Attributes or ANSI/ASQ Z 1.4 The Sampling Procedures and Tables for Inspection by Attributes

Table 3-4 Sampling Plans

Example 1. Assume a lot size of 600 pieces and an AQL of 4.0%. Let us find, step by step, a sampling plan for this lot.

1. Look under the lot or batch size column in Table 3-3 and find the entry that corresponds to a quantity of 600. This will be the line where the lot or batch size is 501 to 1200. Go across this line to sample size code letter column. There is a letter J there.

2. In Table 3-4 look under the sample size code letter column and find the letter J. Go across the J row and into the sample size column. It indicates the sample size of 80. Then continue across the J row until you meet the 4.0 AQL column. Here there are two numbers, 7 and 8, with Ac and Re on top of them in the third top row. This means that if the number of defective samples is 7 or less out of the sample of 80, accept the lot of 600 pieces. If the number of defective samples is 8 or more out of 80 samples, then reject the lot of 600 pieces.

To summarize above, take 80 samples at random out of a lot of 600 pieces. Inspect all 80 pieces. If the number of defective pieces found is 7 or less, then accept the lot of 600 pieces. If the number of defective pieces found is 8 or more, reject the lot of 600 pieces. What has been done is a determination about the quality (acceptability or rejectability) of a lot of 600 pieces based on the inspection of 80 pieces.

Taking a random sample or taking samples at random is very important. A random sampling means that every unit or piece in a lot has an equal chance of being picked as a sample. If samples are not selected randomly, the selected group of samples won't be a good representative of the lot and that could adversely affect acceptance or rejection decision about that lot.

Changing the AQL from 4.0 to 2.5 or 6.5 for the same lot size, that is, 600 pieces in this case, will result in different sets of acceptance or rejection numbers as shown below:

2.5		4.0		6.5	
Ac	Re	Ac	Re	Ac	Re
5	6	7	8	10	11

Example 2. Assuming a lot size of 1500 pieces, let us find sampling plans for each of the following AQLs: 2.5, 4.0, and 6.5. From Table 3-3, we see that the sample size code letter will be K. From Table 3-4, the sample size for the code letter K is identified as 125. In other words, take 125 samples at random from the lot of

1500 pieces. The following are various acceptance and rejection numbers for various AQLs and the sample size of 125:

2.5		4.0		6.5	
Ac	Re	Ac	Re	Ac	Re
7	8	10	11	14	15

As can be seen from the above examples, the higher the AQL used (i. e., 2.5 Vs 4.0 and 4.0 Vs 6.5), the lower the accepted quality level and vice versa.

Please note that a lot will be considered failed when even a single "critical" defect is found. A critical defect is any defect leading to injury or fatal injury or catastrophic economic loss.

What we have discussed so far are single sampling plans. In single sampling plans, the accept/reject decision is taken based on the inspection results of sampling a lot once. There are other sampling plans called double sampling. In double sampling, the accept/reject decision is sometimes based on sampling a lot twice. A supplier feels he has been given a second chance in double sampling.

Acheson (1975), Hahn and Schilling (1975), Grant and Leavenworth (1996) and Stephens (2001) contain an excellent discussion of statistical sampling or acceptance sampling.

3-2-6 Managing Inspection

Inspections can be done at your own distribution centers (DCs) or warehouses and/or at suppliers' facilities, such as factories and/or DCs. A good balance between inspections at your DCs and at suppliers' facilities can be very effective.

3-2-6-1 In-Plant Inspections

In-plant inspections are those inspections conducted on behalf of a retailer at suppliers' facilities. Inspectors can be located strategically in various geographical areas from where they can travel to suppliers' facilities, generally, within their assigned geographical areas. Typically, a central office, such as your QA headquarters receives purchase orders and shipping information from all buyers and suppliers or has access to such information and, based on this information, schedules inspections at supplier facilities. If a supplier is going to have in-plant inspection for the first time, then, the retailer's scheduling office should give the supplier some idea of what to expect and what is involved in in-plant inspection. Each inspector gets his/her inspection schedule weekly from the inspection scheduling office. Inspectors, then, confirm their inspection schedules with suppliers, make their own travel arrangements and arrive at the suppliers' facilities at appointed day and time, perform inspections and pass on the inspection results to the scheduling office, which in turn, passes on this information to the respective buyers.

Your suppliers should know your expectations, both in terms of product quality and cooperation in scheduling and conducting in-plant inspections. It is up to the buyers to let the suppliers know that their merchandise will be inspected at their facilities before shipping. Therefore, suppliers should get in touch with QA to arrange for inspections. Suppliers should contact the in-plant inspection scheduling office and let them know when the merchandise will be ready for shipment. Your merchandise should be ready for shipment and set aside for inspection so that when an in-plant inspector shows up at an appointed time, he/she can start inspection right away by taking random samples from this shipment. Unless your shipment is set aside, the in-plant inspector can not take proper random sample of your shipment. Once the inspector selects the samples, the supplier personnel should help the inspector in bringing those samples to the inspection area, unpack them, and pack them after inspection. The inspection area should be well lighted and clean. The inspector should go over his/her findings of inspection with the supplier management representative so that information is passed on to appropriate supplier personnel for whatever action is necessary. Therefore, it is important that a supplier management representative is available when an in-plant inspection is scheduled.

Most retailers have a policy that if a shipment is not ready for inspection when an in-plant inspector shows up at an appointed time for inspection, the supplier is charged for the inspector's travel expense and part of the wages for wasting time because that inspector was non-productive. Also, most retailers assess a certain charge to the supplier when a shipment fails an inspection. There are two reasons for this. One, most likely the in-plant inspector will have to come back to inspect the rejected shipment after the supplier has taken corrective action. Second, to discourage suppliers from using retailer's inspectors in lieu of their own inspection efforts. If such charges are not assessed, some suppliers may begin to think and develop an attitude "why should I spend my resources inspecting merchandise for my customers since their inspectors will come for inspection anyway?"

If a supplier is being visited the first time for inspection, then, the in-plant inspector should brief the supplier about what is expected of the supplier. An example of a new supplier briefing is in the Appendix II, Standard Operating Procedures.

In-plant inspectors should be located in such a way that they do not spend more than 50 % of their time traveling, otherwise, it would be inefficient use of the resources. In-plant inspectors should be relocated every three years in order to prevent them from becoming complacent and too friendly with the suppliers.

A standard operating procedure (SOP) for conducting in-plant inspections is outlined in the Appendix II. An SOP should be made as detailed or as short and concise as necessary.

The in-plant inspection scheduling function will be necessary even if in-plant inspection is outsourced. A core scheduling staff will be necessary to coordinate inspection work and inspection results with the inspection company as well as the suppliers and the buying/procurement staff.

3-2-6-2 DC (Distribution Center) Inspections

To accomplish inspections at your DCs, typically, the QA supervisor at a DC reviews daily receipt of shipments and decides which shipments to inspect and farm out the inspection work among inspectors. Typically, a shipment is not "received" in the DC inventory until QA releases that shipment. As a check and balance, many retailers have a system, where even if the DC wanted to "receive" a shipment that was not released by QA, the system will not allow the DC to do that. Unless a shipment is "received" by the DC, it will not show up in the inventory. In order to prevent shipments being held for inspection for too long, it may be necessary to have a policy where if a shipment can not be inspected within 48 hours of receipt, it must be released by QA.

Inspection area should be clean, uncluttered, and well lit. Without sufficient light, it is easy to miss defects. A standard operating procedure (SOP) for DC inspections is outlined in the Appendix II.

Typically, inspections at the distribution centers are not outsourced; however, it can be done.

3-2-6-3 Failed/Rejected Shipments

When the inspection results indicate that a shipment did not pass the inspection, is it a failed shipment or a rejected shipment? There is a distinct difference between the terms "failed" and "rejected." This difference stems from the fact that the ultimate decision whether to accept a shipment or not is up to the respective buyer, unless it involves a safety related deficiency. A "failed' shipment may be accepted due to some merchandising considerations. When a decision is made not to accept a "failed' shipment, then it becomes a "rejected' shipment. It is important for everyone in the company to understand this difference and use these terms appropriately.

Along with the information that is conveyed to the buyer about a failed shipment, the buyer should also be notified about various options the buyer has concerning that failed shipment. These options are:

a. Accept the shipment as is
b. Reject the shipment and cancel the purchase order
c. If the shipment is at the retailer's DC

    (i) Ask QA inspectors to screen the failed shipment, i.e., inspect the failed shipment 100% and separate good from the bad. Accept only good pieces and return all bad pieces or write off the bad pieces and charge the supplier for the write-off amount. If a decision is taken to choose this option, bear in mind that while QA inspectors are busy screening this shipment, other shipments will go uninspected in the meanwhile, resulting in reduced inspection coverage (more on inspection coverage in 3-2-6-8). Normally, it is not worthwhile to screen a shipment which has a percent defective higher than 8 to 10 percent. A decision will also have to be made whether to charge the supplier for the screening. What is happening in the screening is that the retailer's QA is doing the work that the supplier should have done. Normally, QA provides a cost estimate to the buyer for screening a failed shipment. The buyer checks with the supplier, and if the supplier is willing to pay for the screening, then only screening is undertaken. Otherwise, the failed shipment is returned to the supplier.

(ii) Ask the supplier to send personnel to the retailer's DC to perform the screening and upon completion of the screening, re-inspect the shipment.

(iii) Return the shipment to the supplier for corrective actions. Re-inspect this shipment after it is received back.

d. If the shipment is at a supplier's facility, ask the supplier to correct the deficiencies and reschedule the in-plant inspection.

3-2-6-4 Standard Inspection Procedures (SIPs)

Standard inspection procedures (SIPs) should be developed for various products inspected. Whether inspection is outsourced or conducted in-house, each inspector should have a copy of applicable SIPs for guidance and quick reference. The SIPs should be periodically reviewed and revised if necessary to reflect changes in product features, standards, regulations, etc. Examples of such SIPs for several products are shown in the Appendix III. These procedures outline step by step how to inspect an item and what to look for. SIPs also help each QA inspector to inspect each item the same way. Such consistency in inspection work is necessary for the accuracy and validity of the inspection results.

Some companies classify product defects as to minor or major. It does not make sense for a retailer to classify defects because from the consumer's point of view, a defect is a defect. If an item has a minor flaw that a consumer may not object to, then it is better not to consider that item defective rather than classifying that flaw as a minor flaw and define how many minor flaws make a major flow, and then trying to decide whether that item is acceptable or not. In order to be effective, it is better to keep defect scoring criteria simple.

While standard inspection procedures (SIPs) should clearly define defects, the inspectors should be trained to ask themselves a question when seeing a fault in an item, "would I buy this item the way it is?" If the answer is "yes," then the item is not defective and it is acceptable. If the answer is "no," then the item is defective and is not acceptable.

In addition to quality, some retailers also monitor supplier performance in terms of whether the supplier is complying with stated requirements or not. These requirements can be color, size breakdown of shipment, labeling, packaging, etc. Any failure to meet one or more of these requirements is considered non-conformance. It is possible that a shipment is acceptable for quality but fails for non-conformance. In such a case, the buyer will have to decide whether non-conformance is something that can be lived with or not. What constitutes defects and what constitutes non-conformance should be spelled out in SIPs.

A copy of applicable SIPs should be given to suppliers and they should be asked to perform inspection of your merchandise using your SIPs. This way, both, your suppliers and your QA inspectors would be accomplishing inspections in the same manner, which will make it easier to compare inspection results. SIPs also facilitate communication.

Also, it is advisable to have your suppliers use the same sampling plans as you to inspect merchandise to be shipped to you but use lower AQL. For example, if you are using an AQL of 4.0, your supplier should use an AQL of 2.5 to inspect merchandise to be shipped to you and if it passes supplier's own inspection, then when your inspector inspects the same merchandise using 4.0 AQL, it will almost always pass the inspection.

Defect characteristics guide for a variety of products are in the Appendix III, Standard Inspection Procedures (SIPs).

Wingate, Gillespie, and Barry (1984) provide a wealth of information on what to look for in a variety of consumer products.

3-2-6-5 Inspection Efficiency

Inspection efficiency can be measured in terms of the number of samples inspected per hour. While reviewing such figures, keep in mind that the time it takes to inspect a sample depends on the product. For example, it takes a lot longer to inspect a stereo system then to inspect a shirt. Therefore, the number of samples inspected per hour will vary a great deal from product to product. Also, bear in mind that it takes time to locate a shipment, select samples, bring samples to the inspection area, unpack samples and repack them after inspection, and filling out an inspection report. Usually, all such times are captured under "administrative time". The time it takes to inspect an item is considered inspection time. Inspection time and administrative time for each DC inspector should be captured every week. In addition to these times, travel time should be captured for in-plant inspectors on a weekly basis. Typically, administrative time should be less than inspection time. If administrative time is higher than inspection time, then, that indicates that inspectors are spending too much time locating, unpacking and packing samples, and filling out inspection reports. This may be due to factors beyond inspectors' control, and it may be time to review inspection process and procedures. While there are no industry averages for the number of samples inspected per hour, the Table 3-5 shows such figures based on this author's experience.

Inspection efficiency is an indication of inspection productivity and therefore, should be of concern to QA management, regardless whether inspection is conducted in-house or outsourced.

Product Category	No. of Samples Inspected per Hour
Ashtrays, Lighters	33
Candy, Cookies, Nuts[1]	30
Liquor and Spirits[1]	23
Carbonated Drinks[1]	27
Oral Hygiene	26
Electrical Hair Care/Hygiene Supplies	23
Shaving Supplies	26
Bath, Toiletries, Soap	26
Cosmetics, Perfumes[2]	15
Laundry Supplies, Foot/Shoe Care Supplies[1]	32
Sanitary Items	11
Toiletries, OTC Drugs[1]	36
Sunglasses, Eyewear	15
Watches	17
Jewelry	12
Leather Goods	12
School/Office Supplies	20
Office Equipment	12
Stationery	50
Seasonal Decorations	17
Men's Clothing	19
Men's Accessories	30
Ladies' Clothing	20
Boys' Clothing	23
Girls' Clothing	23
Infants' & Toddlers' Clothing	21
Footwear	21
Linens & Domestics	11
Dinnerware/Flatware	15
Kitchenware (Non-electrical)	12
Giftware	14
Major Appliances	7
Traffic Appliances	9
Furniture	7
Hardware and Tools	14
Luggage	9
Outdoor Living	14
Home Furnishing	9
Sporting Goods/Camping Supplies	12
Toys, Games, Bicycles	14
Home Electronics	8

Notes:

1- These items may require inspection to see if they leak or have dented containers, or are beyond their expiry date.
2- These items may require taking an item out of the box for inspection and putting it back in the box after inspection. The inspection could be for any leakage from the container, dent or damage to the container, or labels, cautions, instructions, etc.

Table 3-5 Number of Samples Inspected per Hour

3-2-6-6 Inspection Results

Typically, inspection results are captured for each inspector on a weekly basis. Then, they are consolidated by each DC. This gives an idea about productivity of each inspector and each DC. A typical summary may look like the following:

Week of 11 Feb. XX

Weekly Activity Report, Mr./Ms. ________________, DC1

No. of lots inspected	80
No. of lots failed for quality	5
No. of lots failed for non-conformance	2
No. of samples inspected	400
No. of samples defective	50
Percent defective	12.5
$ amount inspected	1,234,000
$ amount failed for quality	300,000
$ amount failed for non-conformance	100,000
No. of inspection hours	30
Administrative hours	8
Personal leave (hours)	2

Table 3-6 Individual Weekly Activity Report

These results can be summarized for each month and for each year.

Inspection results can be summarized to reflect a supplier's performance. A typical inspection summary for a supplier for a given period may look as follows:

ABC Company- Inspection Results for January 1-31, XXXX	
AQL	4.0
Number of lots (shipments) inspected	10
Number of lots (shipments) failed for quality	2
Number of shipments failed for non-conformance	3
% lots failed for quality	20.0
% lots failed for non-conformance	30.0
$ amount inspected	12,864,000
$ amount failed for quality	1,587,435
$ amount failed for non-conformance	2,600,798
% $ amount failed for quality	12.3
% $ amount failed for non-conformance	20.2
Number of samples inspected	800
Number of samples found defective	35
% defective	4.4
Upper Limit %	6.1

Table 3-7 Supplier Quality Summary

3-2-6-7 Upper Limit

Upper limit is a statistical calculation of % defective based on the number of samples inspected and the AQL used, as follows:

$$\text{Upper Limit (UL)} = AQL + 3\sqrt{AQL\,(100-AQL)/n}$$

Where n = number of samples inspected for a given period.

When the % defective is higher than the (UL) upper limit two to three times in a row, it is an indication that the supplier's process is not within statistical control and that there may be assignable causes for defects. By addressing those causes, the process can be brought back within statistical control, and therefore, the resulting shipments will have a higher probability of acceptance than those shipments that came from a process that was not in statistical control.

If % defective is less than the UL, then the process is considered to be in statistical control and the variation is considered normal variation.

Upper limit in other words is a flag or an alarm. For detailed discussion of the concept of the UL, please see Grant and Leavenworth (1996).

While various retailers have different standards to consider who is a poor quality supplier or when to start taking action, in this author's opinion, action is warranted:

a. When more than two shipments from a supplier in a row fail inspection, and/or
b. When the % defective of a supplier for a given period of time exceeds the Upper Limit twice in a row.

QA specialists should be monitoring performance of the suppliers within their respective categories, on a continuous basis and as soon as a supplier meets one of the above conditions, a letter should be sent to the buyer, requesting that the supplier be informed and corrective actions requested. Another alternative is for QA to contact the supplier directly informing him of your concern with his performance and asking for some corrective actions, along with a copy of this letter to the buyer to keep the buyer informed. Having sent such letter(s), the QA specialist should follow-up on it and if necessary elevate matters to higher level.

3-2-6-8 Inspection Coverage

There is always the question of how much to inspect? One way to measure this is called inspection coverage. Inspection coverage is simply how much is being bought in a given category versus how much is inspected, and expressed in percentage. For example, if a retailer is buying $ 1,000 million worth merchandise over a year and out of that $ 400 million worth merchandise is inspected then the overall inspection coverage is 40% (400/1000). However, if out of $ 1,000 million, if inspectable merchandise is worth $ 700 million, then true inspection coverage is 57% (400/700). Inspection coverage is how much inspectable merchandise is inspected out of how much is bought or procured.

Inspectable merchandise is that merchandise which lends itself for visual inspection. For example, clothing, small kitchen appliances, personal care and grooming appliances, sporting and camping goods, home entertainment electronics, toys, shoes, luggage, jewelry, are inspectable. On the other hand, tobacco, cosmetics, health & beauty products, household cleaning supplies, beverages, photo films, are considered not inspectable, except for leakage, labeling and packaging.

Breakdown of this inspection coverage by various categories may look as follows:

	$ Amount in millions		Inspection
	Procured	Inspected	Coverage %
Children's Wear	70	60	85.7
Men's Wear	50	15	30.0
Ladies' wear	100	60	60.0
Linens & Domestic	70	30	42.9
Appliances	200	100	50.0
Sporting Goods	100	50	50.0
Shoes	30	20	66.7
Luggage	30	25	83.3
Jewelry	50	40	0.0
Total	700	400	57.1

Table 3-8 Inspection Coverage by the Category of Merchandise

There is no standard as to how much inspection coverage is good or adequate. Each retailer does what he/she feels comfortable with. To a great degree, inspection coverage depends on the quality of suppliers a retailer deals with. Obviously, poor quality suppliers will require more inspection coverage compared to good quality suppliers. Another factor to consider is the amount of private label and/or house brand merchandise a retailer carries. With higher proportion of private label and house brand merchandise higher inspection coverage makes sense, while with higher proportion of national and well known brand merchandise, lower inspection coverage makes sense. Each retailer finds her/his own comfort level in this regard.

Regardless of the level of inspection coverage, inspection function should be managed effectively to get the most out of money spent for inspections. This means that those suppliers with poor quality should receive more/frequent inspections than those suppliers with better quality. Thus, supplier quality history (quality performance), such as shown in Table 3-7 is very important in scheduling inspections.

3-2-6-9 Inspection Charges to Suppliers

For an inspection program to be effective there has to be a "cause and effect" mechanism in place. It is not unusual for some suppliers to think that "my retail customer is going to inspect merchandise shipped by my company so why should I spend my time and efforts (money) inspecting merchandise?" Therefore, these suppliers slack-off in their quality assurance efforts. To prevent this from happening, most retailers charge their suppliers for their time and efforts when a shipment fails QA inspection. Typically, such charges comprise the wages (including fringe benefits) of the inspector plus some flat fee for cost of administration, i.e., notifying buyer of the failure, preparing paper work to return shipment back to the supplier, scheduling re-inspection, etc. Here is a formula for calculating how much to charge back to the supplier.

[Number of hours it took to inspect a shipment that failed x Hourly wages including fringe benefits of the inspector] + Flat administrative fee = Charge back to the supplier

If the shipment is failed at a supplier's facility, then the travel expense for that inspector is also added to the above charge. Travel expenses will include hotel and meal expenses, airfare, car rental, any highway tolls, parking fee, etc.

If an inspection was scheduled at a supplier's facility and when the inspector shows up, the shipment is not ready for the inspector to inspect, it is a waste of time for that inspector. Many retailers charge their suppliers for such an incident, called a futile visit.

The dollar amount charged back to a supplier for failed shipments can also be an indicator of quality performance of that supplier because the higher the shipment failures, the higher the charges back to the supplier.

For some retailers, the amount charged back to suppliers for quality failures practically pays for the travel expenses of their in-plant inspectors.

3-2-6-10 Comparability Checks

It is very important that quality assurance inspection be consistent from an inspector to inspector, regardless of whether one is an in-plant inspector or a distribution center inspector. This is a difficult task, however, with the training of QA inspectors and use of continuous review of their performance, such consistency can be achieved.

After an inspector finishes inspecting a lot, his/her supervisor should inspect the same lot and use the following formula to see if both of them are in agreement or not. Or, the supervisor should take the inspection results of two inspectors who inspected the same lot, and using the same formula, see if the finding of these two inspectors are comparable (consistent) or not. Such comparability checks should be performed on each inspector at least once a month.

Here is the formula used to determine whether two inspection results are comparable or not.

$$Z = \frac{P_1 - P_2}{\sqrt{[N_1P_1(1-P_1) + N_2P_2(1-P_2)]/N_1N_2}}$$

where

P_1 = % defective found by the supervisor or one inspector
P_2 = % defective found by the inspector or the person being checked
N_1 = sample size of the supervisor or one inspector
N_2 = sample size of the inspector or another person being checked

Comparability Check Formula

If Z = more than 1.96 (regardless of whether it is + or -), there is 95 % probability that comparability between the inspection results of two persons does not exist, or the results are not comparable. If Z = 1.96 or less (regardless of whether it is + or -), there is 95 % probability that comparability between the inspection results of two persons does exist, or the results are comparable.

Example 1: The inspector's sample size is 200 and she found 5 defects. The supervisor's sample size is 200 and she found 20 defects. Are these inspection results comparable?

$P_1 = (20 \div 200) = .10$
$P_2 = (5 \div 200) = .025$
$N_1 = 200$
$N_2 = 200$

$$Z = \frac{.10 - .025}{\sqrt{[20\,(.90) + 5\,(.975)]/200 \times 200}}$$

$$Z = \frac{.075}{\sqrt{(18 + 4.875)/40000}}$$

$$Z = \frac{.075}{\sqrt{.0006}}$$

$$Z = \frac{.075}{.0244949}$$

Z = 3.06 Since Z = 3.06, which is greater than 1.96, there is 95 % probability that the inspection results are not comparable.

Example 2: The inspector's sample size is 200 and she found 14 defects. The supervisor's sample size is 80 and she found 5 defects. Are these inspection results comparable?

$P_1 = (5 \div 80) = .0625$
$P_2 = (14 \div 200) = .07$
$N_1 = 80$
$N_2 = 200$

$$Z = \frac{.0625 - .07}{\sqrt{[12.5\,(.9375) + 5.6\,(.93)]/80x200}}$$

$$Z = \frac{-.0075}{\sqrt{(11.7188 + 5.208)/16000}}$$

$$Z = \frac{-.0075}{\sqrt{.0011}}$$

$$Z = \frac{-.0075}{.033166} = -0.226$$

Since Z = -0.226, which is less than 1.96, there is 95 % probability that the inspection results are comparable.

There are a number of reasons for inspection results to be not comparable.

a. It is quite possible that the inspector did not take a random sample from a shipment.
b. It is possible that the inspector's defect scoring criteria is not the same as others.
c. Combination of the above two.

In the case of non-comparability, the supervisor and the inspector can discuss the areas of improvement for the inspector, by analyzing inspection results, i.e. defects scored and how the samples were selected.

The inspection management should regularly conduct such tests and monitor inspection results of all the inspectors to make sure that some inspectors are not too critical or too lax in defect scoring. The key in managing an inspection function is consistency of defect scoring from an inspector to inspector. It is of utmost importance to "calibrate" defect scoring criteria from inspector to inspector. It also helps to bring all inspectors together once a year for a day or two to go over quality procedures and practices, including specifications. Meeting face to face also fosters team spirit and camaraderie.

3-2-6-11 Inspection Economics

The cost of inspection can be measured in terms of one or more of the following:

a. Average cost of inspecting a sample
b. Average cost of inspecting a shipment
c. Average cost of finding a defective sample
d. Average cost of rejecting a shipment
e. Total defective $ amount prevented from reaching stores per year vs. $ amount expended in inspection efforts per year

3-2-7 Advantages and Disadvantages of End-Item Inspection

One criticism often leveled against the end-item inspection is that while end-item inspection based on statistical sampling is effective in identifying and preventing defective merchandise from reaching stores and in improving quality of merchandise through appropriate feedback of information and corrective actions on suppliers' part, it is after the fact. That is, the merchandise is already made. Therefore, even though defective merchandise is prevented from reaching stores, the retailer is out of that merchandise. Repairing merchandise already made or replacing rejected merchandise is more expensive than making defect-free merchandise in the first place. Therefore, the argument goes, it is better to take a pro-active approach to quality than end-item inspection. What follows are several pro-active approaches.

3-3 Supplier Quality System Audit

An audit is defined as an independent, structured, and reported check to see that something is as it should be. An audit may examine any portion of the management control spectrum, including financial, environmental, and quality aspects of business and government (Arter 2003).

Quality audit is the systematic, independent, and documented process for obtaining audit evidence and evaluating it objectively to determine the extent to which agreed criteria are fulfilled (ISO 9001:2000, 3.9.1).

Supplier quality system audit is performed for a number of reasons as follows:

a. For a prospective supplier, a quality system audit can provide information about the quality procedures and practices and their effectiveness. Such information can be helpful in deciding whether to buy from that supplier or not.

b. If a current supplier has poor quality performance, a quality system audit of this supplier may identify some areas for improvement.

c. If a current supplier is a good quality supplier and is being considered for certification, then it makes sense to audit that supplier's quality system to verify whether good quality is a result of systematic, well thought out efforts or just sheer good luck.

If suppliers have effective process controls in place, then, it stands to reason that resulting products will be good quality products.

3-3-1 Supplier Quality System Requirements

Supplier quality audits are generally performed against one of the following requirements:

Supplier's own quality policy and procedures
A retailer's quality requirements
Some third party requirements such as ISO 9000. ISO 9000 standards are discussed in Chapter 4, Standards and Specifications.

Here are some points to be considered while evaluating a supplier's quality system.

a. Is there an established quality control program? Is it in writing and current? Are production personnel familiar with the program? Is there a requirement for quality training?
b. Are there adequate and appropriate inspection tools, fixtures, gages, and instruments? Are they controlled, inspected, and calibrated in accordance with a written procedure? Are appropriate records kept? Is there traceability for critical materials? Are rejected materials, components, sub-assemblies and finished goods segregated and controlled?
c. What type of in-process quality control procedures does this supplier have in place? Are they adequate?
d. Does the supplier under evaluation exercise control over their supplier's quality? Are there visits made to key materials suppliers and sub-contractors to assure appropriate quality control in place? Are there provisions for identifying materials so that traceability can be maintained?
e. Is there adequate inspection and testing of incoming materials? Are selected suppliers granted certification which exempts their materials from incoming inspection and test so as to reduce the cost of quality. If so, is there adequate surveillance exercised over the quality of such material to assure that the quality level of these suppliers continues to remain at an acceptable level?

There are four phases of a quality system audit.

Preparation
Performance
Reporting, and
Closure

3-3-2 Preparation

Preparation phase starts once a decision is taken to audit the quality system of a supplier. Preparation begins by letting the supplier know about your intentions to visit them to audit their quality system and the reason why, and tentatively deciding mutually convenient date(s), and identifying the lead auditor and the audit team. The audit team consists of two to four individuals depending on the size of the supplier's facility. A copy of supplier's quality manual is requested so that the audit team can review supplier's quality policy and procedures before showing up at the supplier's facilities. Preparation also includes collecting and reviewing data on supplier's quality performance. Audit is never conducted by a single person because a single person can introduce his/her bias into the conduct of audit and audit findings. Having two to four individuals in an audit team helps objectivity of the audit. One of the team members should be designated as the lead auditor. It helps a great deal in performing an effective audit if the lead auditor has auditing experience and some professional qualifications such as a certification in quality auditing from the American Society for Quality or an ISO 9000 auditor certification from a recognized body.

3-3-3 Performance

Performance phase of the audit includes an opening meeting with the supplier management at the facility to be audited, actual conduct of the audit and closing meeting. Audit scope and objectives are discussed in the opening meeting and general schedule or timetable for audit is established. Actual conduct of the audit involves reviewing supplier's quality procedures and practices, reviewing and verifying records and corrective actions, interviewing some employees regarding supplier's quality procedures and practices, etc. Audit findings are presented to the supplier management in the closing meeting and some tentative agreement is reached on when those things that need to be addressed will be addressed including corrective actions. A draft copy of the audit report is given to the supplier management in the closing meeting.

3-3-4 Reporting

The reporting phase of an audit simply involves sending supplier management an official audit report with a cover letter requesting that the supplier address those items that need to be addressed and respond in writing about their plan for addressing those items. Results of an audit are generally reported as finding(s), observation(s), and comment(s). A *finding* is a statement of facts regarding serious non-compliance with established policies, procedures, instructions, drawings or other official documents; a serious control deficiency that has or can result in a condition adverse to quality. An *observation* is an item of objective evidence which suggests a finding; a detected program weakness, which, if not corrected, will result in a degradation of product or service quality. An observation is less serious than a finding. A *comment* is simply an aspect offered for management's attention. It can be good or bad.

3-3-5 Closure

The closure phase of auditing involves evaluating actions taken by the supplier to address audit findings. Such evaluation may include visiting the supplier again to verify that the actions taken and improvements are effective. Once you are satisfied that the supplier has effectively addressed all audit findings an audit is considered "closed" with a letter to the supplier indicating that you are satisfied with the steps they have taken and that this audit is considered closed.

Here are two examples of supplier quality system audits reports. Obviously, the names of the companies and individuals have been changed to protect their identities.

SUPPLIER QUALITY SYSTEM AUDIT REPORT
XX-002

DATES OF AUDIT: April 10-12, XXXX

COMPANY: ABC Corporation
1501 Any Street
Any Town, XY 12345

PRINCIPAL CONTACT: Ms. PQR, Director of Corporate Quality

AUDIT TEAM representing XYZ Corporation: Mr. DEF, Director of Quality Assurance
and Lead Auditor
Ms. JKL, Quality Auditor

PURPOSE OF THE AUDIT: To evaluate the effectiveness of the quality procedures and practices of ABC Corporation.

SCOPE: ABC Corporation's quality system at the facilities in Any Town, XY.

KEY DOCUMENTS: ABC Corporation's Corporate Quality Manual
ANSI/ASQ 9001-XXXX Quality management systems—Requirements
XYZ Corporation's Supplier Quality Assistance Manual

KEY PRODUCTS: Men's shirts and trousers

OVERALL ASSESSMENT: ABC corporation is a privately owned company. Established in 1967 in Any Town, XY, the company has six facilities in Any Town, XY, two in the Dominican Republic, a distribution center in Boom Town, TN, and the marketing office in Atlanta, GA. ABC corporation has one centralized cutting operation in Any Town, XY for the eight sewing facilities. ABC corporation employs approximately 2,400 people spread over ten facilities. ABC corporation's key customers include some large well-known retailers and branded apparel manufacturers.

From December 1, XXXX through March 31, XXXX, XYZ corporation inspected 3489 samples of both short and long sleeve shirts and found 100 samples defective, resulting in a 2.9 % defective rate. The Pareto analysis of the defects found is at the end of this report. The audit team inspected 10 shirts and found one shirt defective.

ABC corporation has all the elements of a quality system in place except cost of quality as evidenced by ISO 9001 registration, enthusiastic and knowledgeable staff who love what they do, and solid top management support and Ms. PQR, the Corporate Quality Director, reports directly to the president of the company. However, the quality system can be made more effective by addressing the following findings.

FINDINGS

1. Review of just one month's end-item daily audit data for the month of March 'XX for XYZ corporation indicates % defective ranging from a low of 5.0% to a high of 35.0%! This is a clear indication of lack of process controls within manufacturing processes. Also, it is interesting to note that this level of defectives is found after 100% end-item inspection at the end of the line.

2. Personnel assigned to 100% inspection at the end of the sewing modules are thread trimmers and 100% inspectors. There are no assigned quality personnel conducting in-process inspections, however, the supervisor inspects five shirts for each operator per day. The current system can be made more effective by assigning quality in-process inspectors to identify manufacturing errors at the point of commission. For example, after 100% inspection, a random sampling of one of the non-conforming product containers contained 23 defective shirts. Eight of the shirts had misaligned pockets. Both pocket and button attachment is performed very early in the process. These operations directly affect the pocket alignment. If these defects were pinpointed before the manufacturing process is completed, rework and/or irregulars could be decreased significantly, consequently reducing the manufacturing costs.

3. Between quality assurance and production, considerable information (data) is captured, summarized, and reviewed on a daily and weekly basis, however, there was no evidence of trend analysis of any of the data. Without trend analysis it is not possible to know whether quality is improving, staying the same, or declining. Also, without trend analysis it is not possible to determine effectiveness of quality improvement efforts. It would be beneficial for ABC corporation to identify no more than four or five elements such as seconds %, repair %, % defective based on end of the line 100% inspection, and % defective based on end of the line audit and plot them on a daily basis on a chart. By doing this for at least a month a trend may emerge which can be very insightful. Sharing this information with the entire workforce by placing these charts on the wall at prominent places within the ABC corporation factory will encourage the workforce to do better.

4. The auditors did not see any evidence of ABC corporation having a cost of quality system in place. An effective cost of quality system can help not only identify areas for improvement but help prioritize them. Without having an effective cost of quality system in place effectiveness of quality improvement efforts cannot be determined.

5. There are some inconsistencies between forms in the quality procedures versus those being used on the floor. For example, in the QOP-QA-0133 Cutting Inspection Report, FM-QOP-QA-0133-1 shows the date 10/1/96 while the same form used on the floor shows the date 11/15/00. In the same QOP, The Cutting Inspection Checklist shows effective date of 5/4/99 while the same form used on the floor shows effective date of 6/28/99. This shows that the forms used on the floor are updated versions of the forms in

the quality procedures. According to the internal QC auditor, this was one of the findings in his internal audit last December, and here it is almost mid April XXXX and it has not been corrected. While not a major problem, this shows lack of adequate internal control and poor response to an internal audit finding. We were informed that this is not a solitary incident.

OBSERVATIONS

1. Shading of fabric rolls is currently performed visually. Evaluating shade of a fabric visually does not provide any hard data, is subjective, and makes communication of shade variance with the fabric supplier very difficult if not impossible. There are a number of instruments available for measuring shade of fabrics which provide quantitative data and takes subjectivity out of shade evaluation. It may be beneficial for ABC corporation in the long run to begin instrumental shade evaluation of fabrics, collect data on shade variation, do a trend analysis, and then, if necessary, approach fabric manufacturers for reduction in shade variation. Also, it would be beneficial to pursue quantitative shade specifications by the ABC corporation.

2. A random sampling of personnel folders indicated documented training by qualified personnel. With this training and current work instructions at each workstations, it is baffling to the auditors why the end-item quality level is not lower. For example, on 11 April XX, at the end-item inspection of a lot (shipment) of shirts for XYZ corporation, 50 shirts were inspected and the lot was rejected with 6 shirts defective resulting in 12.0 % defective.

DEF
Lead Auditor
Director of Quality Assurance
XYZ Corporation

PARETO ANALYSIS
December 1, XXXX through March 31, XXXX

Defect	Quantity	% of Total Defects
Shading	19	18.3
Open seams	18	17.3
Misweaves	13	12.5
Misaligned pockets	9	8.6
Stains	9	8.6
Misplaced pocket flap	8	7.7
Pleat at pocket flap	5	4.8
Uneven shoulder loops	5	4.8
Broken buttons	4	3.9
Uneven collar points	4	3.9
Skipped stitches	4	3.9
Misplaced pencil pocket	2	1.9
Misplaced cuff button	2	1.9
Black thread inside collar	2	1.9
Total	104	100.0

Note: The number of defects are more than the number of defective shirts because a shirt can have more than one defect.

EXPLANATION OF TERMS

FINDING: A statement of fact regarding serious noncompliance with established policy, procedures, instructions, drawings, or other applicable documents; a serious control deficiency that has or can result in a condition adverse to quality.

OBSERVATION: An item of objective evidence which supports a finding; a detected program weakness, which, if not corrected, will result in a degradation of product or service quality. Observation is less serious than a finding.

COMMENT: An aspect offered for management's attention.

Report 3-1 ABC Corporation Quality System Audit Report

SUPPLIER QUALITY AUDIT REPORT
XX-041

DATES OF AUDIT: August 23-25, XXXX

COMPANY: RST, Inc.
Household Products Division
P. O. Box XXX. Highway Y North
Big Town, YZ 38635

PRINCIPAL CONTACTS: Mr. SUV, Quality Assurance Manager
Mr. BCD, Plant Manager

AUDIT TEAM representing XYZ Corporation: Mr. DEF, Director of Quality Assurance and Lead Auditor
Ms. JKL, Quality Auditor
Mr. MRQ, Quality Auditor
Mr. GHI, Quality Auditor

PURPOSE OF THE AUDIT: To evaluate effectiveness of the quality procedures and practices of the Household Products Division, RST, Inc.

SCOPE: RST Inc.'s quality system at the facilities in Big Town, YZ.

KEY DOCUMENTS: RST Inc.'s Corporate Quality Manual
Quality Manual of Household Products Division, RST Inc.
ANSI/ASQ 9001-XXXX Quality management systems—Requirements
XYZ Corporation's Supplier Quality Assistance Manual

KEY PRODUCTS: Kitchen centers, stand mixers, juicers, toasters, humidifiers, and injection molded plastic parts such as housings for these appliances.

OVERALL ASSESSMENT: While elements of a quality system are in place and the Household Products Division of RST Inc. has an excellent quality history as a supplier to XYZ corporation, the quality system can be made more effective by addressing the following findings and observations.

FINDINGS

1. Incoming material inspections (IMI) are not fully effective. Supporting observations from receiving inspection records and suppliers' history records review in IMI follow:

   a. Part # 778330-826 from one supplier was inspected on 3rd, 5th, 13th, and 22nd August by IMI with four lots failed; however, the last two lot failures occurred in-process, after IMI inspections, which accepted those two lots.

b. The sample size used by IMI were incorrect. The QA manual's IMI procedure 4.2.4 require application of a C=0 sampling plan. The proper sample size for the quantity received on the last lot inspected (lot size 2432 each) was 42 each. The sample size used was 32 each.

2. There are no internal quality audits. Internal audits of plant quality system are essential to ensure the system is functioning effectively, that written procedures are followed and that those procedures are effective.
3. Test equipment used in Finished Goods audit for testing hi-pot, leakage current, and power (watts) on humidifiers and blenders were not calibrated. Periodic and regular calibration of test equipment is essential to assure accuracy and reliability of the test results.

4. Currently, there are no written procedures or work instructions for:

   a. Finished goods Audit—Corrective Actions Procedure
   b. In-process Quality Control
   c. Corrective/Preventive Action Assurance
   d. Parts Revision, Pre-Pilot and Pilot Runs
   e. Rework
   f. Molding Shop Operations
   g. Changing an MRT (Material Rejection Ticket) for Non-conforming Purchased Material and Non-conforming Production Material
   h. Handling Failures from Certified Suppliers
   i. In-Line Product Testing
   j. Internal Quality Audits
   k. Calibration, and
   l. Quality Alert

Written procedures or work instructions are essential for consistency and reference as well as training.

OBSERVATIONS

1. On the worksheet used for data collection in the Finished Goods Audit (Finished Goods Audit Procedure QUA-021-00005)

   a. Specifications and tolerances for various characteristics tested are not indicated.

b. No provision is made to note the results of hi-pot and leakage current tests.
c. No provision is made to note the product description or identification such as model or style number and/or serial number.

Looking at this worksheet, one would not know what are the requirements for a given characteristic and whether hi-pot and leakage current tests were performed or not.

2. Material Hold form (Finished Goods Audit Procedure QUA-021-00005) needs improvement to incorporate:

   a. Product identification, and
   b. Results of screening and rework for the group of product held by this form.

   This form then should be routed to QA for collection of data, and become part of quality records for that product shipment or purchase order.

3. The Finished Goods Audit Procedure (QUA-021-00005) calls for an AQL of 1.0 regardless of the nature of defects, i.e., critical, major or minor, while in actual practice AQLs of 0, 0.65 and 2.5 are used for critical, major and minor defects, respectively. Written procedure for Finished Goods Audit needs to be revised to reflect the actual practice.

4. The categories of defects, i.e., critical, major, and minor are not well defined. (Finished Goods Audit, QUA-021-00005).

5. There is some duplication in the description and defect codes, e.g., critical defect code 2, "defective parts" is also a major defect code 2 "defective parts" (Finished Goods Audit, QUA-021-00005). Deficiencies are coded by numbers and it would be valuable for defect data analysis if each deficiency had a unique code number.

6. Scrap Control (QUA-021-00004) procedure requires rewrite. This procedure should be called for when a decision is made to scrap material within the following procedures:

   a. Non-Conforming Purchase Material Control (QUA-021-00003)
   b. Finished Goods Audit (QUA-021-00005)

c. Molding Inspection (QUA-021-00007)
d. Non-Conforming Production Material Control (yet to be written)

7. Drawing received in the Lab and the Molding departments were traced back to Drawing Control with several found with outdated revisions, i.e.,

   a. In the Lab: Drawing # 219722 (Reliability for Toasters) 1/87 Revision A. Drawing Control showed 8/18/94 Revision B was correct.
   b. In Molding Department: Part # 14797 (Base Plate) 6/23/91 Revision AD (found both in mating kit and in the QC file cabinet in the Molding Dept.); Drawing Control showed 6/25/94 revision AH (file hard copy) and 3/14/94 revision AG on microfiche which included a handwritten reference to revision AH. None of these differences revealed any adverse impact on quality—and in fact, Drawing Control was found to be in the process of taking corrective action to update all drawings. It did also have a current master list of all drawings as its corrective action basis.

COMMENTS

1. The QA manual's Molding Inspection Procedure (QUA-021-00007), para 5.4.1 denotes that a process (of a press) must be found stable by the Mold technician before approval to production run the press. It actually means the Mold Technician assures the part is produced right before the run is approved. Paragraph 5.4.1 should be changed to reflect this. A process cannot be declared stable until it runs and is measured for a reasonable time.

2. While Incoming material Inspection Procedure (QUA-021-00002), para 4.5 references Certified suppliers, there are none at this time, although supplier certification procedure does exist.

3. Abolish the Deviation Control Procedure (QUA-021-00006) as a separate procedure and incorporate it within the following procedures:

   a. Non-conforming Purchase material Control (QUA-021-00003)
   b. Finished Goods Audit (QUA-021-00005)
   c. Molding Inspection (QUA-021-00007)
   d. Non-conforming Production Material Control (yet to be written)

4. The quality manual requires various administrative and editorial corrections which were reviewed with Messrs SUV and Danley, the QA manager and quality engineer, respectively.

DEF
Lead Auditor
Director of Quality Assurance
XYZ Corporation

Quality Summary of Household Products Division, RST, Inc.
14 May XXXX through 31 July XXXX

AQL	2.5
Number of Lots Inspected	66
Number of Lots Failed	1
Number of Samples Inspected	1534
Number of Samples Defective	21
% Defective	1.4

EXPLANATION OF TERMS

FINDING: A statement of fact regarding serious noncompliance with established policy, procedures, instructions, drawings, or other applicable documents; a serious control deficiency that has or can result in a condition adverse to quality.

OBSERVATION: An item of objective evidence which supports a finding; a detected program weakness, which, if not corrected, will result in a degradation of product or service quality. Observation is less serious than a finding.

COMMENT: An aspect offered for management's attention.

Report 3-2 RST, Inc. Quality System Audit Report

3-3-6 Value of Quality System Audit

The value of a quality system audit to retailers is that it is a proactive approach to managing quality. By performing quality system audits, retailers can identify areas for improvement in process controls that, when addressed effectively, result in quality improvement. Based on this quality improvement, the retailers can redirect their

QA efforts where needed most. Mehta and Scheffler (1998) and Mehta and Kirby (1998) show how supplier quality audits resulted in quality improvement for one retailer. Because of such improvement a retailer was able to reduce its QA staff from 106 to 40 in about 10 years with substantial cost savings and without any adverse effect on the quality of merchandise. Mehta and Scheffler (1994) also noted traits of those suppliers who welcome audits and those suppliers who do not.

Value of a quality system audit to a supplier is that as such an audit is done by the customer, i.e., the retailer, it brings in an outside, fresh viewpoint. Supplier personnel are sometimes too close to what they do every day so that they can't see things that an outsider can. For the suppliers, quality system audits performed by a retailer is essentially free consulting because a retailer's QA auditors took time to review suppliers' quality system and identified areas of opportunity for quality improvement.

Supplier quality system audits combined with end-item inspections are powerful and effective approaches to quality management.

There are a number of short courses available on quality system auditing, ranging from two days (16 hours) to one week (40 hours). It would be worthwhile to send key QA staff members to such courses and have them in turn provide in-house training to the rest of the QA staffers. It may also be advisable or worthwhile to require key QA staffers to obtain a certification in auditing such as Certified Quality Auditor (CQA) from the American Society for Quality. Courses and examinations for this certification are available in many countries. In the early 90s one large retailer in the U.S. decided to place increasing emphasis on understanding suppliers' processes and process controls with a view to find areas for quality improvement through supplier quality system audits. In order to accomplish this, the QA management encouraged its staffers to become Certified Quality Auditors. Many staff members took up this professional development challenge and become more competent and better qualified in the process of becoming CQA (Mehta 1993).

Arter (2003), Parsowith (1995), Mills (1989), Russell (2000) provide excellent information on how to effectively conduct supplier audits and how to use audits for improving supplier performance.

3-4 Supplier Certification

Some retailers use supplier certification to motivate suppliers to meet quality requirements. According to Maas, Brown and Bossert (1990) "a certified supplier is a source that through previous experience and qualification, can provide material of such quality that it needs little, if any, receiving inspection or test before becoming approved stock or being released into the production process." Supplier certification indicates a retailer's confidence in a supplier's ability to supply defect free merchandise on a continuous basis. It implies that the supplier has an effective quality system in place and supplier's processes are capable of delivering defect free products on a timely basis. To earn supplier certification from a retailer is also a matter of pride for the supplier personnel. Supplier certification also means that the retailer will not have to inspect and/or test every shipment from a supplier, resulting in reduced inspection and/or testing costs on the retailer's part or the retailer can direct its QA resources where they are better needed, thus making QA efforts more effective. It is also beneficial for the supplier because the certified supplier does not have to arrange for inspection of every order before it is shipped, which is savings in administrative costs for the supplier.

Supplier certification works in conjunction with supplier quality system audits.

3-4-1 Certification Criteria

Supplier certification criteria can be as simple as follows:

a. Based on inspection of at least 300 samples, the percent defective should be less than the AQL used for the given category of merchandise.
b. Should have been no test failure within the past year.
c. Should have been no product recall within the past year.
d. Supplier must have an effective quality system in place.

While the results of a, b, and c above are good indicators of an effective quality system in place, it is better to visit the supplier being considered for certification and verify that the supplier has an effective quality system in place by conducting an audit of the supplier's quality system.

Supplier quality system is certified for typically a year or two and if the supplier quality performance continues to be acceptable, the certification is renewed for another period of time. Supplier quality system certification is never for an indefinite period of time.

Supplier certification criteria can also be based on a point system where various elements important to the retailer are given point values and if a supplier earns more than certain points, then he is certified. Here is an example of a point-based system of supplier certification.

Element	Point Value
Percent lots accepted	
100 %	50
99 %	49
Deduct one point from 50 for each 1 % less shipment acceptance from 100 %	
Pass tests 100 %	20
Deduct one point from 20 for each test failure	
On time delivery	
Plus minus 1 day of delivery date	10
Up to and including five days early or two days late delivery	7
More than five days early and/or more than two days late	0
Paper work[1]	
Paperwork in good order	10
Paperwork needs improvement	7
Paperwork unacceptable	0
Supplier attitude and technical support	
Supplier's willingness to cooperate	5
Supplier's technical capability	5

1- Purchasing and QA's assessment of the accuracy and completeness of packing slip, package labeling, invoice, bill of lading, certificate of analysis, and other paperwork.

The maximum points a supplier can get for a period of time is 100. The total point values can be rated as follows:

Rating	Total Points
Excellent	91-100
Outstanding	81-90
Good	71-80
Fair	61-70
Poor	51-60
Unacceptable	0-50

Any supplier receiving "Excellent" rating is a candidate for certification. For any suppliers receiving a rating of outstanding or less should not be considered for certification. It is better to use such rating system to help suppliers improve their performance by pinpointing their deficiency and allowing reasonable time to take corrective and preventive actions, rather than use such rating system to punish those suppliers who are not meeting the requirements.

In case, a supplier is awarded certification, it is best to present the certificate to the senior management of the supplier at the supplier facility in the presence of the workers because the workers actually earned this honor through their hard work and diligence and supplier certification is actually recognition of the supplier's personnel.

Public recognition can be a tremendous motivator to continue to perform well. For example, GE Appliance has found that it can motivate suppliers by going public with its commendations. Suppliers are encouraged to publicize their awards and to use them as a way of generating new business from other customers (Burt 1989).

According to an APQC (American Productivity and Quality Center) best practice report on international purchasing (APQC 1999), best practice companies certify suppliers in-house, sometimes in conjunction with ISO standards or third party qualification.

According to another report on supply chain management and partnership (Best Practices, LLC 2000) supplier certification is a first step toward developing meaningful supplier partnerships. Among excellent supply chain management companies, certification is not regarded as an end in itself; it is viewed as a means to achieving key performance results and strategic objectives. Certification establishes a common language for communication. This in turn fosters an increased level of trust and understanding between partners. Certification also raises confidence in supplied services and materials, giving a company the freedom to rapidly-or even immediately place those supplies in its own lines. Excellent companies often certify suppliers at different levels, reflecting the strength, depth and maturity of the relationship.

Maass, Brown and Bossert (1990) provide excellent in-depth discussion of the supplier certification process. Supplier certification practices as described in this book have been repeatedly demonstrated to work and work well. Some of the contributors to the original discussions in this book have cut inspection of purchased material by 40 % or more.

A variety of training courses are available on supplier certification. It would be worthwhile to have some QA staff members go through such training before embarking on a supplier certification program.

3-4-2 De-Certification Criteria

It is important to continuously monitor quality performance of certified suppliers and take appropriate action(s) when their performance slips. In case, some certified suppliers can not maintain their performance at a level to justify maintaining their certification, there should be some criteria to decertify them after giving them reasonable opportunities to address quality problems.

3-5 Supplier Surveys

Supplier survey is generally done on a prospective supplier. Survey typically involves using a checklist of items in the form of "yes" or "no" answers to collect information without going into much detail and therefore it is less formal and takes less time. Form 3-1 shows an example of a supplier survey. Information gathered from a supplier survey can be helpful in deciding whether to buy from that company or not.

XYZ Corporation Supply Survey					
Supplier Contact Information			Factory Contact Information		
Quality Control					
Observations	YES	NO	Observations	YES	NO
Written QA procedures maintained			End of line inspectors inspect only		
Supplier Has an in-process QA System			Incoming components inspected		
No. of in-process QA Stations ______			Tests performed on components		
Adequate?			Tests performed on end items		
Records maintained at stations			Records of test results maintained		
Records analyzed by management			Corrective actions taken to prevent		
Tests are performed by			repeated discrepancies		
In-house Lab ____ Outside Lab ____			Rejected product controlled		
Necessary testing, measuring or			Standard maintained at each station		
Inspection equipment maintained			Acceptance & rejection criteria		
Calibration records maintained on			defined at each station		
test equipment			QA organizationally separate form		
End item audits performed to deremine			production		
outgoing quality level			End of line inspection performed		
Overall QA system considered			100% ____ Sampling ____		
satisfactory					
Remarks					
Signature of the Surveyor			Date:		

Form 3-1 Supplier Survey

3-6 Factory Evaluation

Some retailers perform factory evaluation before letting a factory start production of their merchandise or awarding a contract to manufacture their merchandise. One retailer is so particular about which factory makes their private label merchandise that if a factory passes the evaluation, it is designated to make only certain private labels depending on how many points the factory received in factory evaluation.

Factory evaluation involves evaluating manufacturing technology and practices, including quality assurance/control practices with a view to how they may affect end-item quality. Those retailers who do factory evaluation have their own criteria and scoring system. If a factory receives more than a certain score, then that factory is approved for making products for that retailer. It is possible that a supplier may have more than one factory but only some of them may have passed factory evaluation. Retailers generally give some time to those factories that fail factory evaluation to address those areas that need to be improved and those factories are reevaluated.

Here is an example of a factory evaluation system for apparel manufacturers. Similar factory evaluation systems can be developed for other product manufacturers or industries.

Factory Evaluation

Factory Name ____ Date ________
Address ____
____
____

1.0 Marker Making

a. Is marker making automatic or manual?
Automatic ______(5) Manual ______

Manual marker making lends itself for making mistakes and would require thorough checking before releasing markers to cutting. Therefore, automatic marker making is better. Automatic marker making improves productivity also.

2.0 Receiving

a. Is fabric inspection performed in receiving?
Yes ______(5) No ____

On all suppliers? Yes ___ (5) No ___
Only on problem suppliers? Yes ___ (3) No ___

It is important to inspect fabric and catch any defective fabric before it is spread for cutting.

b. Is fabric inspection accomplished using fabric inspection machine(s)?
Yes ______(5) No ______

Using fabric inspection machine facilitates fabric inspection resulting in more effective fabric inspection.

c. What defect scoring system is used?

4 Point System ____(5) 10 Point System ______(3)
Graniteville "78" System ___(3) Factory's own ___(3) Customer's ___ (3)

4 point defect scoring system is most widely used fabric defect scoring system and therefore, using this system will facilitate comparison and communication of fabric inspection results with other parties.

In case of either factory's or customer's system, please describe the scoring criteria.

Are examples of standard fabric defects (either actual or photographs) available to the inspector for guidance? Yes _____ (5) No _____

Having either actual or photographs of fabric defects to inspectors as reference takes subjectivity out of scoring fabric defects and makes inspection results more reliable.

d. Are supplier results of fabric inspection relied upon instead of the factory performing its own inspection?

Yes ____(3) No ____

e. Are fabric rolls shaded and grouped according to the shade?

Yes ____(3) No ____ Not Applicable ____
By the factory _____ By the supplier ______

Grouping fabric rolls by their shades is important in order to prevent shading in garment parts.

f. Is shade sorting based on instrumental data? Yes _____ (5) No ____

g. Is shade sorting accomplished visually? Yes ____(3) No ____

Instrumental shade sorting is more accurate and is more effective in preventing shading problems later on because there is no subjectivity in instrumental shade sorting, and also, it makes communication regarding shading and shade variation easier.

h. Is incoming fabric tested for the following or relied upon supplier to furnish test results with each shipment? Or neither _____

i. Fabric weight ____ tested in-house/tested by outside lab/relied upon fabric supplier (1)

j. Shrinkage
washing _____ tested in-house/tested by outside lab/relied upon fabric supplier (1)
dry cleaning ___ tested in-house/tested by outside lab/relied upon fabric supplier (1)

k. Colorfastness ____ tested in-house/tested by outside lab/relied upon fabric supplier
Colorfastness to: washing _____(1) dry cleaning _____(1) perspiration ______(1)
chlorine bleach _____(1) sunlight _____(1)
fumes/gases ___(1)
In case of beachwear/swimwear, is fabric tested for protection to ultra-violate light?
Yes _____(1) No ____

It is important to test incoming fabric shipments to verify that what is being received is what was bought and to prevent performance problems later on.

l. Is fabric supplier quality history maintained and used as a basis for quality improvement?

Yes ____ (3) No _____

m. Are rejected/defective fabric rolls labeled as such and kept in a segregated area so that they may not be used inadvertently?

Yes _____(3) No _____

n. Is fabric stored in such a way that it is prevented from being damaged in any way?

Yes _____ (3) No _____

o. Are accouterments and accessories such as buttons, zippers and other trim items inspected upon receipt?

Yes _____(3) No _____

p. Accouterments and accessories are not inspected upon receipt but the suppliers' certificate of compliance (CoC) is relied upon for quality of these items.

Yes _____ (3) No _____

q. Are buttons, snaps, hooks, zippers, sewing threads, etc. tested upon receipt or the suppliers are relied upon to furnish test results either with each shipment or on demand?
Or neither _____

Buttons ___ tested in-house/tested by outside lab/relied upon supplier (1)
Snaps ____ tested in-house/tested by outside lab/relied upon supplier (1)
Hooks ____ tested in-house/tested by outside lab/relied upon supplier (1)
Zippers ___ tested in-house/tested by outside lab/relied upon supplier (1)
Sewing threads ______ tested in-house/tested by outside lab/relied upon supplier (1)

r. Are incoming inspection records maintained in such a way that enables one to review supplier quality history?

Yes _____ (3) No _____

s. Are the receiving function and assignment of fabric storage location computerized? Yes _____ (5) No _____

3.0 Spreading

a. Is spreading manual, semi-automatic or automatic?
Automatic ____ (5) Semi-automatic _____ (3) Manual _____

b. Is fabric inspection accomplished during spreading?
Yes _____ (3) No ____

c. Is each spread checked?
Yes _____ (6) No _____

4.0 Cutting

a. Is cutting automatic? Yes ______ (5) No _____ If the answer is yes, note the equipment being used.

Cutting quality is better with automatic cutting.

b. How are small parts cut?
Die cut ______(5) Knife cut ______(3)

Die cutting is more accurate than knife cutting.

c. Is every cut checked after cutting is accomplished?
Yes ______(6) No ______

5.0 Sewing

a. Does the factory use

Bundle production system ______ Unit production system ______(5)

b. Are seams, stitches, and needles used appropriate for the item being sewn?

Seams: Yes ___(2) No _____ Stitches: Yes ___(2) No ___
Sewing threads: Yes ____(2) No _____ Needles: Yes _____(2) No ____

c. Are microprocessors used on sewing machines to automatically control such things as presser foot lift, backtack, thread trim, fullness, number of stitches, etc.?
Yes _____(5) No ______

d. Are simple automatics in use such as

Buttonholers Yes ____(2) No ____ Button sewers Yes ____(2) No _____
Bar tack machines Yes ___ (2) No ___ Label sewers Yes ____(2) No ____

e. Are operations such as following mechanized?

Patch pocket setting Yes ___ (2) No ___
Stitching collars or flaps Yes ___ (2) No ___ Long seam joining Yes ___ (2) No ___
Making jetted pockets Yes ___ (2) No ___ Serging trousers Yes ___ (2) No ___

f. Are work aids and attachments such as following used?

Guides Yes ___ (2) No ___ Compensating foot Yes ___ (2) No ___
Special presser feet Yes ___ (2) No ___ Stitching jig Yes ___ (2) No ___
Folders Yes ___ (2) No ___ Undertrimmer Yes ___ (2) No ___

g. Is sewing work inspected at various points throughout the production of an item?

Yes _____(6) No _____

h. For a given item that is being sewn, are there written sewing specifications available to the sewing operators and supervisors?

Yes _____ (6) No _____

6.0 Fusing

a. If fusing is used, is it flat bed or continuous?

Flat bed _____(5) Continuous _______(5) Fusing is not used _______

b. Is fusing press/machine operation monitored for quality by periodic peel strength or bond strength tests? Yes ____ No _____

Once a day/shift _____ (1)Twice a day/shift _____(3)Thrice a day/shift _____(6)

Checking fusing operation several times a day through peel strength or bond strength testing is important to make sure that the fusing operation is consistent throughout the day.

7.0 Finishing

a. How is finishing accomplished?

Ironing _______ (3) Steam finishing _______(5)

b. Are completed garments inspected before they go on to finishing?

Inspected 100 % _____(5) Inspected on a sampling basis ____(3)
Not inspected at all ____

If the inspection is done on a sampling basis, describe the sampling plan.

c. Are garments inspected after finishing operation(s) to evaluate quality of finishing operations?

Yes _____(5) No _____

8.0 Final inspection

a. Are garments put through metal (needle) detector? Yes _____ (5)
No _____

b. Is final inspection conducted before garments are packed? Yes _____
No _____

What does the final inspection consist of?

Garment inspection on A sampling basis ______ (8) 100% basis _____(5)
Size measurements (measurements of critical garment dimensions) _____(5)

Form fitting (putting garments on proper size mannequins to see if they properly fit the labeled size) ______(5)
Live modeling (having models try garments to see if they fit the labeled size) ____(5)

c. Is packing operation checked?

Yes ____ (5) No _____

d. Does the factory have written quality/workmanship standards in general?
Yes _____ (8) No _____

e. Are quality procedures written? And are they easily available to workers for reference?

Yes ____(5) No ____ Yes _____(5) No ______

9.0 Are final garments tested for?

a. Shrinkage in washing Yes _____(1) No _____
dry cleaning Yes ____ (1) No _____

b. Durable press performance if applicable Yes _____ (1) No _____

c. Overall appearance retention Yes _____(1) No _____

d. Seam strength Yes _____(1) No _____

10.0 Does the factory have performance standard against which test results can be compared?

Yes ____ (5) Factory has its own set of performance standards _____
Factory relies on its customers' performance standards ____
Industry standards (such as ASTM standards) are relied upon _____

No ____

11.0 Before going into full production, does the factory make a small lot (pilot lot) of the garments to be produced and work out all the details? Yes ____(5) No ____

12.0 Maintenance

Are maintenance records kept? Yes _____(5) No ______

If yes, review some maintenance records and get some feel for how well plant machinery and equipment are maintained? Record your comments below.

13.0 Are employees adequately trained? Yes _____ (5) No _____
Are employee training records maintained? Yes _____(5) No _____

14.0 Who is responsible for quality? And who does that individual report to?

QC Inspector ______
QC Supervisor ______(1)
QC Manager ________(2)
Plant/Factory Manager _____(3)
Director of Quality ______ (4)
VP Quality ______(5)

Quality Manager _______
Plant/Factory Manager _____(1)
Director of Manufacturing _____(2)
VP Manufacturing/Operations ___(3)
SVP/EVP/Exec. Director _______(4)
CEO/COO/President/Managing Director______(5)
Owner/Proprietor _____(6)

While everyone in a factory should be responsible for producing quality goods, there should be an individual, independent of production, that manages quality function and reports to the highest level of management.

15.0 What is the highest level at which factory quality performance is reviewed? How frequently?

Plant/Factory Manager ______ (1)
Director of Manufacturing _____ (2)
Director of Quality ______ (3)
VP Quality _________(4)
VP Manufacturing/Operations ______(5)
SVP/EVP/Exec. Director _______(6)
CEO/COO/President/Managing Director ______(7)
Owner/Proprietor _____(8)

Daily ______(5)
Weekly ______(4)
Monthly ______(3)
Quarterly _____(2)
Yearly _______(1)

16.0 Inspect a sample of 32 garments taken at random and record the number of defective garments found. For each defective garment, list the defects found. Calculate % defective.

% defective = (Number of garments found defective/32) x 100

17.0 General Conditions

Lighting Excellent________(5) Fair _______(3) Poor _______

Spacing Excellent________(5) Fair________(3) Poor ______

Logical flow of material Excellent _______(5) Fair_______(3) Poor ______

18.0 Cleanliness and orderliness of the factory.

Cleanliness		Orderliness	
Excellent ________	(5)	Excellent ________	(5)
Fair ____________	(3)	Fair ____________	(3)
Poor ________		Poor __________	

Business Technology

		Yes (5)	No (0)
1.0	Is factory able to label, track and respond to product orders in real time on the basis of style, color, fabric, and size?	_____	_____
2.0	Is factory able to exchange (send and receive) information concerning current status of a customer's products on an electronic basis?	_____	_____
3.0	Is factory able to provide goods to a customer's distribution centers that can be efficiently moved to stores, that is, containers or packages marked with bar codes concerning contents; shipment of products ready for display in retail stores?	_____	_____
4.0	Is factory able to perform transactions such as receive a purchase order, receive payment, send advance shipment notice, etc. electronically?	_____	_____
5.0	Does factory have an ERP system installed to be able to track and communicate production in real time?	_____	_____

6.0 Is factory able to acknowledge electronically:

a. That the purchase order from your customer is not only received but actually entered into your system, therefore, becoming a "real order?" _____ _____

b. That a pick-ticket for that order has been generated along with a double-check of what is listed on that pick-ticket? _____ _____

c. Ultimately what has been packed for that order? _____ _____

d. That the order has been turned over to the carrier? _____ _____

Notes/Remaeks

Form 3-2 Factory Evaluation—Apparel Manufacturers

The number in the parenthesis in the above factory evaluation form represent score for that element. At the end of the factory evaluation add all the applicable score points and that would be the score that factory received. The maximum score (points) a factory can get is 361. Then, a criteria can be set that, for example, a factory must receive at least 90% score (or 325 points) in order to pass the factory evaluation, or whatever level the retailer feels comfortable with. A "gradual" criteria can also be established. For example,

a. A factory must receive at least 70% score in order to be considered for manufacturing "regular" private label merchandise for a retailer.
b. A factory must receive at least 80% score in order to be considered for manufacturing better than "regular" private label merchandise for a retailer.
c. A factory must receive at least 90% score in order to make 'premium" private label merchandise for a retailer.
d. Any factory receiving less than 70% score will not be considered for doing business with.

It is up to the retailer whether to help a factory improve it's score over a period of time by pointing out areas for improvement and working with a factory (supplier development) or simply to move on to the next factory.

3-7 Supplier Quality Assistance

Some companies may not have a quality system in place and yet it may be necessary to do business with those companies. In that case the retailer may offer assistance in the quality area even though those companies may be producing quality products. Without any quality system in place there is no guarantee that they will continue to supply quality products. Typically, assisting a supplier in the quality area consists of:

a. Helping supplier develop quality procedures including statistical sampling plans.
b. Train supplier personnel in inspection procedures, which includes use of statistical sampling plans, defect scoring criteria, acceptance and rejection criteria; use of appropriate test methods; record keeping; and data collection and analysis.
c. Inform supplier personnel of applicable standards, regulations, and laws.
d. Provide supplier a list of resources from where suppliers can buy test equipment and accessories, can have testing done, obtain copies of applicable test methods standards and regulations, and send their personnel for training.

Many companies do not devote necessary resources to help develop suppliers and the result is a huge gap in their cost competitiveness. You cannot optimize your cost performance without having good supplier performance (Sheridan 1998).

Retailers are increasingly looking to their suppliers to ensure that processes down the supply chain effectively provide products that meet customer needs and expectations. Smart retailers do this by offering guidance to suppliers in improving their operations to enhance its own customer satisfaction, thus continuously improving its own competitive position via quality and productivity improvement.

Key Points

- Testing and end item inspection are important to assure that shipments accepted are safe and have acceptable level of quality.
- Packaging quality is just as important as product quality for mail order and internet merchandise.
- While end item inspection is not considered pro-active by some quality experts, it is still better than no inspection at all and can provide some valuable information about product quality and supplier quality performance.
- Even a single "critical" defect found in a lot should be grounds for rejecting that lot.
- Supplier quality system audit, supplier quality system certification, and factory evaluation are pro-active ways to assure quality of merchandise.

References

American Association of Textile Chemists and Colorists 2002. *Technical Manual.* Vol. 77. Research Triangle Park, NC.

American Productivity and Quality Center. 1999. *International Procurement: Selecting, Engaging, and Managing World's Best Suppliers.* Consortium Benchmarking Study, Best Practices Report.

American Productivity and Quality Center. 1997. *Partnering for Profit: Building and Managing Global Supplier Relationships.* Consortium Benchmarking Study, Best Practices Report.

ANSI/ASQC Z 1.4-1998. *Sampling Procedures and Tables for Inspection by Attributes.* American Society for Quality, Milwaukee, WI.

Annual Book of ASTM Standards. 2002. Volumes 07.01 and 07.02. American Society for Testing and Materials, International. West Conshohocken, PA.

Arter, Dennis R. 2003. *Quality Audits for Improved Performance.* American Society for Quality. Milwaukee, WI.

ASTM D-1776. Standard Practice for Conditioning Textiles for Testing. *Annual Book of ASTM Standards, Vol. 07.01.* American Society for Testing and Materials, International. West Conshohocken, PA.

Best practices, LLC. 2000. *Best Practices in Supply Chain Management and Partnerships.* Report # OP-70. Chapel Hill, NC.

Burt, D.N. 1989. Managing Suppliers Up to Speed. *Harvard Business Review,* July-August: 127-135. Cambridge, MA.

Duncan, Acheson J. 1975. An Introduction to Acceptance Sampling Plans. *ASTM Standardization News*, September. pp. 10-14, 50. American Society for Testing & Materials, International. West Conshohocken, PA.

Federal Trade Commission (FTC). 2001. Guides for the Jewelry, Precious Metals, and Pewter Industries, Effective April 10. Paragraph 23.11 Definition and misuse of the word "diamond." www.ftc.gov/bcp/guides/jewel-gd.htm

Glossary & Tables for Statistical Quality Control. 1996. ISBN 0-87389-354-9. American Society for Quality. Quality Press. Milwaukee, WI

Grant, Eugene L. and Leavenworth, Richard S. 1996. *Statistical Quality Control*, 7th Edition. ISBN 0-07-844354-7. Quality Press. Milwaukee, WI.

Hahn, Gerald J. and Schilling, Edward G. 1975. An Introduction to the MIL-STD-105D Acceptance Sampling Scheme. *ASTM Standardization News.* September. pp. 20-30. American Society for Testing & Materials, International, West Conshohocken, PA.

ISO 9000-2000 Quality management systems—Fundamentals and Vocabulary. American Society for Quality. Milwaukee, WI.

ISO 2859-1:1999. *Sampling procedures for inspection by attributes—part 1: Sampling schemes indexed by acceptance quality limit (AQL) for lot-by-lot inspection.* International Organization for Standardization, Geneva, Switzerland.

Juran, Joseph M. 2003. *Architect of Quality*. October. McGraw-Hill.

Kadolph, Sara J. 1998. *Quality Assurance for Textiles and Apparel.* ISBN 156367-144-1. Fairchild Publications, New York, NY.

Maass, Richard A.; Brown, John A.; Bossert, James L. 1990. *Supplier Certification: A Continuous Improvement Strategy.* American Society for Quality. Milwaukee, WI.

Matlins, Antoinette L. and Bonanno, A. C. 1995. *Jewelry & Gems: The Buying Guide. How to Buy Diamonds, Pearls, Colored Gemstones, Gold & Jewelry with Confidence and Knowledge.* Gemstone Press. Woodstock, VT.

Mehta, Pradip V. 1992. *An Introduction to Quality Control for the Apparel Industry*. American Society for Quality, Milwaukee, WI.

Mehta, Pradip V. 1993. Implementing Supplier Quality Assistance Program. A paper presented at the Annual Conference of the Customer-Supplier Division of the American Society for Quality. November, Dayton, OH. American Society for Quality, Milwaukee, WI

Mehta, Pradip V. and Bhardwaj, Satish K. 1998. *Managing Quality in the Apparel Industry*. New Age International (P) Ltd., New Delhi, India.

Mehta, Pradip V. and Kirby, Lee. 1998. Down to the Last Detail. *American Jewelry Manufacturer.* February. pp. 38-41.

Mehta, Pradip V. and Scheffler, Joan. 1998. Getting Suppliers in on Quality Act. *Quality Progress.* January. American Society for Quality. Milwaukee, WI.

Mehta, Pradip V. and Scheffler, Joan. 1994. Supplier Quality Assistance Program Results. A paper presented at the Annual Conference of the Customer-Supplier Division of the American Society for Quality. Milwaukee, WI.

Mills, Charles A. 1989. *The Quality Audit: A Management Tool.* McGraw-Hill, New York, NY.

Parsowith, B. Scott. 1995. *Fundamentals of Quality Auditing.* American Society for Quality, Milwaukee, WI.

Russell, J. P. Editor. 2000. *The Quality Audit Handbook.* American Society for Quality, Milwaukee, WI.

Stephens, Kenneth S. 2001. *The Handbook of Applied Acceptance Sampling: Plans, Procedures, and Principles.* Quality Press. Milwaukee, WI

Wingate, Isabel B., Gillespie, Karen R., and Barry, Marry E. 1984. *Know Your Merchandise for Retailers and Consumers.* ISBN 0-07-071016-3. McGraw-Hill, New York, NY.

Bibliography

Andrade, G.F., Bossert, J.L., Braun, L.F., Krahula, J., Lawrimore, B., Silver, B. 1990. Customer and Supplier: The Capitalism Connection. *44th Annual Quality Congress Proceedings.* May. San Francisco, CA. pp. 957-967. American Society for Quality, Milwaukee, WI.

Bhote, Keki R. 1992. Most Vendor Certification Methods Are Trivial. *46th Annual Quality Congress Proceedings.* May. Nashville, TN. pp. 230-236. American Society for Quality, Milwaukee, WI.

Maass, Richard A. 1988. Supplier Certification—A positive response to JIT. ASQC Quality Congress Transactions, Dallas, TX. Pp 88-92. American Society for Quality Control, Milwaukee, WI.

Vendor-Vendee Technical Committee. 1977. *How to Conduct A Supplier Survey.* American Society for Quality, Milwaukee, WI.

Vendor-Vendee Technical Committee. 1981. *How to Establish Effective Quality Control for the Small Supplier.* American Society for Quality, Milwaukee, WI.

4

Standards and Specifications

4-1 Introduction

It is hard to imagine achieving quality without standards. The New American Webster Dictionary (1972) defines a standard as a basis of comparison, a criterion; measure. A standard is also something that is established by authority, custom or general consent as a model or example to be followed. It is also something established for use as a rule or basis of comparison in measuring or judging capacity, quantity, content, extent, value, quality, etc. According to ISO (International Organization for Standardization), standards are documented agreements containing specifications or other precise criteria to be used consistently as rules, guidelines, or definitions of characteristics, to ensure that materials, products, processes and services are fit for their purpose (www.iso.ch). A specification is a detailed statement of requirements.

Almost everything we use today is made to some standard(s). Standards not only enable mass production but also ensure compatibility, safety, performance, communication and better quality. Standards can be used in marketing strategy to promote purchase of products that meet nationally recognized requirements, especially when conformance is backed by a certification program.

The benefits of standards literally surround us. Clothes fit and do not fade or fall apart in just one laundering or dry-cleaning, buildings stand, cars run, tape recorders record, and planes fly because each is made to conform to technical standards for material, design, and performance. Civilization or industrial progress as we know it today would have not been possible without the order standards create. According to W. Edwards Deming the convenience of 110 volts and uniform outlets everywhere in the northern hemisphere would be difficult to express in words (Lamprecht 2000). Much of what we take for granted in every day life is the result of standardization. Some other benefits of standards are:

a. Standards facilitate communication and prevent misunderstanding.
b. Standards make parts interchangeability possible and as a result, mass production is possible.
c. Standards can be used in marketing strategy to promote purchase of products that meet nationally recognized requirements, especially, when conformance is backed by a certification program.

Another reason why standards and specifications are important is that increasingly consumer products are made in several countries and exported all over the world as our markets become more global. Therefore, it becomes important that the consumer goods are made to comply with specifications and meet at least minimum safety standards.

Lamprecht (2000) mentions a vivid example of the value of standards as follows.

> "The material and socioeconomic costs associated with such a lack of standardization was clearly demonstrated during the Chicago fire of 1871 when fire engines from other cities which had come to provide assistance, could not connect to the fire hydrants because of a difference in screw threads."

There are voluntary standards and mandatory standards. *Voluntary* standards are developed through participation of all interested stakeholders such as producers, importers, retailers, users, consumers and representatives of government and academia. *Mandatory* standards or regulatory standards are those incorporated in regulations and laws and for which the government has enforcement authority. Some standards initially developed as voluntary standards can become mandatory or regulatory standards.

Standards can be company, consortium, industry, government, or consensus standards. *Company* standards are those developed or adapted and used by a company only either within the company and/or in purchasing goods and services. *Consortium* standards are those standards developed and used by a small group of like minded companies formed to undertake an activity that is beyond the resources of any one member of the consortium. *Industry* standards are those standards developed by an industry association or trade association. *Government* standards can be either written/developed by the government officials or developed by private sector and then adopted by reference as government standards. For example, a number of ASTM standards for consumer products have become CPSC requirements or standards. *Consensus* standards are those standards developed by representatives of all sectors that have interest in participating in the development and/or use of the standards. These sectors include producers, importers, retailers, users, consumers, representatives of government and academia.

4-2 Sources of Standards

Various standards developing organizations at the international level and the national level are sources of a variety of standards. There are many standards development organizations throughout the world. Here is a brief overview of some of these organizations.

4-2-1 American Association of Textile Chemists and Colorists (AATCC) www.aatcc.org

Founded in 1921, the American Association of Textile Chemists and Colorists has grown from a group of 270 charter members into the world's largest textile chemistry membership society, with close to 7,000 members in the U.S. and 60 countries. AATCC is a source of test methods in areas of colorfastness, wet processing, fiber identification, and textile chemistry. AATCC has published more than 175 test methods in these areas, which are contained in AATCC's Technical Manual published every year. AATCC test methods are developed through the consensus process by research committees composed of industry experts. Research committees are the working force behind AATCC test methods. Many people donate their time by serving on one or more committee(s). Extensive investigation and interlaboratory comparisons, often covering several years' work, are conducted. Simplicity, reproducibility, applicability, and cost performing the test and the time required to perform the test are all important considerations in each development. AATCC Test Methods that may be of interest to retailers are listed in the section 4-5 of this chapter.

4-2-2 ANEC www.anec.org

Consumer participation in standards development is very important. Therefore, an association to represent consumer interests was established in Europe in 1995, called ANEC, the European Association for the Coordination of Consumer

Representation in Standardization. ANEC represents consumers from all European Union and European free trade area countries. ANEC is directly represented in the three European standards bodies (CEN, CENLEC and ETSI) and has very close links to ISO and IEC. ANEC's aims are:

a. Ensuring that the interests of the European consumers are given their full weight at political level in the work of the standards bodies and institutions dealing with standards.
b. Improving participation at national level.
c. Enhancing professionalism and effectiveness of consumer observers through training and access to expertise, e.g., comparative testing results, product safety research accident data and consultants.

4-2-3 American National Standards Institute (ANSI) www.ansi.org

Founded in 1918 by five engineering societies and three government agencies, the ANSI remains a private, nonprofit membership organization supported by a diverse constituency of private and public sector organizations. The ANSI represents the interest of its nearly 1,400 company, organization, government agency, institutional and international members.

ANSI does not itself develop American National Standards (ANSs). ANSI facilitates communication and information exchange between members. ANSI's membership councils, standards boards and planning panels are neutral forums where members identify, discuss, and agree upon solutions to standards and conformity assessment issues. ANSI accredits qualified organizations to develop standards in the technical area in which they have expertise. ANSI's role is to administer the voluntary consensus standards system, providing a neutral forum for the development of policies on standards issues and serving as an oversight body to standards development and conformity assessment programs and processes. The Institute ensures that its guiding principles—consensus, due process and openness—are followed by more than 175 distinct entities currently accredited under one of the ANSI's three methods of accreditation (organization, committee or canvass). Today there are more than 13,000 ANSI-approved American national Standards. These documents provide dimensions, ratings, terminology and symbols, test methods, performance and safety requirements for products and services ranging from electric motors to screw threads, computers and robots to medical instruments. American national standards are voluntary.

ANSI-approved standards become mandatory when, and if, they are adopted or referenced by the government or when market forces make them imperative.

ANSI is the sole U.S. representative and dues-paying member of the two major non-treaty international standards organizations, the International Organization for Standardization (ISO), and via the U.S. National Committee (USNC), the International Electrotechnical Commission (IEC).

ANSI was a founding member of the ISO and plays an active role in its governance. ANSI is one of five permanent members to the governing ISO Council, and one of four permanent members of ISO's Technical Management Board. U.S. participation, through the U.S. National Committee (USNC), is equally strong in IEC. The USNC is one of the 12 members on the IEC's governing Committee of Action.

Through ANSI, the United States has immediate access to the ISO and IEC standards development processes. ANSI participates in almost the entire technical program of both the ISO (78 % of all ISO technical committees) and the IEC (91 % of all IEC technical committees) and administers many key committees. As a part of its responsibilities as the U.S. member body to the ISO and the IEC, ANSI accredits U.S. Technical Advisory Groups (U.S. TAGs) or USNC Technical Advisors (TAs). The U.S. TAG's (or TA's) primary purpose is to develop and transmit, via ANSI, U.S. positions on activities and ballots of the international technical committee. In many instances, U.S. standards are taken forward, through ANSI or its USNC, to the ISO or IEC where they are adopted in whole or in part as international standards. Since the work of international technical committees is carried out by volunteers from industry and government, not ANSI staff, the success of these efforts often is dependent upon the willingness of U.S. industry and the U.S. government to commit the resources to ensure strong U.S. technical participation in the international standards process.

The ANSI Consumer Interest Council (CIC) facilitates the representation of consumer interests in the voluntary standards process and enhances the effectiveness and credibility of the ANSI Federation. According to ANSI, consumers are defined as those individuals who use goods or services to satisfy their individual needs and desires, rather than to resell them or to produce other goods or services with them (CIF 2002). The CIC consists of knowledgeable representatives from consumer organizations, producers, retailers, distributors, industry councils, and government. Membership on the Council is open to consumer representatives who are willing to participate in its work and who express an interest in membership. CIC's goals are:

- Outreach and networking: build stronger relationships among ANSI and national and international organizations to:
  1. Increase standards awareness among consumer representatives, including increased participation in CIC and ANSI by government, consumers, business, and trade associations;
  2. Build dialogue on key issues by providing a primary forum and information source on consumer interest issues related to voluntary standards and conformity assessment;
  3. Develop effective information exchanges among consumer professionals;
  4. Provide consumer feedback to the ANSI Federation;
  5. Represent consumers before COPOLCO and other international standards related activities.
- Policy development: facilitate enhanced consumer interest participation throughout the ANSI process and organization.
- Consumer participation: encourage consumer participation in the development of standards for consumer products and services to identify and meet consumer concerns and needs.

The CIC is the US link to the COPOLCO (Consumer Policy Committee of the International Organization for Standardization). COPOLCO offers a unique opportunity to identify and influence issues developing in the international consumer community. COPOLCO provides a forum for the exchange of information and experience on consumer participation on current work within ISO and IEC affecting the consumer, on the implementation of standards in the consumer field and on any other question of interest for consumers in national and international standardization.

ANSI has a standards education web site www.standards-learn.org with a free online standards introduction "why standards matter."

4-2-4 American Society for Testing and Materials International (ASTM Intl) www.astm.org

Organized in 1898, ASTM International has grown into one of the largest voluntary standards development systems in the world. ASTM is a not-for-profit organization that provides a forum for producers, users, ultimate consumers, and those having a general interest (representatives of government and academia) to meet on common ground and write standards for materials, products, systems, and services. From the work of 132 standards-writing committees, ASTM publishes standard test methods, specifications, guides, classifications, and terminology. ASTM's standard development activities encompass metals, paints, plastics, textiles, petroleum, construction, energy, the environment, consumer products, medical services and devices, computerized systems, electronics, and many other areas. ASTM headquarters has no technical research or testing facilities; such work is done voluntarily by 35,000 technically qualified ASTM members located throughout the world. More than 9,100 ASTM standards are published each year in the 71 volumes of the Annual Book (or CD-ROM) of ASTM Standards. These standards and related information are sold throughout the world.

ASTM develops six principal types of full-consensus standards as follows (ASTM 1999):

Standard Test Method—a definitive procedure for the identification, measurement, and evaluation of one or more qualities, characteristics, or properties of a material, product, system, or service that produces a test result.

Standard Specification—a precise statement of a set of requirements to be satisfied by a material, system, or service that also indicates the procedures for determining whether each of the requirements is satisfied.

Standard Practice—a definitive procedure for performing one or more specific operations or functions that does not produce a test result.

Standard Terminology—a document composed of terms, definitions of terms, descriptions of terms, explanations of symbols, abbreviations, or acronyms.

Standard Guide—a series of options or instructions that do not recommend a specific course of action.

Standard Classification—a systematic arrangement or division of materials, products, systems, or services into groups based on similar characteristics such as origin, composition, properties, or use.

ASTM International offers web-based training for its members on standards and other related technical information.

A list of ASTM standards and specifications as well as volumes that may be of some interest to retailers are listed in the section 4-4 of this chapter.

4-2-5 British Standards Institution (BSI) www.bsi-global.com

The British Standards Institution (BSI) is the national standards body for the UK, independent of government, industry and trade associations. The BSI became the world's first national standards body after it was established in 1901 as the Engineering Standards Committee. The BSI pioneered international collaboration on standards writing as early as 1910 and by 1946 was instrumental in the formation of the international standards body, ISO. In 1979 the BSI produced the world's first management systems standard BS 5750. This standard formed the prototype for the ISO 9000 series. The BSI launched the world's first environmental management standard, BS 7750, which was adopted as ISO 14000 in 1976.

BSI produces independent standards through a committee process. The committee process used to draft standards was devised to avoid conflict of interest and to allow all relevant groups to participate in the formulation of a standard. When consensus is reached by a committee, a draft standard is put forward for public debate. To be certain that a standard meets the needs of all interested parties, from manufacturers to retailers to end users, all interests need to be represented in its development. Technical committees developing British standards are made up of volunteers—people of all ages and professions, including consumer representatives.

British standards are national guidelines for products ranging from toys to digital audio equipment, for services like complaint management and data protection. Most standards are voluntary although they can be made mandatory by law or regulation. If industry asks for a standard to be reviewed, BSI can facilitate this process. All standards are reviewed every five years, and if a standard is unworkable or no longer relevant it can be redrafted or replaced.

BS 6476:1984 British Standard Guide to Garment quality and relevant British Standards may be of some interest to retailers.

4-2-6 Canadian Standards Association (CSA) www.csa.ca

The Canadian Standards Association is a not-for-profit membership-based association serving business, industry, government and consumers in Canada and the global marketplace. CSA is accredited by the Standards Council of Canada (SCC) as a standards developing organization (SDO). CSA works closely with the International Association of Electrical Inspectors (IAEI), the Electrical Safety Foundation International (ESFI), Health Canada, provincial regulators, and the U. S. Consumer Product Safety Commission (CPSC) to promote standards for consumer safety in North America and around the world. The CSA marks mean a product has been tested and meets applicable standards for safety and/or performance, including the applicable standards written or administered by the American National Standards Institute (ANSI), Underwriters Laboratories (UL), Canadian Standards Association (CSA), National Sanitation Foundation International (NSF), and others.

4-2-7 European Committee for Standardization (CEN) www.cenorm.be

CEN, headquartered in Brussels, Belgium, is an independent, non-profit making European regional scientific and technical organization. It was started in 1961. CEN's mission is to promote voluntary technical harmonization in Europe in conjunction with worldwide bodies and its partners, such as ISO, IEC and the European Committee for Electrotechnical Standardization (CENELEC). CEN members are national standards bodies from Austria, Belgium, Czech Republic, Denmark, Finland, France, Germany, Greece, Iceland, Ireland, Italy, Luxembourg, Malta, Netherlands, Norway, Portugal, Spain, Sweden, Switzerland, and United Kingdom. Formal adoption of European standards is decided by a weighted majority vote of all CEN national members and is binding on all of them.

4-2-8 International Electrotechnical Commission (IEC) www.iec.ch

Founded in 1906 and currently headquartered in Geneva, Switzerland, IEC is the leading global organization that prepares and publishes international standards for all electrical, electronic and related technologies. These serve as a basis for national standardization and as reference when drafting international tenders and contracts. IEC is a counterpart (of sorts) to the ISO, but focuses on electrical and electronic components and products.

IEC's international standards facilitate world trade by removing technical barriers to trade. A component or system manufactured to IEC standards and manufactured in one country can be sold and used in other countries.

European standards (EN) that may be of interest to retailers are listed in the section 4-8 of this chapter.

4-2-9 International Organization for Standardization (ISO) www.iso.ch or www.iso.org

The International Organization for Standardization (ISO) is a worldwide federation of national standards bodies from some 120 countries, one from each country. ISO is a non-governmental organization established in 1947. The mission of ISO is to promote the development of standardization and related activities in the world with a view to facilitating the international exchange of goods and services, and to developing cooperation in the sphere of intellectual, scientific, technological and economic activity. ISO's work results in international agreements which are published as International Standards. At any one time there are about 7,000 projects and around 200,000 people contributing to ISO standards development.

ISO is a word derived from Greek isos, meaning "equal," which is the root of the prefix "iso" that occurs in a host of terms, such as "isometric" (of equal measure or dimensions) and "isonomy" (equal of laws, of people before the law). From "equal" to "standard," the line of thinking that led to the choice of "ISO" as the name of the organization is easy to follow. In addition, the name ISO is used around the world to denote the organization, thus avoiding the plethora of acronyms resulting from the translation of "International Organization for Standardization" into the different national languages of members.

The differences in the standards from country to country and region to region can contribute to so called "technical barriers to trade". Export oriented industries have always felt the need to agree on world standards to help international trade. This was the origin of the establishment of ISO. International standardization is now well established for very many technologies in such diverse field as information processing and communications, textiles, packaging, distribution of goods, energy production and utilization, shipbuilding, banking and financial services. It will continue to grow in importance for all sectors of industrial activity for the foreseeable future.

In order for consumers to provide input in standards development, ISO has a committee on consumer policy, COPOLCO (Consumer Policy Committee). At present it has 75 members distributed throughout the world. This committee has the following objectives:

a. To study means of helping consumers to benefit from standardization, and means of improving consumer participation in national and international standardization.
b. To provide a forum for the exchange of information on the experience of consumer participation in the development and implementation of standards in the consumer field, and on other questions of interest to consumers in national and international standardization.
c. To advise the ISO council as to the consolidated viewpoints of consumers on matters relevant to ISO's current and potential standardization and conformity assessment work.
d. To advise the ISO council on the need for new or revised policies or actions within ISO as they relate to consumers' needs.

Among various priority areas of interest to consumers identified by COPOLCO the following may be of interest to retailers:

- domestic appliances (safety and performance, including ergonomic aspects);
- child-related products (including toys and child resistant devices);
- sports and leisure goods (including personal and protective equipment);
- bicycles;
- furniture;
- safety of consumer products.

COPOLCO's task is to secure, through a procedure it has established, that standards development in the above priority areas progresses satisfactorily from the consumers' point of view, with adequate representation of consumer interests in the relevant technical bodies.

As of this writing, Standards Australia International, Ltd. (SAI), the national standards body of Australia has floated a proposal to COPOLCO for a new technical committee on safety of household products. According to SAI, consumer products are often manufactured according to the specifications of large importers, which are

not necessarily identical with those of small importers. Therefore, the absence of international standards may result in higher costs to importing nations with small markets and particular specifications regarding safety of consumer products. COPOLCO members agreed to form an ad hoc committee comprised of national interests that would consider various aspects of the proposal in more detail.
ISO provides a well-established process and organization to protect the integrity with which International Standards (IS) are developed, validated and approved and by which compliance is assessed and certified. Compliance with international standards is normally voluntary unless adopted into legislature framework of a country, in which case they become mandatory.

COPOLCO also recently recommended to ISO the development of international standards in the field of second-hand (used) goods. Specific product areas of concern are used tires, used vehicles, used electrical appliances, tools, machinery and equipment, and used clothing. It is believed that the proposed ISO standards would serve to supplement national regulations, particularly in developing and transitional economies where consumer protection laws may be less developed or non existent.

An excellent overview of how ISO standards are developed is available on the ISO website www.iso.org/iso/en/stdsdevelopment/whowhenhow/how.html

A number of ISO standards of interest to retailers are listed in the section 4-7 of this chapter as well as in other appropriate chapters of this book.

4-2-10 Standards Council of Canada (SCC)

www.scc.ca

The Standards Council of Canada (SCC) is a federal Crown corporation with the mandate to promote efficient and effective standardization in Canada by coordinating and overseeing the efforts of the national Standards System, which includes organizations and individuals involved in voluntary standards development, promotion and implementation in Canada. More than some 14,000 Canadian volunteers contribute to committees that develop national or international standards. Some 250 organizations have been accredited by the Standards Council. Some of these develop standards, others are conformity assessment bodies which determine the compliance of products or services to a standard's requirements. Accredited standards development organizations may submit standards to the Standards Council for approval as National Standards of Canada. This designation indicates that the given document meets criteria that are important to many standards users.

The Standards Council coordinates the contribution of Canadians to the ISO and IEC. Located in Ottawa, the Standards Council has a 15-member governing Council and a staff of approximately 70. The organization reports to Parliament through the Ministry of Industry.

4-2-11 Underwriters Laboratories (UL) www.ul.com

Underwriters Laboratories (UL) is an independent, not for profit organization providing global conformity assessment programs and services. In addition to being a leader in product safety certification and conformity assessment services, UL is a world leader in standards development. UL's standards for safety are used to evaluate and certify products and systems. These standards are used by manufacturers to help design products and systems to meet requirements of certification, by regulatory authorities who reference the standards for products and systems used in their jurisdictions, by code development organizations that adopt and reference UL standards for safety, and by certification organizations that apply UL requirements for product evaluations. UL uses several standards development methods that have been approved by the American National Standards Institute (ANSI) to achieve recognition of a UL standard as an ANSI/UL standard. Therefore, many of the UL standards become American National Standards. UL standards on consumer products are listed in the section 4-6 of this chapter.

4-3 Developing Standards and Specifications

There are many advantages of participating in standards development activities. One advantage is that you can bring a retailer's view point or consumers' voice in standards development so standards are realistic and consumer friendly. Another advantage is that by getting involved in standards development, you will keep abreast of various developments in products, services and their standards. You will be up-to-date and know what is coming in future trends, changes in requirements or specifications, and therefore, be able to prepare in advance to meet those trends or requirements. Retailers' involvement in the development of standards, and the processes that evaluate whether products comply with standards, increases the likelihood that products will be accepted in the marketplace. Since consumers are the ultimate end users of the products which are based on these standards and retailers sell these products, retailers are ideally suitable to participate in standards development activities.

In 2003 Canadian government asked CSA (Canadian Standards Association) to undertake a specific study to assess current processes for consumer and public involvement in CSA standards work in energy efficiency and offer recommendations about how to enhance consumer involvement in this area of standards work. The research included surveys of participants as well as a benchmarking study on various models of public participation in standards development and rule making.

The results showed that active and informed consumer participation in the standards process can bring a considerable number of benefits to standards work and helps to create demanding standards that meet real consumer expectations.

While the research focused on energy efficiency standards, the findings provide valuable information that can be applied to other voluntary standards work (Bank 2003).

Various standards developing organizations, including ISO, have ways to get consumer representatives (retailers, consumer advocates, educational institutions, etc.) involved in standards development through something like the a Consumer Advisory Council or Consumer Interest Council.

Quality assurance staff are often called upon to specify performance standards and product specifications. If a decision is to use existing standards such as from ASTM, AATCC, UL, etc., then the job is that much easier. However, sometimes, there are no standards or a retailer may want to develop its own standards and specifications for its private label merchandise. When a decision is made to have private label items such as clothing, health and beauty products, appliances, table tops (dishes, placemats, flatware, etc.), etc., the buyer has a general idea as to how he/she expects those items to compete in the market place. Knowing this, development of standards and specifications is a matter of reverse engineering, i.e., testing competing products for various properties and characteristics and then deciding where you want to place your product in terms of those values.

The GMM (General Merchandise Manager) of a large retailer asked it's QA division to develop specifications for it's private label men's short sleeve woven sports shirts and identified private labels of three department stores in the area as competing brands. The QA specialist for men's wear bought competing shirts from those three stores, measured them and tested them. The results are in Tables 4-1 through 4-6.

	Brand A	Brand B	Brand C
Style	XYZ	ABC	LMN
Made In	Sri Lanka	Jamaica	Bangladesh
Price	$ 20.00	$22.00	$13.99
Fiber Content	55% cotton and	55% cotton and	35% cotton
	45% polyester	45% polyester	65% polyester
Fabric Weight (oz/yd^2)	2.8	2.9	2.7
(Ends x Picks)/inch	108 x 68	109 x 72	101 x 69
Type of Weave	Plain	Plain	Plain
Care Instructions	Machine wash cold with like colors. Only non-chlorine bleach when needed. Tumble dry low. Steam iron.	Machine wash warm normal cycle. Use non-chlorine bleach when needed. Wash separately or with like colors. Tumble dry low. Press with warm steam iron.	Machine wash warm. Tumble dry. Only non-chlorine bleach when needed. Warm iron when needed.
Shrinkage in Three Laundering %	Length – 2.0 Width – 1.0	Length – 1.5 Width – 1.0	Length – 1.0 Width – 0.5
Fabric Strength (lbs)			
Length	68.0	70.1	81.5
Width	41.8	44.7	53.6
Seam Strength (lbs)			
Arm Opening	50.0^{+}	48.1^{+}	64.6^{+}
Side Seam	40.5^{+}	46.4^{+}	49.1^{+}
Shoulder Seam	73.4^{+}	63.4^{+}	77.5^{+}
Yoke seam	69.7^{+}	64.1^{+}	73.2^{+}
	+ Indicates fabric rupture	+ Indicates fabric rupture	+ Indicates fabric rupture
Pilling resistance @ 5000 Rubs	5	5	5
Abrasion Resistance	442 Rubs	487 Rubs	525 Rubs
Colorfastness to Washing			
Staining	5	5	5
Change in Shade	5	5	5
Colorfastness to Light (40 hours)	5	4	5
Colorfastness to Rubbing	5.0 – Dry 4.5 - Wet	5.0 – Dry 4.0 - Wet	4.5 – Dry 4.0 - Wet
Colorfastness to Perspiration	5	4.5	4.5
Durable Press Rating			
Fabric	2.9	3.3	3.4
Collar	3.0	3.3	3.8
Arm Hole Seam	2.6	3.1	3.6
Side Seam	2.5	2.9	3.6
Yoke Seam	2.8	3.7	3.9
Cuffs	3.1	3.4	3.7
Pocket	2.7	2.8	3.3
Front Placket	2.2	2.0	2.6
Overall	2.7	3.0	3.5

Notes:

1. In pilling resistance, a rating of 5 indicates no pilling and a rating of 1 indicates heavy pilling.
2. In colorfastness to washing, a rating of 5 indicates no staining and/or change in shade, while a rating of I indicates heavy staining and/or change in shade.
3. In colorfastness to light, a rating of 5 indicates no fading and a rating of 1 indicates heavy fading.
4. In colorfastness to rubbing and perspiration, a rating of 5 indicates no color transfer and a rating of 1 indicates heavy color transfer.
5. In durable press, a rating of 5 indicates no need for ironing and a rating of 1 indicates need for heavy ironing.

Table 4-1 Comparative Performance of Men's Short Sleeve Woven Sports Shirts

Tables 4-2 through 4-6 show comparative measurements of these shirts from three retailers.

Size	Small	Small
Brand	B	C
	Inches	Inches
Length	31 ¼	30 3/8
Chest Width	42 ½	41 ¾
Crossback Width	18 1/2	16 5/8
Sleeve Length		
Crossback	19 3/8	18 ¾
Top	9 7/8	10 1/8
Bottom	7 3/8	7 ¼
Sleeve Cuff	16 ¾	14 ¼
Arm Hole	21	19
Neck	15 3/8	15

Table 4-2 Measurements of Men's Woven Short Sleeve Sports Shirts, Size Small

Size	Medium	Medium	Medium
Brand	A	B	C
	Inches	Inches	Inches
Length	31 1/8	31 ¼	30 5/8
Chest Width	44 ½	44 5/8	46 1/8
Crossback Width	18 7/8	19	18
Sleeve Length			
Crossback	21 5/8	20	19 5/8
Top	12 1/8	10 ¼	10 ½
Bottom	8 ¼	7 1/2	7
Sleeve Cuff	17 3/8	17 ¼	15 ¼
Arm Hole	21 ½	22	20
Neck	16 3/8	16	15 3/4

Table 4-3 Measurements of Men's Woven Short Sleeve Sports Shirts, Size Medium

Size	Large	Large	Large
Brand	A	B	C
	Inches	Inches	Inches
Length	32 ¼	33 ¼	31 ¾
Chest Width	48 ¾	47	49 1/8
Crossback Width	19 3/8	19 ¾	19 1/4
Sleeve Length			
Crossback	21 7/8	21 1/8	20 5/16
Top	12	11 1/8	10 3/8
Bottom	8 ¼	6 7/8	7 1/2
Sleeve Cuff	18 3/8	17 ¼	16
Arm Hole	22 7/8	22 ¾	20 7/8
Neck	17 ½	17 ¼	17

Table 4-4 Measurements of Men's Woven Short Sleeve Sports Shirts, Size Large

Size	X-Large	X-Large	X-Large
Brand	A	B	C
	Inches	Inches	Inches
Length	33 ½	33 3/8	32
Chest Width	51 ½	50 1/8	52
Crossback Width	19 7/8	20 ½	20 3/8
Sleeve Length			
Crossback	22 7/8	21 7/8	20 3/4
Top	12 ¾	11 5/8	10 5/8
Bottom	8 ¼	6 7/8	7 1/4
Sleeve Cuff	19 ½	18	16 3/4
Arm Hole	23	24	21 5/8
Neck	18	17 7/8	18 1/4

Table 4-5 Measurements of Men's Woven Short Sleeve Sports Shirts, Size X-Large

Size	XX-Large	XX-Large
Brand	A	B
	Inches	Inches
Length	34 1/16	33
Chest Width	54	54 5/8
Crossback Width	20 5/8	21 5/8
Sleeve Length		
Crossback	23 ¼	22 7/8
Top	12 13/16	12 1/16
Bottom	8 ¾	7
Sleeve Cuff	19 ¼	18 1/2
Arm Hole	24	26 1/8
Neck	19 ½	18 1/2

Table 4-6 Measurements of Men's Woven Short Sleeve Sports Shirts, Size XX-Large

Based on the above results, Tables 4-7 and 4-8 show performance standards or specifications and size measurements, respectively, for the private label men's woven short sleeve sports shirts that were provided to the GMM requesting development of such specifications.

	Private Label	Test Method
Style		
Fiber Content	55% cotton and	AATCC 20A
	45% polyester	
Fabric Weight (oz/yd^2)	2.8 minimum	ASTM D 3776
(Ends x Picks)/inch	100 x 68 minimum	ASTM D 3775
Type of Weave	Plain	Visual
Care Instructions	Machine wash warm with like colors. Only non-chlorine bleach when needed. Tumble dry low. Remove promptly and iron if necessary.	ASTM D 3938
Shrinkage in Three Laundering %	Length – 3.0 max. Width – 3.0 max.	AATCC 150
Fabric Strength (lbs)		ASTM D 5034
Length	65.0 minimum	
Width	55.0 minimum	
Seam Strength (lbs)		ASTM D 1683
Arm Opening	30.0 minimum	
Side Seam	30.0 minimum	
Shoulder Seam	30.0 minimum	
Yoke seam	30.0 minimum	
Pilling resistance @ 5000 Rubs	4.5 minimum	ASTM D 3514
Abrasion Resistance	450 Rubs minimum	ASTM D 3886
Colorfastness to Washing		AATCC 61
Staining	3 min.	
Change in Shade	3 min.	
Colorfastness to Light (40 hours)	3 min.	AATCC 16E
Colorfastness to Rubbing	3.0 – Dry min. 3.0 – Wet min.	AATCC 8
Colorfastness to Perspiration	3.0 min.	AATCC 15
Durable Press Rating	3.0 min. in all areas	AATCC 88B,C and 124

Table 4-7 Suggested Performance Standards for Men's Private Label Short Sleeve Woven Sports Shirts

Size	S	M	L	XL	XXL	Tolerances
Brand						
	Inches	Inches	Inches	Inches	Inches	Inch
Length	32	32 ½	33	33 ½	34	± 1
Chest Width	44	46	48	52	56	± 1
Crossback Width	19	19 ½	20	20 ¾	22	± 1/2
Sleeve Length						
Crossback	19 ½	20 ¼	21	21 ¾	22 ½	± 1/2
Top	10	10 ¾	11 ½	12 ¼	13	± 1/2
Bottom	7 ½	8	8 ½	9	9 ½	± 1/2
Sleeve Cuff	16 ½	17	17 ½	18 ½	19	± 1/2
Arm Hole	21	22	23	24	25	± 1/2
Neck	15	16	17	18	19	± 1/2

Table 4-8 Suggested Size Specifications for Men's Private Label Short Sleeve Woven Sports Shirts

On the following pages are some examples of fabric performance specifications used by several organizations.

Conformance Property	Minimum Requirements	Test Method
General Fabric Qualities		
Defects	No appreciable major defects	ASTM D 3990
Color uniformity	Uniform color within a garment panel. Uniform color from section to section	Visual
Strength Properties		
Breaking Strength (W & F)	11.3 Kg (25lbs)	ASTM D 5034
Tear Strength (W & F)	680 g (1.5 lbs.)	ASTM D 1424
Wearing Qualities (Abrasion Resistance)		
Surface Wearing Qualities	75 rubs	ASTM D 3886
Edge Wearing Qualities	75 rubs @ 8mm radius	ASTM D 3885
Pilling Resistance	No appreciable pilling @ 7000 rubs	ASTM D 3514
Resistance to Seam Slippage	10 lbs. @ 1/8 in. opening	ASTM D 434
Dimensional Stability (W & F)	3.0 % Max.	AATCC Test Method 96
Colorfastness Properties		
In Washing	Class 4.0	AATCC Test Method 61
In Crocking (Dry & Wet)	Class 4.0	AATCC Test Method 8
In Perspiration	Class 4.0	AATCC Test Method 15
To Light	10 hours	AATCC Test Method 16A
Durable Press Qualities		
Fabric	Class 3.5	AATCC Test Method 124
Seams & Stitching	Class 3.5	AATCC Test Method 88B
Seam Strength	11.3 Kg (25 lbs.)	ASTM D 1683
Flammability (Flannel)	Class 1.0	AATCC Test Method 33

Table 4-9 Fabric Performance Standards of an Outerwear Manufacturing Firm

Conformance Property	Minimum/Maximum	Test Method
Cold water bleeding	4 (3 for indigo denim)	AATCC 107
Colorfastness to Crocking		AATCC 8
Pigment printed and black	3 Dry, 2 Wet	
All other fabrics	4 Dry, 3 Wet	
Colorfastness to Washing		AATCC 61 IIA
Pigment printed and black	3 Change, 2.5 Stain	
All other fabrics	4 Change, 3.5 Stain	
Colorfastness to Light	4 Change	AATCC 16 (16 hours minimum)
Colorfastness to Sublimation	4 Change/Stain	AATCC 133
Colorfastness to Ozone	4 Change	AATCC 109 (2 cycles)
Burst Strength	60 lbs.	ASTM D 3786
Stretch (5 lbs.)	Min. Max.	ASTM D 6614
1 x 1 and 2 x 2 Ribs	100 % 140 %	
Interlock	60 % 140 %	
Jersey, Pique, Terry	40 % N/A	
1 x 1 Rib containing Lycra	150 % N/A	
Fleece (Unprinted)	20 % N/A	
Printed Fleece	12 % N/A	
Growth	20 % (80 % Recovery)	ASTM D 6614
Needle Cutting	None	ASTM D 1908
Shrinkage		ASTM D 3776
1 x 1 and 2 x 2 Ribs	12 % x 12 %	
Jersey, Pique, Terry, Interlock	7 % x 7 %	
Fleece	12 % x 7 %	
Mesh	4 % x 4 %	
Weight	Specified + or - 5 %	ASTM D 3776
Flammability	State & Fed. Reg.	CS 191-53 & ASTM D 1230 see also 16 CFR Parts 1610,1615 or 1616
Stripe Bow and Bias	See Attachment	Physical Inspection
Random Tumble pilling	3.0	ASTM D 1375 (30 minutes)

Note: The average result of samples tested from each shipment must meet minimum standards. Sample sizes range from 2 to 5, depending on the shipment size and severity of sampling required.

Table 4-10 Knit Fabric Quality Standards of a Children's Wear Manufacturer

Conformance Property	Minimum/Maximum	Test Method
Cold water bleeding	4 (3 for indigo denim)	AATCC 107
Colorfastness to crocking		AATCC 8
Indigo denim	3 Dry, 2.5 Wet	
Black	3 Dry, 2 Wet	
Pigment printed or dyed	3 Dry, 2 Wet	
All other fabrics	4 Dry, 3 Wet	
Colorfastness to Washing		AATCC 61 IIA
Indigo denim and black	3 Change, 2.5 Stain	
All other fabrics	4 Change, 3 Stain	
Colorfastness to Light	4 Change	AATCC 16 (16 hours minimum)
Colorfastness to Sublimation	4 Change/Stain	AATCC 133
Resistance to Yarn Slippage @ 1/4 in.		ASTM D 434
9 oz and heavier	25 lbs.	
Shirts, dresses and less than 9 oz	20 lbs.	
Tensile		ASTM D 1683 (Grab)
9 oz and heavier	50 lbs.	
Shirts, dresses, less than 9 oz	30 lbs.	
Tear		ASTM 1424 (Elmendorf)
Above 10 oz	6 lbs.	
Less than 9 oz for bottom, shorts and corduroy	3 lbs.	
Shirts and dresses	2 lbs.	
Shrinkage	4 % x 4 %	ASTM D 3776
Weight	Specified + or - 5 %	ASTM D 3776
Flammability	State & Fed. Reg.	CS 191-53 & ASTM D 1230 see also 16 CFR Parts 1610,1615 or 1616
Stripe Bow and Bias	See Attachment	Physical Inspection

Note: The average result of samples tested from each shipment must meet minimum standards. Sample sizes range from 2 to 5, depending on the shipment size and severity of sampling required.

Table 4-11 Woven Fabric Quality Standards of a Children's Wear Manufacturer

Property	Test Method	100 % Polyester	Shirting and blends	Tubular single knits	Cotton velour
Appearance	AATCC-124, IIB (3 washes)	4.0	4.0	-	-
Crease Retention	AATCC-88C, IIC (3 washes)	3.0	3.0	-	-
Bursting Strength	ASTM-231 (Mullen)	60	40	40	-
Shrinkage					
Pressing & Curing	Appropriate cycles	2% x 2%	3% x 3%	-	-
Washing	AATCC 135, IIB (3 washes)	3% x 3%	3% x 3%	8% x 8%	12% x 12%
Total		4% x 4%	5% x 5%		
Restorable to	AATCC-96, IIE-2 (Restoration procedure)			5% x 5%	6% x 6%
Growth % after 1 hour recovery	ASTM D 6614	4%	4%	4%	4%
Crockfastness	AATCC-8				
Dry		4	3-4	-	3-4
Wet		3	2-3	-	2-3
Colorfastness to Abrasion	AATCC-119	4	3-4	-	-
Colorfastness to Sublimation 30 seconds, dry contact heat @ 350°F	AATCC 133	4	3-4	-	-
Colorfastness to Laundering	AATCC-61, IIA				
Shade Change		4	3-4	-	3-4
Staining		4	3-4	-	3-4

Table 4-12 Minimum Fabric Performance Standards for Knit Fabrics made by the Apparel fabric Division of a Large Mill in the USA

Property	Test Method	End Use Jeans	End Use Casuals
Washed Appearance	AATCC-124, IIB (3 washes)	3.5	3.5
Crease Retention	AATCC-88C, IIC (3 washes)	4	4
Seam Slippage	ASTM D 434	35 lbs.	25 lbs.
Shrinkage	AATCC-135, IIB (3 washes)		
Pre-curred, warp x fill		2% x 2%	2% x 2%
Post-curred, warp x fill		2% x 2%	2% x 2%
Pressing & Curing	Appropriate Cycles	2% x 2%	2% x 2%
Washing		2% x 2%	2% x 2%
Total (press, cure, & wash)		3.5 % x 3.5%	3.5% x 3.5%
Non-permanent Press[1]	AATCC-96, IIE-3 (3 washes)	3% x 3%	3% x 3%
Tear Strength (Elmendorf)	ASTM D 1424	3.5 lbs.	3.0 lbs.
Tensile Strength (grab)	ASTM D 1682	60 lbs.	50 lbs.
Crockfastness[2]	AATCC-8		
Dry		3-4	3-4
Wet		2-3	2-3
Colorfastness to Abrasion	AATCC-119	3-4	3-4
Colorfastness to Sublimation	AATCC 133		
30 seconds, dry contact heat @ 350°F		3	3
Colorfastness to Laundering	AATCC-61, IIA		
Shade Change		3-4	3-4
Staining		3-4	3-4

1- Non-permanent press fabrics tested for shrinkage in a home washing machine and tumble dryer must be hand steam ironed sufficiently to restore to a wearable level of smoothness before measuring shrinkage.

2- Crocking of dark colors and reds cannot be guaranteed because of limitations in the current state of technology.

Table 4-13 Minimum Fabric Performance Standards for Men's and Boys' Woven Sportswear Fabrics made by the Apparel Fabrics Division of a Large Mill in the USA

Test Description	Specification	Test Method[1]
Fabric Weight	Specified ± 10%	101
Construction		
Ends/Inch	Specified ± 5 %	103
Picks/Inch	Specified ± 5 %	103
Tensile Strength		
Warp (lbs.)	50.0 min.	201
Filling (lbs.)	40.0 min.	201
Tear Strength		
Warp (lbs.)	3.5 min.	203
Filling (lbs.)	3.0 min.	203
Flat Abrasion (cycles)	300 min.	205
Random Tumble Pilling (30 min.)	4.0 min.	212
Seam Failure (lbs.)	32.0 min.	213/4
Dimensional Stability		
Length (%)	3.0 max.	305
Width (%)	3.0 max.	305
Appearance Retention	Satisfactory	306
Color Permanency to		
Light (20 AFU)	4.0 min.	401
Accelerated Washing/Dry-cleaning		
Shade Change	4.0 min.	402/3
Staining	3.0 min.	402/3
Home Laundering		
Shade Change	4.0 min.	410
Staining	4.0 min.	410
Crocking		
Dry	4.0 min.	404
Wet	3.5 min.	404
Perspiration		
Shade Change	4.0 min.	405
Stain	4.0 min.	405
Chlorine Bleach	4.5 min.	412
Non-chlorine Bleach	4.5 min.	419
Flammability	Pass – Class 1	16 CFR Parts 1610, 1615 or 1616

1- These are this organization's test methods.

Table 4-14 Woven Fabric Performance Specifications for Premium Apparel of a Large Retail Organization—Predominantly Cotton Fabric Weight ≥ 3.5 oz./sq.yd.

Test Description	Specification	Test Method[1]
Fabric Weight	Specified ± 10 %	101
Construction		
Wales/Inch	Specified ± 5 %	103
Courses/Inch	Specified ± 5 %	103
Bursting Strength (lbs.)	40.0 min.	208
Random Tumble Pilling (30 min.)	4.0 min.	212
Dimensional Stability		
Length (%)	5.0 max.	305
Width (%)	5.0 max.	305
Appearance Retention	Satisfactory	306
Color Permanency to		
Light (20 AFU)	4.0 min.	401
Accelerated Washing/Dry-cleaning		
Shade Change	4.0 min.	402/3
Staining	3.0 min.	402/3
Home Laundering		
Shade Change	3.5 min.	410
Staining	3.5 min.	410
Crocking		
Dry	4.0 min.	404
Wet	3.0 min.	404
Perspiration		
Shade Change	3.5 min.	405
Staining	3.5 min.	405
Chlorine Bleach	4.5 min.	412
Non-chlorine Bleach	4.5 min.	419
Flammability	Pass – Class 1	16 CFR Parts 1610, 1615 or 1616

1- These are this organization's test methods.

Table 4-15 Knit Fabric Performance Specifications for Premium Apparel of a Large Retail Organization—Predominantly Manmade Fabric Weight < 4.0 oz./sq.yd.

Test Description	Specification	Test Method[1]
Fabric Weight	Specified ± 10%	A-8
Construction		
Ends/Inch	Specified ± 5 %	A-7
Picks/Inch	Specified ± 5 %	A-7
Tensile Strength		
Warp (lbs.)	35.0 min.	A-9
Filling (lbs.)	35.0 min.	A-9
Tear Strength		
Warp (lbs.)	1.5 min.	A-11
Filling (lbs.)	1.5 min.	A-11
Flat Abrasion (cycles)	300 min.	A-13
Resistance to Pilling @ 5000 Rubs	3.0 min.	A-14
Seam Strength (lbs.)	20.0 min.	A-12
Dimensional Stability (3-5 Laundering or Dry-cleaning)		
Length (%)	5.0 max.	A-6
Width (%)	3.0 max.	A-6
Appearance Retention	Satisfactory	AATCC 143
Smoothness of Seams after Repeated Home Laundering	3.0 min.	A-15
Color Fastness to		
Light (20 AFU)	4.0 min.	A-4
Accelerated Washing/Dry-cleaning		AATCC 61
Shade Change	3.0 min.	
Staining	3.0 min.	
Home Laundering		
Shade Change	3.0 min.	A-6
Staining	3.0 min.	A-6
Crocking		
Dry	3.0 min.	A-2
Wet	3.0 min.	A-2
Perspiration		
Shade Change	3.0 min.	A-3
Staining	3.0 min.	A-3
Chlorine Bleach	4.0 min.	AATCC 3
Non-chlorine Bleach	4.0 min.	AATCC 172
Flammability	Pass – Class 1	16 CFR Parts 1610, 1615 or 1616

1- These are this organization's test methods.

Table 4-16 Woven Fabric Performance Specifications for Standard Apparel of a Retail Organization

Test Description	Specification	Test Method[1]
Fabric Weight	Specified ± 10 %	A-8
Construction		
Wales/Inch	Specified ± 5 %	A-7
Courses/Inch	Specified ± 5 %	A-7
Bursting Strength (lbs.)	50.0 min.	A-10
Resistance to Pilling @ 5000 Rubs	4.0 min.	A-14
Dimensional Stability (3-5 Laundering or Dry-cleaning)		
Length (%)	5.0 max.	A-6
Width (%)	5.0 max.	A-6
Appearance Retention	Satisfactory	AATCC 143
Color Fastness to		
Light (20 AFU)	4.0 min.	A-4
Accelerated Washing/Dry-cleaning		AATCC 61
Shade Change	3.0 min.	
Staining	3.0 min.	
Home Laundering		
Shade Change	3.0 min.	A-6
Staining	3.0 min.	A-6
Crocking		
Dry	3.0 min.	A-2
Wet	3.0 min.	A-2
Perspiration		
Shade Change	3.0 min.	A-3
Staining	3.0 min.	A-3
Chlorine Bleach	4.0 min.	AATCC 3
Non-chlorine Bleach	4.0 min.	AATCC 172
Flammability	Pass – Class 1	16 CFR Parts 1610,1615 or 1616

1- These are this organization's test methods.

Table 4-17 Knit Fabric Performance Specifications for Standard Apparel of a Large Retail Organization

The following table shows an example of specifications for dinnerware.

Item Description	Requirements	Standard/Test method
Packaging/labeling	Manufacturer's name, stamp, country of origin and product identification must appear on the package	16 CFR 500[1]. Visual Examination
Use & care Instructions	Must be complete and adequate	Visual Examination
Capacity	Within ± 5 % of claim	Measure the capacity
Lead & Cadmium Leaching	Not to exceed limits	U.S. FDA CPG 7117.06-07
Lead & Cadmium leaching in Lip & Rim (Mugs only)	Not to exceed limits	ASTM C 927
Lead Content in Surface Paint (if applicable)	Not to exceed limits	16 CFR 1303
Washability	Must be dishwasher safe	Minimum 5 wash cycles without break, crack or change in shade or fading of design/color. Visual Examination.
Microwaveability	Must be microwave safe otherwise it must be clearly stated	For microwave safe items, fill tap water up to 80% of the capacity and heat at 1000 watts setting for 5 minutes. No crack or breakage accepted. Visual Examination.
Thermal Shock	Must be able to handle thermal shocks	Heat up to 350^0 F for an hour in convection oven. No breakage, crack or change in appearance. Visual Examination.
Environmental Exposure	Must be able to withstand environmental exposure	Expose at 60^0 C and 95 % relative humidity for 48 hours. No change in appearance. Visual Examination.
Manufacturer Marking	Must be permanently printed on the back of the item	Visual examination
Construction and Workmanship	Must be free of bubbles, nicks, dents, scratches, and free of impurities	Visual Examination

1- Title 16 Commercial Practices, Chapter I—Federal Trade Commission, Part 500—Regulations Under Section 4 of the Fair Packaging and Labeling Act.

Table 4-18 Performance Specifications for Dinnerware (Porcelain, China, Stoneware)

Test Description	Requirements	Standards
Candle Performance		
Flame Length	Maximum 1 ½, Minimum ¼ inch	1 ½ inch
Burning Characteristics	Wax pool temperature (if applicable)	180° F
	Max. container temperature—all area	160° F
	Wick length before burn	¼ to ¾ inch
	Wax overflow and/or dripping	None or minimal
	Wick mushroom/blooming	Minimal
	Wick ash	Minimal
	Wick afterglow smoking	10 seconds
	Ignition of decorative components	None
	Re-ignition of wick once extinguished	None
	Soot deposit and/or smoke	None
	Wick placement-centering	Within 1/8" of center
	Wick drowning out	None
Burn Time (Life of Candle)	90% of the advertised or labeled claim	
Construction/Workmanship		
Lead Content	<0.06 % by weight for painted candles only Wick core should be free of lead	
Candle	Wick must be secure No dents, scratches, cracks, or distortion of wax Candle base must be flat and stable	
Candle Holder/Container	No dents, scratches, or cracks Base must be flat and stable	
Labeling and Packaging	Must have following information on the candle Country of origin Name and place of the manufacturer, Packer, or distributor including city, State, and zip code Net weight and dimension Net quantity of contents for packaged candles Life of candle (burn time)	16 CFR 500 Fair Packaging and Labeling Act
	Warning	ASTM F 2058 Standard Specification of Cautionary Labeling For Candles

Recommended warning label by ASTM

> ⚠ WARNING
>
> To prevent fire
>
> - Keep burning candle within sight
> - Keep out of reach of children and pets
> - Never burn a candle on or near anything that can catch fire

Table 4-19 Performance Specifications for Candles

Here is an example of jewelry specifications.

XYZ Corporation
Jewelry Specifications

A sample will be inspected in its entirety, i.e. quality of diamond(s) and/or stone(s), quality of mounting, precious metal content, stamping and tagging. Diamonds shall be graded for clarity and color based upon the Gemological Institute of America's (GIA's) diamond grading scale.

The Following jewelry specifications are the minimum acceptable requirements. All jewelry shall either meet or exceed the following:

1. REQUIREMENTS FOR DIAMONDS:

A. Acceptable Carat Weight Ranges:

Carat Wt.		Range	Carat Wt.		Range
1/4	=	0.23 to 0.29	1 1/2	=	1.45 to 1.62
1/3	=	0.30 to 0.36	2	=	1.90 to 2.22
1/2	=	0.45 to 0.58	2 1/2	=	2.45 to 2.62
3/4	=	0.70 to 0.83	3	=	2.90 to 3.19
7/8	=	0.84 to 0.94			
1	=	0.95 to 1.15			
1 ¼	=	1.16 to 1.29			
1 1/3	=	1.30 to 1.44			

		Best	Better	Good
B.	Clarity:	VS_2 or better	SI_2 or better	I_3 or better
C.	Color :	G or better	J or better	M or better

D. Cut: Must be well cut and proportioned. Fancy shaped diamonds with unattractive or unbalanced cuts will be unacceptable.

2. ALL DIAMONDS:

A. No knife-edge girdles or extremely thick girdles in the diamond.
B. No dark centers in the diamond which are the result of light leakage caused by too deep of a pavilion.
C. Round diamonds must have a table percentage between 52% and 67%.
D. Round diamonds must have crown angles no less than 30 degrees or greater than 38 degrees.
E. Diamonds must be good or better symmetry and polish.
F. No chips, breaks or fractures in the stone.
G. No laser drilled diamonds.
H. No treated (clarity enhanced) diamonds including fracture filled treatment.
I. No diamonds will have strong fluorescence.
J. Culet size on diamond must be None—Medium.
K. On all items containing more than one diamond, the diamonds shall face up approximately the same size and color.
l. Diamonds must be properly seated, securely set and not loose.

3. COLORED STONES:

A. All colored stones shall be of natural origin unless specified in the contract as being synthetic, simulated, or imitation.
B. Colored stones shall not have any eye-visible damage.
C. No colored stones which are enhanced by a non-permanent or superficial process shall be accepted. Oiling of emeralds is acceptable as it is industry practice.
D. In any jewelry item containing more than one of the same colored stone, all stones shall be matching in color and size unless the design of the piece of jewelry is purposely made for variation.

4. REQUIREMENTS FOR MOUNTING

A. All mountings should be with six prongs and must have minimum finished pennyweight as follows:

Carat Weight of Stone(s)	Minimum Finished Penny weight (DWT)[1]
1/4	1.20
1/3	1.25
1/2	1.55
3/4	1.55
1	1.65
1 1/2	1.80
2	1.80
2 1/2	1.85
3	1.90

1- One penny weight = 1/20 ounce or 24 grains

B. All items shall be plumb gold as defined by the National Gold & Silver Stamping Act 15 U.S.C. 291, et seq and the Federal Trade Commission (FTC), unless otherwise specified. Reference: FTC Guides for the Jewelry, Precious Metals and Pewter Industries, 16 C.F.R. Part 23 Section 23.4.

C. Porosity shall not be acceptable if it affects the aesthetic value or durability of the item.

D. Castings shall be free of stress damage, breaks and fractures, and excess metal flashing. All castings shall be complete and strong.

E. All items shall be properly constructed and strong. Indentations, holes, excessive or incomplete amounts of solder which affect appearance or product durability are not acceptable.

F. All items shall be smooth and uniformly polished. File marks, scratches, nicks, protrusions and rough edges are not acceptable.

G. All white gold shall be rhodium plated.

H. All items must have the stone settings securely and accurately soldered so that they are straight, balanced and even in position on the item.

I. All stones shall be properly seated and securely set, i.e., stones shall not be loose. All prongs or heads shall be uniform, straight and flush with the stone. The prongs shall not have sharp edges or points. Excessive prong coverage which detracts from the appearance of the item shall not be accepted. Insufficient prong coverage or over polished prongs which affect the durability of the prong or security of the stone are not acceptable. Stone pavilions shall not protrude into the finger area.

J. All rings for stock shall be furnished in size(s) specified on the purchase order and must be within 1/4 size of the size stated on the purchase order.

K. Earring backs shall be of sufficient strength to withstand normal wear without bending or coming loose. Earring backs shall be a minimum weight of 0.20 grams with a 0.033" post hole. Earring posts shall be a minimum of 0.033" thick by 7/16" in length.

5. REQUIREMENTS FOR STAMPING:

A. All jewelry shall be stamped with the following information:

1. Hallmark: Karat gold shall be stamped with 10 kt, 14kt, or 18 kt per the National Stamping Act:
2. Supplier's trademark: Stamping of the supplier's trademark shall be placed as close to the hallmark as possible. The hallmark and trademark shall be equal in size.
3. The item shall be stamped with XYZ Corporation's item identification number.

B. All information to be stamped in rings must be placed in a position in the shank as to not interfere with the possibility of resizing the item.

6. REQUIREMENTS FOR PRETICKETING:

A. All merchandise must be pre-ticketed with a tag. The tag should have

a. Carat weight of the diamond
b. Clarity and color of the diamond
c. XYZ Corporation's Style Number
d. Karat gold
e. Sell price
f. Universal Product Code (UPC)

B. The tags will be supplied to the supplier by the XYZ Corporation along with a copy of the purchase order(s).

A defect characteristic guide for jewelry is in the Appendix III, Standard Inspection Procedures.

4-4 ASTM Standards, Specifications and Test Methods

Listed here are standards, specifications and test methods developed by ASTM International that may be of interest to retailers.

In the serial designations prefixed to the following titles, the number following the dash indicates the year of original adoption as standard or, in case of revision, the year of last revision. Thus, standards adopted or revised during the year 1999 have as their final number, 99. A letter following this number indicates more than one revision during that year, that is, 99a indicates the second revision in 1999, 99b indicates third revision, etc. Standards that have been reapproved without change are indicated by the year of last reapproval in parentheses as part of the designation number, for example, (1999). A superscript epsilon (e) indicates an editorial change since the last revision or reapproval-ε1 for the first change, ε2 for the second change, etc.

Consumer Products Specifications

F	400-97	Consumer Safety Specification for Lighters
F	404-99a	Consumer Safety Specification for High Chairs
F	406-99	Consumer safety Specification for Play Yards
F	833-98	Consumer Safety Specification for Carriages and Strollers
F	834-84 (1994)	Consumer Safety Specification for Toy Chests
F	839-83 (1998)	Specification for Cautionary Labeling of Portable Gasoline Containers for Consumer Use
F	$852\text{-}99^{\varepsilon 1}$	Specification for Portable Gasoline Containers for Consumer Use
F	833-97	Performance Specification for Padlocks
F	919-95a	Specification for Slicing Machines, Food, Electric
F	952-94	Specification for Mixing Machines, Food, Electric
F	963-03	Consumer Safety Specification on Toy Safety
F	966-96	Consumer Safety Specification for Full-Size and Non-Full Size Baby Crib Corner Post Extension
F	976-99	Specification for Portable Kerosine Containers for Commercial Use
F	977-97	Consumer Safety Specification for Infant Walkers

F	1004-98	Consumer Safety Specification for Expansion Gates and Expandable Enclosures
F	1047-95	Specification for Frying and Braising Pans-Tilting Type
F	1126-97	Specification for Food Cutters (Electric)
F	1148-98c	Consumer Safety Specification for Home Playground Equipment
F	1169-99	Specification for Full Size Baby Crib
F	1217-92(1997)	Specification for Cooker, Pressure
F	1235-98	Specification for Consumer Safety for Portable Hook-On Chairs
F	1250-89 (1995)	Consumer Safety Specification for Stationary Exercise Bicycles
F	1360-93 (1999)	Specification for Ovens, Microwave, Electric
F	1371-93a	Specification for Vegetable Peeling Machines, Electric
F	1427-96	Consume Safety Specification for Bunk Beds
F	1447-98	Specification for Protective Headgear Used in Bicycling
F	1495-93	Specification for Ovens, Combination, Electric
F	1561-96	Performance Requirements for Plastic Chairs for Outdoor Use
F	1568-94	Specification for Food Processors, Electric
F	1604-95	Specification for Freezers, Ice cream, Soft Serve, Shake
F	1615-95	Specification for Cautionary Labeling for Five Gallon Open-head Plastic Containers (Buckets)
F	1816-97	Specification for Drawstrings on Children's Upper Outerwear
F	1821-97	Consumer Safety Specification for Toddler Beds
F	1822-97	Consumer Safety Specification for Non-Full-Size baby Cribs
F	1838-98	Performance Requirements for Child's Plastic Chairs for Outdoor Use
F	1898-98	Specification for Bicycle Helmets Used by Infants and Toddlers
F	1912-98	Specification for Bean Bag Chairs
F	1917-99	Consumer Safety Performance Specification for Infant Bedding and Related Accessories
F	1967-99	Consumer Safety Specification for Infant Bath Seats
F	1972-99	Guide for Terminology Relating to Candles and Associated Accessories Items
F	2058	Standard Specification for Cautionary Labeling for Candles Burned in a Home
F	2115	Standard Specification for Motorized Treadmills

F	2179	Standard Specification for Annealed Soda-Lime-Silicate Glass Containers that Are Produced for Use as Candle Containers
PS	59-02	Provisional Specification for Fire Safety for Candles
PS	96-98	Provisional Performance Requirements for Plastic Chaise Lounges, With or Without Moving Arms, with Adjustable Backs, for Outdoor Use
PS	110-98	Safety Specification for Chests, Door Chests and Dressers

Consumer Products Test Methods

F	1784-97	Test method for the Performance of a Pasta Cooker
F	1785-97	Test Method for Performance of Steam Kettles
F	1786-97	Test Method for Performance of Braising Pans
F	1787-98	Test Method for Performance of Rotisserie Ovens
F	2106	Standard Test methods for Evaluating Design and Performance Characteristics of Motorized Treadmills

Clothing and Textiles

Specifications for:

D	6458-99	Body Measurements for Boys, Sizes 8 to 14 Slim and 8 to 20 Regular
D	5826-95	Body Measurements for Children, Sizes 2 to 6x/7
D	6192-98	Body Measurements for Girls, Sizes 7 to 16
D	4910-99	Body Measurements for Infants, Sizes 0 to 24 Months
D	6420-98	Body Measurements for Men Sizes Thirty-Four to Sixty (34 to 60) Regular
D	4522-86(1993)$^{\varepsilon 1}$	Feather-Filled and Down-Filled Products
D	3996-95	Knit Swimwear Fabrics
D	4035-95	Knitted Necktie and Scarf Fabrics
D	3782-95	Men's and Boys' Knitted Dress Suit Fabrics and Knitted Sportswear Jacket, Slack, and Trouser Fabrics
D	4110-95	Men's and Boys' Knitted Bathrobe, Dressing Gown, and pajama Fabrics
D	4119-95	Men's and Boys' Knitted Dress Shirt Fabrics
D	4154-95a	Men's and Boys' Knitted and Woven Beachwear and Sportswear and Sports Shirt Fabric

D	3784-95a	Men's and Boys' Woven Bathrobe and Dressing Gown Fabrics
D	3477-00	Men's and Boys' Woven Dress Shirt Fabrics
D	3780-95a	Men's and Boys' Woven Dress Suit Fabrics and Woven Sportswear Jacket, Slack, and Trouser Fabrics
D	3819-95a	Men's and Boys' Woven Pajama Fabrics
D	3820-95a	Men's and Boys' Woven Underwear Fabrics
D	4232-95a	Men's and Women's Dress and Vocational Career Apparel Fabrics
D	3995-95	Men's and Women's Knitted Career Apparel Fabrics
D	4156-95	Women's and Girls' Knitted Sportswear Fabrics
D	4235-95	Women's and Girls' Knitted Blouse and Dress Fabrics
D	4234-95	Women's and Girls' Knitted Robe, Negligee, Nightgown, Pajama, Slip, and Lingerie Fabrics
D	4233-95	Women's and Girls' Knitted and Woven Brassiere Fabrics
D	4116-95a	Women's and Girls' Knitted and Woven Corset-Girdle-Combination Fabrics
D	4038-95a	Women's and Girls' Woven Dress and Blouse Fabrics
D	3779-95a	Women's and Girls' Woven Rainwear and All-Purpose, Water-Repellent Coat Fabrics
D	4117-95a	Women's and Girls' Woven Robe, Negligee, Nightgown, Pajama, Slip, and Lingerie Fabrics
D	4115-95a	Women's and Girls' Woven Sportswear, Shorts, Slacks, and Suiting Fabrics
D	3562-99	Woven Drycleanable Coat Fabrics
D	3783-95a	Woven Flat Lining Fabrics for Men's and Boys' Apparel
D	4114-95a	Woven Flat Lining Fabrics for Women's and Girls' Apparel
D	3785-95	Woven Necktie and Scarf fabrics
D	3994-95a	Woven Swimwear Fabrics
D	3657-88(1998)$^{\varepsilon 1}$	Zipper Dimensions
D	4465-97	Performance for Zippers for Denim Dungrees

Test Methods for:

D	3775-98	Fabric Count of Woven Fabric
D	6413-99	Flame Resistance of Textiles (Vertical Test)
D	1230-94	Flammability of Apparel Textiles
D	4151-92 (1998)$^{\varepsilon 1}$	Flammability of Blankets
D	204-97	Sewing Threads

D	434-95	Resistance to Slippage of Yarns in Woven Fabrics Using a Standard Seam
D	629-99	Quantitative Analysis of Textiles
D	737-96	Air Permeability of Textile Fabrics
D	1424-96	Tearing Strength of Fabrics by Falling –Pendulum Type (Elemendorf) Apparatus
D	1908-89	Needle –Related Damage Due to Sewing in Woven Fabrics
D	2051-86(1997)	Durability of Finish of Zippers to Laundering
D	2052-85(1996)	Colorfastness of Zippers to Drycleaning
D	2053-99	Colorfastness of Zippers to Light
D	2054-99	Colorfastness of Zipper Tapes to Crocking
D	2057-96	Colorfastness of Zippers to Laundering
D	2058-87(1997)	Durability of Finish of Zippers to Drycleaning
D	2059-87(1997)	Resistance of Zippers to Salt Spray (Fog)
D	2060-95	Measuring Zipper Dimensions
D	2061-93(1998)	Strength Tests for Zippers
D	2062-87(1997)$^{\varepsilon 1}$	Operability of Zippers
D	2594-99a	Stretch Properties of Knitted Fabrics Having Low Power
D	2724-87(1995)	Bonded, Fused, and Laminated Apparel Fabrics
D	3511-99a	Pilling Resistance and Other Related Surface Changes of Textile Fabrics Brush Pilling Tester
D	3512-99a	Pilling Resistance and Other Related Surface Changes of Textile Fabrics Random Tumble Pilling Tester
D	3514-99	Pilling Resistance and Other Related Surface Changes of Textile Fabrics Elastomeric Pad
D	4970-99	Pilling Resistance and Other Related Surface Changes of Textile Fabrics (Martindale Pressure Tester)
D	3882-99	Bow and Skew in Woven and Knitted Fabrics
D	3884-92	Abrasion Resistance of Textile Fabrics (Rotary Platform, Double-head Method)
D	3885-99	Abrasion Resistance of Textile Fabrics (Flexing and Abrasion Method)
D	3886-99	Abrasion Resistance of Textile Fabrics (Inflated Diaphragm Method)
D	4157-92	Abrasion Resistance of Textile Fabrics (Oscillatory Cylinder Method)
D	4158-92	Abrasion Resistance of Textile Fabrics (Uniform Abrasion Method)
D	4966-98	Abrasion Resistance of Textile Fabrics (Martindale Abrasion Tester Method)

D	5034-95	Breaking Strength and Elongation of Textile Fabrics (Grab Test)
D	5362-97	Snagging Resistance of Fabrics (Bean Bag)
D	3939-97a	Snagging Resistance of Fabrics (Mace Test Method)
D	4846-96	Resistance to Unsnapping of Snap Fasteners
D	5430-93 (2000)	Visually Inspecting and Grading Fabrics

Practices For:

D	6321-98	Evaluation of Machine Washable T-Shirts
D	4721-89 (2000)	Evaluation of the Performance of Machine Washable and Drycleanable Bedcoverings and Accessories
D	4720-87 (2000)	Evaluation of the Performance of Soft Window Coverings
D	3692-89 (1995)	Selection of Zippers for Care-Labeled Apparel and Household Furnishings

Guides for:

D	5489-98a	Care Symbols for Care Instructions on Textile Products
D	3938-96	Determining or Confirming Care Instructions for Apparel and Other Textile Consumer Products
D	6322-98	International Test methods Associated with Textile Care Products

Terminology for:

D	4523-85 (1993) $^{\varepsilon 1}$	Feather-Filled and Down-Filled Products
D	5219-99	Body Dimensions for Apparel Sizing
D	3136-00	Care Labeling for Apparel, Textile, Home Furnishing, and Leather Products
D	5253-96	Writing Care Instructions and General Refurbishing Procedures for Textile Floor Coverings and Textile Upholstered Furniture

Packaging

D	4169	Practice for Performance Testing of Shipping Containers and Systems
D	642	Compression Test for Shipping Containers
D	999	Vibration Testing of Shipping Containers

Annual Book of ASTM Standards

Vol. 07.01 and 07.02 Textiles

15.04	Soaps and Other Detergents; Polishes; Leather; Resilient Floor Coverings
15.07	Sports Equipment; Safety and Traction for Footwear; Consumer Products
15.08	Sensory Evaluation; Vacuum Cleaners
15.09	Paper; Packaging

4-5 Standard Test Methods Developed by the American Association of Textile Chemists and Colorists (AATCC)

Listed here are test methods developed by AATCC that may be of interest to retailers. Each test method is designated by a number followed by a date which indicates the year in which the method was issued, last revised or reaffirmed.

Test Method Number	Title
120-1999	Color Change Due to Flat Abrasion (Frosting): Emery Method
101-1999	Colorfastness to Bleaching with Hydrogen Peroxide
23-1999	Colorfastness to Burnt Gas Fumes
8-1996	Colorfastness to Crocking. AATCC Crockmeter Method
132-1998	Colorfastness to Drycleaning
133-1999	Colorfastness to Heat: Hot Pressing
61-1996	Colorfastness to Laundering, Home and Commercial: Accelerated
16-1998	Colorfastness to Light
172-1997	Colorfastness to Non-Chlorine Bleach in Home Laundering
15-1997	Colorfastness to Perspiration
188-2000	Colorfastness to Sodium Hypochlorite Bleach in Home Laundering
162-1997	Colorfastness to Water: Chlorinated Pool
106-1997	Colorfastness to Water: Sea
143-1996	Appearance of Apparel and Other Textile End Products after Repeated Home Laundering

88C-1996	Appearance: Retention of Creases in Fabric after Repeated Home Laundering
88B-1996	Appearance of Seams in Durable Press Items after Repeated Home Laundering
150-2000	Dimensional Changes in Automatic Home Laundering of Garments
135-2000	Dimensional Changes in Automatic Home Laundering of Woven or Knit Fabrics
96-1999	Dimensional Changes in Commercial Laundering of Woven and Knitted Fabrics Except Wool
158-2000	Dimensional Changes on Drycleaning in Perchloroethylene: Machine Method
86-2000	Drycleaning: Durability of Applied Design
176-1996	Skewness Change in Fabric and Garment Twist Resulting from Automatic Home Laundering
130-2000	Soil release: Oily Stain Release Method
22-1996	Water Repellency-Spray Test
127-1998	Water Resistance: Hydrostatic Pressure Test
128-1999	Wrinkle Recovery of Fabrics: Appearance Method

AATCC has a series of CD-ROMs designed to explain and demonstrate AATCC test methods and evaluation procedures. The Color Assessment CD contains Evaluation Procedures 1,2,6,7,8, and 9. These relate to the use of Gray Scales for color change and staining, the 9-step Chromatic Transference scale, the fundamentals of Visual Assessment, and the use of color instruments in assessment. There is also a practical demonstration of the correct use of each of the color scales. These evaluation procedures are vital for assessing color in product design and development as well as manufacturing and quality control.

4-6 UL Standards for Consumer Products

Listed here are safety standards developed by the Underwriters Laboratories, Inc. that may be of interest to retailers.

UL 30	Metal Safety Cans
UL 32	Metal Waste Cans
UL 45	Portable Electric Tools
UL 62	Flexible Cord and Fixture Wire
UL 73	Motor Operated Appliances

UL 112	Portable Wood Ladders
UL 136	Pressure Cookers
UL 141	Garment Finishing Appliances
UL 153	Portable Electric Lamps
UL 184	Portable Metal Ladders
UL 298	Portable Electric Hand Lamps
UL 466	Electric Scales
UL 474	Dehumidifiers
UL 482	Portable Sun/Heat Lamps
UL 484	Room Air Conditioners
UL 499	Electric Heating Appliances
UL 507	Electric Fans
UL 647	Unvented Kerosene-Fired Room Heaters and Portable Heaters
UL 696	Electric Toys
UL 697	Toy Transformers
UL 745-1	Portable Electric Tools
UL 749	Household Dishwashers
UL 817	Cord Sets and Power-Supply Cords
UL 826	Household Electric Clocks
UL 858	Household Electric Ranges
UL 859	Household Electric Personal Grooming
UL 923	Microwave Cooking Appliances
UL 1005	Electric Flatirons
UL 1017	Vacuum Cleaners, Blower Cleaners, and Household Floor Finishing Machines
UL 1023	Household Burglar-Alarm System Units
UL 1026	Electric Household Cooking and Food Appliances
UL 1028	Hair clipping and Shaving Appliances
UL 1056	Fire Test of Upholstered Furniture
UL 1082	Household Electric Coffee Makers and Brewing-Type Appliances
UL 1083	Household Electric Skillets and Frying-Type Appliances
UL 1410	Television Receivers and High-Voltage Video Products
UL 1431	Personal hygiene and Health Care Appliances
UL 1447	Electric Lawn Mowers
UL 1448	Electric hedge trimmers
UL 1594	Sewing and Cutting Machines
UL 1662	Electric Chain Saws
UL 1786	Nightlights

UL 2054	Household and Commercial Batteries
UL 2157	Electric Clothes Washing Machines and Extractors
UL 2158	Electric Clothes Dryers

4-7 ISO/IEC Standards

Here are some ISO/IEC standards that may be of some interest to retailers. The entire listing of ISO and IEC standards is available on ISO and IEC web sites www.iso.org/iso/en/stddevelopment/tc/tclist/TechnicalCommitteeStandardsListPage and www.iec.ch/cgi-bin//procgipl/www/iecwww.p?wwwlang=e&wwwprog=dirlst.p&committee=ALL
under each technical committee, respectively

ISO/IEC Draft Guide 14	Purchase information on goods and services intended for consumers, giving recommendations on the provision of information concerning products and services before purchase, enabling consumers to compare and choose products or services. Furthermore, the guide gives general recommendations on the creation and implementation of product information systems and purchase information bodies.
ISO/IEC Guide 37 (1995-01)—	Edition 2.0 Instructions for use of products of consumer interest
IEC 62079	Preparation of instructions—Structuring, content and presentation
ISO/IEC Guide 41	Packaging—recommendations for addressing consumer needs. This guide will help assess the most suitable type of packaging for products before they are put on the market for consumer use. It gives the general recommendations to be taken into consideration when determining packaging in order to protect goods and maximize benefits for consumers.
ISO/IEC Guide 46	Comparative testing of consumer products and related services—General Principles
ISO/IEC Guide 50	Child safety and standards—General guidelines
ISO/IEC Guide 51	Guidelines for inclusion of safety aspects in standards
ISO/IEC Guide 71	Guidelines for standards developers to address the needs of older persons and persons with disabilities

ISO 3758	Textiles—Care labeling code using symbols
ISO 4481:1997	Cutlery and flatware—Nomenclature
ISO/DIS 5395	Power lawn-mowers—Definitions, safety requirements and test procedures, defining terms, safety requirements and test procedures applicable to power rotary and cylinder lawn-mowers
ISO/DIS 8442-5	Materials and articles in contact with foodstuffs—Cutlery and table hollowware—Part 5: Specific cutting test
ISO 8124-1	Safety of Toys Part 1 Safety Aspects Related to Mechanical and Physical Properties
ISO 8124-2	Safety of Toys Part 2 Flammability
ISO 8124-3	Safety of Toys Part 3 Migration of Certain Elements
IEC 61558-2-7	Safety of Power Transformers, Power Supply Units and Similar—Part 2 Particular Requirements for Transformers of Toys
ISO 9994	Lighters-Safety Specification
ISO 8098	Cycles
ISO/TR 10219:1989	Batteries for watches—Dimensions, requirements and marking
ISO/TR 10220:1989	Batteries for watches—Leakage tests
ISO/DIS 11393-4	Protective clothing for users of hand-held chain-saws-Part 4 test methods and requirements for protective gloves, specifying requirements and test methods for gloves that are intended to provide protection against cuts by a hand-held chain-saw, including requirements for identification marking and information for the user.
ISO 12819:1999	Methods of evaluation of the battery life of a battery-powered watch
ISO 7175-1:1997	Children's cots and folding cots for domestic use—Part 1: Safety Requirements
ISO 7175-2:1997	Children's cots and folding cots for domestic use—Part 2: Test methods
ISO 8191-1:1987	Furniture—Assessment of the ignitability of upholstered furniture—Part 1: Ignition source: smoldering cigarette
ISO 8191-1:1988	Furniture—Assessment of ignitability of upholstered furniture—Part 2: Ignition source: match-flame equivalent
ISO 9098-1:1994	Bunk beds for domestic use—Safety requirements and tests—Part 1: Safety requirements
ISO 9098-2:1994	Bunk beds for domestic use—Safety requirements and tests—Part 2: Test methods

ISO 9221-1:1992	Furniture-Children's high chairs—Part 1: Safety requirements
ISO 9221-2:1992	Furniture—Children's high chairs—Part 2: Test methods
ISO 8653:1986	Jewellery—Ring-sizes—Definition, measurement and designation
ISO 8654:1987	Colors of gold alloys—Definition, range of colors and designation
ISO 9202:1991	Jewellery—Fineness of precious metal alloys
ISO 10713:1992	Jewellery—Gold alloy coatings
ISO/TR 11211:1995	Grading polished diamonds—Terminology and classification
ISO/FDIS 11211-1	Grading polished diamonds—Part 1: Terminology and classification
ISO/FDIS 11211-2	Grading polished diamonds—Part 2: Test methods
IEC 60335-1 (2001-05)	Edition 4.0—Household and similar electrical appliances—Safety—Part 1: General requirements
IEC 60335-2-3 (2002-03)	Edition 5.0—Household and similar electrical appliances—Safety—Part 2-3: Particular requirements for electric irons
IEC 60335-2-5 (2002-03)	Edition 5.0—Household and similar electrical appliances—Safety—Part 2-5: Particular requirements for dishwashers
IEC 60335-2-9 (2002-03)	Edition 5.0—Household and similar electrical appliances—Safety—Part 2-9: Particular requirements for grills, toasters, and similar portable cooking appliances
IEC 60335-2-25 (2002-03)	Edition 5.0—Household and similar electrical appliances—Safety—Part 2-25: Particular requirements for microwave ovens, including combination microwave ovens
IEC 60335-2-27	Edition 4.0—Household and similar electrical appliances—Safety—Part 2-27: Particular requirements for appliances for skin exposure to ultraviolet and infrared radiation
IEC 60335-2-29	Edition 4.0—Household and similar electrical appliances—Safety—Part 2-29: Particular requirements for battery chargers

IEC 60335-2-30 Edition 4.0—Household and similar electrical appliances—Safety—Part 2-30: Particular requirements for room heaters

IEC 60335-2-44 Edition 3.0—Household and similar electrical appliances—Safety—Part 2-44: Particular requirements for ironers

IEC 60335-2-80 Edition 2.0—Household and similar electrical appliances—Safety—Part 2-80: Particular requirements for fans

IEC 60335-2-100 Edition 1.0—Household and similar electrical appliances—Safety—Part 2-80: Particular requirements for hand-held mains-operated garden blowers, vacuums and blower vacuums

IEC 60436 (1981-01) Methods for measuring the performance of electrical dishwashers, 2nd edition

4-8 EN Standards [European Committee for Electrotechnical Standardization (CENELEC)]

EN 774 Garden Equipment—Handheld, integrally powered hedge trimmers—Safety

EN 786 Garden Equipment—Electrically powered walk-behind and hand-held lawn trimmers and lawn hedge trimmers—Mechanical safety

EN 836 Garden Equipment—Powered lawnmowers

EN 847-1 Tools for woodworking—Safety requirements—Part 1: Milling tools and circular saw blades

EN 50088:1996(R2003) Safety of electric toys

EN 50144-1:1999(R2002) Safety of handheld electric motor-operated tools—Part 1: General requirements

EN 50144-2-1:2000 Safety of handheld electric motor-operated tools—Part 2-1: Particular requirements for drills

EN 50144-2-2:2000 Safety of handheld electric motor-operated tools—Part 2-2: Particular requirements for screwdrivers and impact wrenches

EN 50144-2-4:2000	Safety of handheld electric motor-operated tools—Part 2-4: Particular requirements for sanders
EN 50144-2-5:2000	Safety of handheld electric motor-operated tools—Part 2-5: Particular requirements for circular saws and circular knives
EN 50144-2-6:2001(R2002)	Safety of handheld electric motor-operated tools—Part 2-6: Particular requirements for hammers
EN 50144-2-7:2000	Safety of handheld electric motor-operated tools—Part 2-7: Particular requirements for spray guns
EN 50144-2-8:1996	Safety of handheld electric motor-operated tools—Part 2-8: Particular requirements for sheet metal shears and nibblers
EN 50144-2-9:1996	Safety of handheld electric motor-operated tools—Part 2-9: Particular requirements for tappers
EN 50144-2-10:2001	Safety of handheld electric motor-operated tools—Part 2-10: Particular requirements for jigsaws
EN 50144-2-11:1997	Safety of handheld electric motor-operated tools—Part 2-11: Particular requirements for saber saws and double-blade reciprocating saws
EN 50144-2-14:2001	Safety of handheld electric motor-operated tools—Part 2-14: Particular requirements for planers
EN 50144-2-15:2001	Safety of handheld electric motor-operated tools—Part 2-15: Particular requirements for hedge trimmers
EN 50144-1:1999(R2002)	Safety of handheld electric motor-operated tools—Part 1: General requirements

A copy of any of the standard can be obtained from the respective standards development organizations. While searching for standards, one web site worth visiting is www.standardsmall.com. This web site has a free "search" feature where one can search standards by either title word or document number. The search can be for all databases or for a particular database such as ISO, ASTM, AATCC, etc. There are also other standard databases such as www.his.com and www.ili-info.com.

4-9 ISO 9000 Series Standards

The ISO 9000 family of standards are international quality management standards. They provide a model for quality management function. These standards were first published in 1987 and revised in 1994 and 2000. These standards are revised every 5 years. These standards are:

ISO 9000:2000, Quality management systems—Fundamentals and vocabulary
This standard defines the terms and definitions used in the ISO 9000 family of standards and establishes a starting point for understanding the standards.

ISO 9001:2000, Quality management systems—Requirements
This is the main standard which outlines requirements of ISO 9000 quality management system.
This standard is used to assess an organization's ability to meet customer and regulatory requirements and is the standard against which third party registration or certification can be achieved.

ISO 9004:2000, Quality management systems—Guidelines for performance improvement
This standard provides guidance for continual improvement of quality management system. It builds on ISO 9001:2000, Quality management system.

ISO 10005:1995, Quality management—Guidelines for quality plans
This standard provides guidelines to assist in the preparation, review, acceptance and revision of quality plans.

ISO 10013:1995, Guidelines for developing quality manuals
This standard provides guidelines for the development and maintenance of quality manuals

ISO/TR 10014:1998, Guidelines for managing the economics of quality
This technical report provides guidance on how to achieve economic benefits from the application of quality management system.

ISO 10015:1999, Quality management—Guidelines for training
This standard provides guidance on the development, implementation, maintenance and improvement of strategies and systems for training that affects the quality of products.

ISO/TR 10017:2003, Guidelines on statistical techniques for ISO 9001:2000.

The ISO 9000 family or series of standards are based on eight quality management principles as follows, which can be used to improve the performance of an organization (www.iso.ch):

1. *Customer focus*—Organizations depend on their customers and therefore should understand current and future customer needs, should meet customer requirements and strive to exceed customer expectations.
2. *Leadership*—Leaders establish unity of purpose and direction of the organization. They should create and maintain the internal environment in which people can become fully involved in achieving the organization's objectives.
3. *Involvement of people*—People at all levels are the essence of an organization and their full involvement enables their abilities to be used for the organization's benefit.
4. *Process approach*—A desired result is achieved more efficiently when activities and related resources are managed as a process.
5. *Systems approach to management*—Identifying, understanding and managing interrelated processes as a system contributes to the organization's effectiveness and efficiency in achieving its objectives.
6. *Continual improvement*—Continual improvement of the organization's overall performance should be a permanent objective of the organization.
7. *Factual approach to decision making*—Effective decisions are based on the analysis of data and information.
8. *Mutually beneficial supplier relationships*—An organization and its suppliers are interdependent and a mutually beneficial relationship enhances the ability of both to create value.

ISO 9001:2000, Quality management system—Requirements, outlines following elements of quality management system.

4 Quality management system

4.1 General requirements
4.2 Documentation requirements
4.2.1 General
4.2.2 Quality manual
4.2.3 Control of documents
4.2.4 Control of records

5 Management responsibility

5.1 Management commitment
5.2 Customer focus
5.3 Quality policy
5.4 Planning
5.4.1 Quality objectives
5.4.2 Quality management system planning
5.5 Responsibility, authority and communication
5.5.1 Responsibility and authority
5.5.2 Management representative
5.5.3 Internal communication
5.6 Management review
5.6.1 General
5.6.2 Review input
5.6.3 Review output

6 Resource management

6.1 Provision of resources
6.2 Human resources
6.2.1 General
6.2.2 Competence, awareness and training
6.3 Infrastructure
6.4 Work environment

7 Product realization

7.1 Planning of product realization
7.2 Customer related processes
7.2.1 Determination of requirements related to the product
7.2.2 Review of requirements related to the product
7.2.3 Customer communication
7.3 Design and development
7.3.1 Design and development planning
7.3.2 Design and development inputs
7.3.3 Design and development outputs
7.3.4 Design and development review
7.3.5 Design and development verification
7.3.6 Design and development validation

7.3.7 Control of design and development changes
7.4 Purchasing
7.4.1 Purchasing process
7.4.2 Purchasing information
7.4.3 Verification of purchased product
7.5 Production and service provision
7.5.1 Control of production and service provision
7.5.2 Validation of processes for production and service provision
7.5.3 Identification and traceability
7.5.4 Customer property
7.5.5 Preservation of product
7.6 Control of monitoring and measuring devises

8 Measurement, analysis and improvement

8.1 General
8.2 Monitoring and measurement
8.2.1 Customer satisfaction
8.2.2 Internal audit
8.2.3 Monitoring and measurement of product
8.3 Control of nonconforming product
8.4 Analysis of data
8.5 Improvement
8.5.1 Continual improvement
8.5.2 Corrective action
8.5.3 Preventive action

There is always the question of whether or not to go for ISO 9000 registration. In North America (the United States, Canada, and Mexico) it is called registration while in Europe and some parts of Asia it is called certification. ISO 9000 registration means that a company had it's quality management system assessed by a third party, i.e. a registrar, against ISO 9000 requirements and subsequent issuing of a certificate to confirm that it is in conformance with the standard's requirements. This process is called registration or certification and the company receiving ISO 9000 registration or certification is called an ISO 9000 registered or certified company. Registration is good for three years from the date it is granted. During this time the registrar can carry out surprise checks once or twice a year, and continued registration depends on the findings of these audits. At the end of three years a renewal audit is performed before the registration is continued.

ISO 9001:2000 and its eight principles can be used to manage quality without ever getting registered. It is a myth that use of ISO 9001-2000 standard calls for registration.

Although there is no conclusive research on the advantages and disadvantages of registration, there is plenty of anecdotal evidence to make a case for or against ISO 9000. Critics say that the registration process is bureaucratic, increases paperwork, causes considerable expense and offers no guarantee of better quality.

On the other hand, registration can help force a company to review its processes, streamline its paperwork, instill discipline in the workforce, and bring together various activities—resulting in noticeable savings, as shown in the following examples:

- In the UK, many CEOs believe it has transformed their company values, putting a focus on serving the customer and understanding the strategic nature of quality as a competitive weapon (Perry 1993).
- A UK-based, medium sized chemicals manufacturer used ISO 9002 as a springboard for developing a Total Quality Management (TQM) approach (Askey Dale, 1994)[1].
- The certification process helped a company in the US understand its own infrastructures—the network of individuals, systems, and processes that allowed it to function as a whole—even though many were located on different continents (Ingman and Schroff, 1996).
- Honda of America Manufacturing Inc.'s drive to attain ISO 9002 helped improve its quality assurance system (Martin and Ann Meyer, 1997)[1].
- Efficiencies resulting from the registration efforts of the United Airlines' (UAL) Engine Maintenance division included reductions in average engine overhaul cycle time from 120 to 60 days, and pieces-parts cycle time from 52 to 26 days (O"Neil, 1998).
- The Indian Merchants' Chamber achieved a total improvement in service quality by upgrading its working practices against a quality system such as ISO 9002 (Bhardwaj, 1999)[1].

1- Before 2000 there were three ISO 9000 standards as follows:
ISO 9001 Quality systems—Model for quality assurance in design, development, production, installation, and servicing
ISO 9002 Quality systems—Model for quality assurance in production, installation, and servicing
ISO 9003 Quality systems—Model for quality assurance in final inspection and test

The 2000 revision of these standards resulted in elimination of ISO 9002 and 9003 leaving only ISO 9001 as an updated version.

The ISO 9000 registration process provides a company with the opportunity to:

- Better understand and anticipate customer requirements.
- Improve its understanding of business processes and control them in a logical, systematic way.
- Reduce paperwork by doing away with forms and reports that do not add any value to the processes or products.
- Foster internal discipline leading to streamlined production, reduced cycle times, and quality improvements.
- Create an environment where quality can be managed more effectively.

The aim of ISO 9000 is to help organizations create quality management systems that improve customer satisfaction by preventing defects or nonconformities in products and services. ISO 9001:2000 requirements are common-sense business requirements.

According to a report covering 15 economies and 5398 firms in North America, Europe, and Asia the main motivations for seeking ISO 9000 certifications are "quality improvements" and "corporate image," and to a slightly lesser extent, "marketing advantage" and "customer pressure" (Corbett, Luca, and Pan, 2003).

While no retailer requires its suppliers to be ISO 9000 registered, some retailers encourage their suppliers to follow ISO 9000 quality management system. Mehta (2000) provides an excellent example of how a multi-billion dollar retailer uses ISO 9000 standards for quality improvement.

4-10 IFAN (www.ifan-online.org)

The International Federation of Standards Users is an independent, non-profit international association of national organizations for the application of standards, companies, professional and trade associations, and government agencies, concerned with the use of standards. It was founded in 1974. IFAN objectives are:

a. To promote uniform implementation of standards without deviation and develop solutions to standards users' problems without itself drawing up standards.

b. To consolidate standards users' interests and views on all aspects of standardization and conformity assessment, and to cooperate with international and regional standardization bodies in order to communicate user views to these organizations.
c. To promote networking in the field of international standardization and conformity assessment.

IFAN holds an international conference every three years.

Key Points

- Standards and specifications are very important for product quality.
- Clear specifications set clear expectations of suppliers which goes a long way towards meeting retailers' quality requirements or regulatory requirements.
- Standard test methods are necessary for consistency of testing and comparability of results.
- It is beneficial for retailers to be actively involved in appropriate standards development activities.
- A copy of any of the standards can be obtained from the respective standards development organizations. While searching for standards, one web site worth visiting is www.standardsmall.com. This web site has free "search" feature where one can search standards by either title word or document number. The search can be for all the databases or for a particular database such as ISO, ASTM, AATCC, etc. There are other standards databases also such as www.his.com and www.ili-info.com.
- While using or referring to a standard it is very important that you refer to the latest edition of that standard. Almost all standards development organizations (SDOs) offer subscription service where by the subscribers are notified as and when any standard is revised, reaffirmed, or discontinued. It pays to subscribe to such service.

References

Askey, J. M. and Dale, B. G. 1994. From ISO 9000 Series Registration to Total Quality Management: An Examination. *Quality Management Journal.* July. Volume 1, Issue 4. pp.67 American Society for Quality, Milwaukee, WI.

Bank, Jeanne. 2003. Canadian Standards Association. Unpublished paper. Consumer involvement in standards work for energy efficiency.

Bhardwaj, Geeta. 1999. TPI Model in a Commerce Chamber: Indian Experience. *53rd Annual Quality Congress Proceedings*, May 24-26. pp. 244-251. Anaheim, CA.

Consumer Interest Forum (CIF). 6 November 2002. Operating Guidelines, American National Standards Institute (ANSI), New York, NY.

Corbett, Charles J.; Luca, Anastasia M.; and Pan, Jeh-Nan. 2003. Global Perspectives on Global Standards. January-February. *ISO Management Systems*. pp. 31-40. International Organization for Standardization, Geveva, Switzerland.

Ingman, Richard W. and Schroff, Udo O. 1996. Positioning for Global Markets. *Industry Week*, July 15. pp. 34.

Mehta, Pradip V. 2000. Using ISO 9000 Series Standards for Quality Improvement 20-21 March. A paper presented at the 7th Annual ISO 9000 Conference. Dallas. TX.

Martin, Andrew T. and Ann Meyer, Brenda. 1997. Bottom-Up ISO 9000 at Honda's Anna Engine Plant. *51st Annual Quality Congress Proceedings*, May 5-7. pp. 356-361. Orlando, FL.

Perry, Mike. 1993. Company-wide Quality Using ISO 9000. *ASQC Quality Congress Transactions*. May 24-26. pp. 280-286. Boston, MA.

O'Neil, James P. 1998. Using ISO 9000 to Go Beyond Industry Norms. *Quality Progress*, December. Vol. 31, No. 12. pp. 43-44. American Society for Quality. Milwaukee, WI.

The New American Webster Dictionary, 1972. New American Library, Times Mirror *What Is ASTM*, A Brochure published by ASTM, 1999. West Conshohocken, PA www.iso.ch About ISO. Introduction. What Are Standards? www.iso.ch/9000e/iso9000family.htm

Bibliography

Spivak, S. M. and Brenner, Cecil F. 2001 *Standardization Essentials: Principles and Practice*, Marcel Dekker, Inc. www.dekker.com

Media Tips and Case Studies. Standards Overview: Avoiding Surprises-Some Thoughts on Standards. American National Standards Institute. www.ansi.org/public/news/media_tips/standards_overview_cont.html

How Standardization Helps Consumers www.ansi.org/consumer_affairs/overview.aspx?menuid=5

The consumer and standards: Guidance and principles for consumer participation in standards development. ISO/IEC. March 2003.

The discrete charm of International Standards: ISO in everyday life. *ISO Bulletin*, October 1998.

Through History with Standards
www.ansi.org/consumer_affairs/history_standards.aspx?menuid=5

Williams, Steve. 2003. The consumer's voice from developing countries in the standardization process—how can it be heard? *ISO Bulletin*, August. pp. 26-28.

5

Product Safety

Increasingly, consumers are concerned about safety of the products they use everyday, particularly, those products meant for children. Therefore, it is common sense that safety should be an integral part of quality. No matter how good attributes a product has, if it is unsafe, they are of no consequences. An unsafe product will always be considered a poor quality product.

For example, according to a Consumer Product Safety Commission (CPSC) press release (2003):

- Old electrical power tools (made before the 1980s) may not have modern safety features to prevent electrocution. Old power tools were made with metal housing, while newer tools are made with plastic housings to provide double-insulation against electric shock. Old power tools also may not have proper grounding or may have frayed wires or other hazards.
- Old extension cords, power strips and surge protectors may have undersized wires, loose connections, faulty components, improper grounding, or non-polarized plugs, resulting in unsafe condition of use.
- Window blinds may have pull cords that end in a loop or inner cords that can form a loop if pulled by children. This can cause strangulation.
- Halogen torchie floor lamps can cause fire when combustibles such as drapes come too close to the bulb.
- Old cribs can entrap, strangle, or suffocate children. Old cribs with more than 2-3/8 inches between crib slats; corner posts; or cut-outs on the headboard or footboard present suffocation and strangulation hazard. Cribs with broken or missing parts or corner posts higher than 1/16 inch also present a risk of death.
- Hairdryers without immersion protection devices to prevent electrocution pose a significant electrocution hazard if they fall into water.

- Disposable and novelty lighters that are not child-resistant pose a significant fire hazard.
- Drawstrings around the neck on children's jackets and sweatshirts can catch and strangle children.
- Gas grills with leaking fuel at the tank connection or delayed ignition or with overfilled tanks or with leaking hoses and valves can cause fire.
- Overheating due to motor failure, the flammability of thermoplastic enclosures, and overheating due to cord failure are three main issues related to fire accidents associated with portable electric fans.

Safety becomes even more important where some "second hand" or "used" retail merchandise is traded in or exported to developing countries.

Therefore it would be beneficial to look at some areas that may pose risks and hazards and review what efforts are made to address consumer product safety.

The best way for the retailers to address product safety is not to buy unsafe products. This can be done through pre-purchase testing in an effort to identify unsafe products to begin with.

One retailer periodically sends out a policy letter to its buyers reminding them of the items that require testing prior to purchase. Exhibit 5-1 shows an example of such a letter. Another retailer has put in place a system where by if certain products have not been cleared by QA the system will not process the purchase orders for those items.

Memorandum For: All Buyers

Subject: Pre-Purchase Testing

Certain products that are inherently prone to safety risk are mandatory for pre-purchase testing by Quality Assurance.

The purchase of the following items will be coordinated with Quality Assurance so that they can be reviewed or pre-purchase tested.

a. Electrically operated toys (110/220VAC), all age groups.
b. Battery powered toys for children up to 3 years of age.
c. All toys intended for children up to 3 years of age including but not limited to, stuffed toys, squeeze toys, ride-on toys, crib mobiles, projectile toys, mouth activated toys, and rack toys.

d. Toys included with other products, such as gifts with purchase (GWP) or purchase with purchase (PWP), i.e., teddy bear received as GWP when the customer purchased a bottle of fragrance.
e. Children's sleepwear.
f. Easter baskets with toys or children's items.
g. Juvenile furniture including cribs, walkers, carriers, car seats, playpens, highchairs, strollers, etc.
h. Baby accessories including baby rattles, pacifiers, teethers, bath accessories, and other baby items.
i. Children's playwear with any ornamentation/toy items attached to it.
j. Electrical personal care appliances, including battery operated products.
k. Small kitchen appliances/traffic appliances.
l. All candles
m. Subsistence carrying items, unless they are brands such as Noritake, Dalton, Wedgewood, etc.
n. Health and beauty care items supplied by non-branded suppliers.

Buyers of the above listed products should contact Quality Assurance as early in the buying cycle as possible so that there is enough time for pre-purchase testing.

Senior Vice President
Purchasing

Exhibit 5-1 Periodic letter to the buyers urging them to have pre-purchase testing done

There can be no discussion of consumer product safety without an overview of the U. S. Consumer Product Safety Commission (CPSC).

5-1 U. S. Consumer Product Safety Commission (CPSC)

The United States Consumer Product Safety Commission (CPSC) an independent federal regulatory agency was created in 1972 by the U. S. Congress through the Consumer Product Safety Act (CPSA). In that law, Congress directed the Commission to "protect the public against unreasonable risks of injuries and deaths associated with consumer products." (CPSC).

Section 15(a) of the CPSA defines the term "substantial product hazard" as "a failure to comply with an applicable consumer product safety rule which creates a substantial risk of injury to the public, or a product defect which, (because of the pattern of defect, the number of defective products distributed in commerce, the severity of the risk, or otherwise) creates a substantial risk of injury to the public."

For the purpose of the Consumer Product Safety Act, "consumer product" means any article or component part there of produced or distributed (i) for sale to a consumer for use in or around a permanent or temporary household or residence, a school, in recreation, or otherwise, or (ii) for the personal use, consumption or enjoyment of a consumer in or around a permanent or temporary household or residence, a school, in recreation, or otherwise.

CPSC accomplishes it's mission by:

a. Developing voluntary standards within industry
b. Issuing and enforcing mandatory standards or banning consumer products if no feasible standard would adequately protect the public
c. Obtaining the recall of products or arranging for their repair
d. Conducting research on potential product hazards
e. Informing and educating consumers through the media, state and local governments, private organizations, and by responding to consumer inquiries

CPSC has jurisdiction over about 15,000 types of consumer products such as automatic drip coffee makers, cribs, high chairs, play yards, toy chests, baby walkers, bicycles, bicycle helmets, bunk beds, toys, cigarette lighters, lawn mowers, carpets and rugs, fabric flammability, children's sleepwear, matchbooks, pacifiers, etc. These items are regulated under one or more of the following acts:

a. Consumer Product Safety Act—This act applies to all consumer products as defined in the Consumer Product Safety Act (Public Law 92-573; 86 Stat. 1207, Oct. 27, 1972).

b. Federal Hazardous Substance Act—This act applies to hazardous household substances and children's products. Some substances must be labeled as hazardous; some are banned. Some of the hazards addressed under this Act are toxicity, flammability, and corrosiveness (Public Law 86-613; 74 Stat. 372, July 12, 1960, as amended).

c. Flammable Fabrics Act—This act applies to products such as clothing, mattresses, and carpets (Public Law 83-88; 67 Stat. 111, June 30, 1953, as amended).

d. Poison Prevention Packaging Act—This act requires child-resistant packaging for certain drugs and other hazardous household substances, such as furniture polish and turpentine (Public Law 91-601; 84 Stat. 1670, December 30, 1970, as amended).

e. Refrigerator Safety Act—This act applies to household refrigerators. Refrigerator doors must be easy to open from the inside to prevent children from becoming trapped (Public Law 84-930; 70 Stat. 953, August 2, 1956).

CPSC maintains a list of regulated products on it's web site at www.cpsc.gov/businfo/regsbyproduct.html. After going to this site click on "Regulated Products" and you will see a list of products there. This list also indicates the act under which a product is regulated and applicable standard(s). If you can not find specific guidance for a product under "Regulated Products," then, that means the product is not covered by CPSC.

Items such as aircraft, alcohol, ammunition, amusement rides (fixed sites), automobiles, boats, car seats, cosmetics, drugs, electronic product radiation, firearms, foods, industrial/commercial/farm products, medical devices, pesticides, rodenticides, fungicides, radioactive materials, tires, tobacco, tobacco products, trucks, and veterinary medicines do not come under CPSC's jurisdiction.

There are some reporting requirements under CPSA (Consumer Product Safety Act) as follows:

a. Any manufacturer, importer, distributor, or retailer of consumer products must notify CPSC immediately if it could be concluded that one of its products: (a) has a defect that creates a substantial risk of injury to the public; (b) creates an unreasonable risk of serious injury or death ; or (c) violates a consumer product safety standard or ban of the product. (15 U.S.C. 2064)
b. A manufacturer must report to CPSC when any of its products has been involved in three or more law suits in a two-year period, where an alleged death or grievous bodily injury occurred and resulted in a settlement or a court judgment in favor of the person who filed the suit. (15 U.S.C. 2085)
c. A manufacturer, distributor, retailer, or importer of marbles, small balls, latex balloons, or toys or games that contain such items must

report to CPSC any incidents of children chocking on those items. (15 U.S.C. 2064 note)

CPSC has an online form to report any of the above conditions. This form can be accessed at www.cpsc.gov/sec15html. Or CPSC can be contacted at

e-mail hazard@cpsc.gov
Phone (800) 638-2772
Fax (800) 809-0924, or by writing to
CPSC
Washington, DC 20207

CPSC has brought lawsuits against companies for failing to make required reports concerning dangerous consumer products.

CPSC has published a "Corrective Actions Handbook." This is a guide for manufacturers, importers, distributors, and retailers on reporting under Section 15 of the Consumer Product Safety Act and preparing for, initiating and implementing product safety corrective action plans. This handbook is available to any business free of charge from CPSC.

In the course of administering the United States' consumer product safety laws, the CPSC has identified safety practices that tend to result in the manufacture and marketing of safe products. These practices are:

1. Building safety into product design.
2. Doing product safety testing for all foreseeable hazards.
3. Keeping informed about and implementing latest developments in product safety.
4. Educating consumers about product safety.
5. Tracking and addressing your products' safety performance.
6. Fully investigating product safety incidents.
7. Reporting product safety defects promptly.
8. If a defect occurs, promptly offering a comprehensive recall plan.
9. Working with CPSC to make sure your recall is effective.
10. Learning from mistakes—yours and others!

Good corporate product safety practices not only further public safety—obviously a worthy objective in itself-but also fuel consumer confidence, a crucial element in today's remarkable economic prosperity. Responsible companies adopt

superior safety practices and continually work to improve them. For more on this topic, visit the web site www.cpsc.gov/businfo/pscconcept.html
Safety tips in the form of Product Safety Fact Sheets are available from CPSC at no charge. Here is a partial listing of fact sheets. A complete listing of fact sheets is on CPSC web site www.cpsc.gov. Once in this web site search for "Fact Sheets" and the whole listing will appear.

Baseball Safety
Bunk Bed
Crib Sheets
Electric Space Heaters
Extension Cords
Power Lawnmowers
Skateboard Safety
Toy Hazards
Bicycle
Children's Furniture
Dangers of Electric Toys
Electrical Safety
Gas Grills
Riding Lawnmowers
Toy Safety

Information from these fact sheets can be very useful in developing standard inspection procedures (SIPs) and test criteria for various items.

Copies of relevant federal laws and regulations can be found in the U.S. Code www.gov/uscode/about.html The U.S. Code does not include regulations issued by executive branch agencies, decisions of the Federal courts, treaties, or laws enacted by State or local governments. Regulations issued by executive branch agencies are available in the Code of Federal Regulations www.gpoaccess.gov/cfr/about.html Proposed and recently adopted regulations may be found in the federal register www.gpoaccess.gov/fr/about.html

Individual government agency web sites also provide comprehensive information about their activities including links to relevant statutes.

Six U. S. federal agencies with vastly different jurisdictions have joined together to create a single web site for all recalls initiated by them. This web site is www.recalls.gov. Once in this website, follow the tabs to obtain the latest recall information, to report a dangerous product, or to learn important safety tips.

5-2 Food and Drug Administration (FDA)

FDA is an agency within the Department of Health and Human Services. FDA's mission is to promote and protect the public health by helping safe and effective products reach the market in a timely way, and monitoring products for continued safety after they are in use through the enforcement of Federal Food, Drug, and Cosmetic Act. Items such as television sets, microwave ovens, cell phones, which emit radiation fall within the jurisdiction of FDA for the radiation characteristics, for all other safety issues these products are within the CPSC jurisdiction. For example, so far as radiation is concerned, all TV sets and microwave ovens regardless of place of manufacture must meet certification and labeling requirements for Electronic Products—General, in accordance with the Code of Federal Regulations (CFR) 21, Part 1010. All TV receivers must also meet requirements of CFR 21 Part 1020.10—Performance Standards for Ionizing Radiation Emitting Products. Microwave oven must meet requirements of CFR 21 Part 1030.10—Performance Standards for Microwave and Radio frequency Emitting Products. Also, cosmetics fall within jurisdiction of FDA. FDA monitors cosmetic products to be sure that they are safe and properly labeled. But these products and their ingredients are not reviewed or approved by FDA before they are sold to the public, and FDA cannot require safety testing of these products. Heavy metal leaching from subsistence carrying vessels is regulated by FDA. For more information on FDA, visit it's web site www.fda.gov

5-3 Electrical Product Safety

Electrical product safety testing is very complicated and involves expensive test equipment and highly trained and qualified technical staff. Therefore, many retailers depend on independent testing laboratories for safety testing and depend on certain marks on products as evidence that not only are those products tested but are safe and continue to be made in compliance with certain safety requirements. In other words, many retailers rely on third party safety certification of electrical products before they consider buying them.

The most ubiquitous certification mark in the world is the UL Mark, Figure 5-1. UL stands for Underwriters Laboratories Inc. UL is an independent, not for profit organization that offers product safety testing and certification programs to determine that products meet nationally recognized safety standards.

A UL Listing mark on a product means that representative samples of the product have been tested and evaluated to UL safety standards with regard to fire, electrical shock and related safety hazards. Some of the UL standards have become American National Standards. It also means that UL Listed products continue to be manufactured in compliance with UL's safety requirements. The requirements are based on UL's published standards for safety. UL field representatives make regular unannounced visits to production facilities worldwide. They check production controls, witness testing, conduct inspections and periodically select samples for further testing at a UL laboratory.

Other safety marks are ETL, Figure 5-2 and CSA, Figure 5-3, respectively. ETL mark is given by the Intertek Testing Services (ITS), a testing, inspection, and certification company focused on products and commodities. CSA mark is given by CSA International, a leading provider of product testing and certification services. Just like UL Mark, both of these marks indicate that representative samples of the product have been tested and evaluated to nationally recognized safety standards with regard to fire, electrical shock and related safety hazards. It also means that ETL and CSA Listed products continue to be manufactured in compliance with applicable national and international safety requirements. ETL and CSA International field representatives make regular unannounced visits to production facilities worldwide. They check production controls, witness testing, conduct inspections and periodically select samples for further testing at ETL and CSA International laboratories.

Figure 5-1 Figure 5-2 Figure 5-3

Reproduced with the permission of the Underwriters Laboratories, ETL SEMKO and CSA International, respectively.

For information on testing and certification services and services to retailers provided by these organizations, please visit their websites www.ul.com, www.itsglobal.com, and www.CSA-International.com.

Some other safety marks are FI mark (FIMKO, Finland), S mark (SEMKO, Sweden), N mark (NEMKO, Norway), D mark (DEMKO, Denmark), TUV Rheinland mark, TUV Rheinland GS mark (www.us.tuv.com/downloads/test.shmtl), VDE and VDEGS marks (www.vde.com/pzi/html/zeichen/zeichen.htm)

According to Federspiel (2003) ISO/CASCO (ISO Committee on Conformity Assessment) has produced a draft standard ISO/FDIS 17030, Third party marks of conformity and their use, which was put out for electronic balloting in summer 2003. In this international standard there are sets of rules for monitoring and surveillance, protection of the mark from unauthorized use, publicly available information about meaning of the mark and the issuer, etc. While the standard provides the requirement for third party marks, it may also be used as guidance on the use of marks of conformity in other than third party activities.

A website www.safetylink.com provides a wealth of links to various sites on electrical product safety.

5-4 CE Mark

Figure 5-4 CE Mark

You have probably heard the phrase CE mark and even seen it on a number of products. The letters "CE" are the abbreviation of French phrase "Conformite Europeene" which means European conformity. CE mark on an item or a product is the manufacturer's assertion that the product complies with the applicable requirements of the European directives, called Product Directives. These directives contain the essential requirements and/or performance levels and harmonized standards to which the products bearing CE mark must conform. Harmonized standards are technical specifications which are established by several European standards development organizations, such as, CEN (European Committee for Standardization) and CENELEC (European Committee for Electrotechnical Standardization). These directives are related to health, safety, environment, and consumer protection. CE marking was adopted in 1993 (EC Directive 93/68/EEC). For those products that come under European Directives they must bear a CE mark for them to be marketed in the European Economic Area (EEA), which consists of the following 18 countries.

Austria	Greece	Spain
Belgium	Ireland	Sweden
Denmark	Italy	United Kingdom
Finland	Luxembourg	Iceland
France	The Netherlands	Liechtenstein
Germany	Portugal	Norway

One common misconception about CE marking is that it is a quality seal. Although it may be indirectly related to quality, the mark is actually concerned with safety, in particular, user safety. CE mark is not an approval mark, certification or quality mark.

Two European Union (EU) directives of interest to retailers are the directive 88/378/EEC on toys and the Low-Voltage Directive (LVD) 73/23/EEC. The Low-Voltage Directive relates to electrical product safety. It applies to products with 50 to 1,000 VAC or 75 to 1,000 VDC input. Products may include components, information technology equipment, household products, power tools, laboratory equipment, test and measurement equipment and power supplies.

Effective 15 January 2004 products, or their particular pre-and post-market safety aspects, not covered by specific EU safety legislation will have to comply with the revised General Product Safety Directive (GPSD) 2001/95/EC. Examples include pushchairs, child-appealing products such as novelty slippers, child appealing Christmas decorations or children's fashion jewelry whose safety is not covered by specific EU Directives (Labtest News 2004).

European Union's consumer policy strategy may be found at
http://eurpoa.eu.int/comm/consumers/overview/cons_policy/index_en.htm

5-5 Toys

Toys can present a variety of hazards such as sharp edges and sharp points, which can be laceration hazard; small part, which can be a ingestion and chocking hazard, electric shock, dirty or non-sanitary stuffing materials in stuffed toys, which can pose not only health hazard but also chocking hazard. Toys can break easily resulting in either small parts, which can be chocking hazard or parts with sharp edges or points, which can be laceration hazard. Items such as bubble solutions, liquids contained within toys, paints and ink, playdoughs, play gels, crayons, glues and adhesives can present toxicological hazards.

Toy safety in the United States is addressed by the Consumer Product Safety Commission (CPSC) regulations under the Federal Hazardous Substance Act, CFR (Code of Federal Regulation) 16 Part 1500 as follows:

1500.18	Banned toys and other banned articles intended for use by children
1501	Requirements for Toy Small Parts hazard
1505	Requirements for Electrically Operated Toys or other Electrically Operated Articles Intended for Use by Children
1510	Requirements for Infant Rattles
1511	Requirements for Pacifiers

In addition to the above requirements, toys sold in the United States must meet the requirements of ASTM 963-03 Standard Consumer Safety Specification on Toy Safety.

Adult and children's costumes and masks are covered by four flammability standards administered by the CPSC under the authority of the Flammable Fabrics Acts. The Standard for the Flammability of Clothing Textiles (16 CFR 1610), and the Standard for the Flammability of Vinyl Plastic Film (16 CFR 1611) apply to clothing and textiles intended to be used for costume or masks. Costumes that are considered or would be used as children's sleepwear must comply with the more stringent Standard for the Flammability of Children's Sleepwear: Sizes 0 through 6X (16 CFR 1615) or the Standard for the Flammability of Children's Sleepwear Sizes 7 through 14 (16 CFR 1616).

European Standards for toy are as follows:

EN 71 Part 1 Mechanical and physical properties
Part 2 Flammability
Part 3 Migration of certain elements
Part 4 Experimental sets for chemistry and related activities
Part 5 Chemical toys (sets) other than experimental sets
Part 6 Graphical symbols for age warning labeling
Part 7 Finger paints
Part 8 Swings, slides and similar activity toys for indoor and outdoor family domestic use

EN 50088 Safety of Electric Toys

Toys are also covered by an EU directives 88/378/EEC and 93/378/EEC safety of toys. According to this directive "toy" is any product or material designed or clearly intended for use in play by children of less than 14 years of age. This directive also has a list of products not regarded as toys for the purpose of this directive.

International standard for toys is in three parts as follows:

ISO 8124-1:2000 Safety Aspects Related to Mechanical and Physical Properties
ISO 8124-2:1994 Flammability
ISO 8124-3:1997 Migration of Certain Elements

5-6 Juvenile Furniture

This category includes items such as bath seats, carriages and strollers, full size and non-full size cribs, high chairs, play yards, gates and enclosures, portable hook-on chairs, toddler beds, and walkers.

Safety is of paramount concern while using these items. These items are covered by the following Federal Regulations as well as ASTM standards administered by CPSC.

16 CFR Part 1508 Standards for Full Size Baby Cribs
16 CFR Part 1509 Standards for Non-Full Size Baby Cribs
16 CFR Part 1513 CPSC Requirements for Bunk Beds

ASTM F 404-99a	Consumer Safety Specification for High Chairs
ASTM F 406-02	Consumer safety Specification for Non-Full-size baby Cribs/Play Yards
ASTM F 833-01	Consumer safety Specifications for Carriages and Strollers
ASTM F 834-84 (1994)	Consumer safety Specification for Toy Chests
ASTM F 966-00	Consumer Safety Specification for Full-Size and Non-Full Size baby Crib Corner Post Extension
ASTM F 977-00	Consumer Specification for Infant Walkers
ASTM F 1004-02	Consumer Safety Specification for Expansion gates and Expandable Enclosures
ASTM F 1148-00	Consumer Safety Specification for Home Playground Equipment
ASTM F 1169-99	Specification for Full Size Baby Cribs

ASTM F 1235-98	Specification for Consumer safety for Portable Hook-On Chairs
ASTM F 1427-96	Consumer safety Specification for Bunk beds
ASTM F 1821-97	Consumer Safety Specification for Toddler Beds
ASTM F 1822-97	Consumer safety Specification for Non-Full-Size Baby Cribs
ASTM F 1838-98	Performance requirements for Child's Plastic Chairs for Outdoor Use
ASTM F 1917-00	Consumer safety Specification for Infant Bedding and Related Accessories
ASTM F 1967-01	Consumer safety Specification for Infant Bath seats
ASTM F 2012-00a	Standard Consumer Specification for Stationary Activity Center
ASTM F 2088-01	Standard Consumer Safety Specification for Stationary Activity Center
ASTM F 2167-01	Standard Consumer Safety Specification for Infant Bouncer Seats
ASTM F 2194-02	Standard Consumer Safety Specification for Bassinets and Cradles
ASTM F 2085-01	Standard Consumer Safety Specification for Portable Bed Rails
ASTM F 2050-01	Standard Consumer Safety Performance Specification for Hand-Held Infant Carriers

Juvenile Products Manufacturers Association (JPMA) has developed a product certification program for juvenile products. To become JPMA certified, a product must be tested by an independent testing facility for compliance with the specific ASTM standards. If a product passes the tests, JPMA allows the manufacturer to label it with JPMA Certified Seal, Figure 5-5.

Figure 5-5 JPMA Certification Seal
Reproduced with the permission of the Juvenile Products Manufacturers Association

For a list of JPMA certified products and suppliers see JPMA web site www.jpma.org

5-7 Drawstrings on Children's Outerwear

Drawstrings on children's clothing are a hazard that can lead to deaths and injuries when they catch on such items as playground equipment, bus doors, or cribs. From January 1985 through September 1995, the U. S. Consumer Product Safety Commission (CPSC) received reports of 17 deaths and 42 non-fatal incidents involving the entanglement of children's clothing drawstrings.

Over two-thirds of the deaths and non-fatal incidents involved hood/neck drawstrings, Figure 5-6 (CPSC 1996). The majority of these cases involved playground slides. Typically, as the child descended the slide, the toggle or knot on the drawstring got caught in a small space or gap at the top of the slide. Examples of catch points include a protruding bolt or a tiny space between the guardrail and the slide platform. As the child hung by the drawstring, suspended part way down the slide, the drawstring pulled the garment up taut to the neck, strangling the child. Victims of these cases ranged in age from 2 through 8 years old. In one case, a five-year-old girl strangled after the draw strings on her jacket hood caught on the slide at her school. One incident involved a fence. A four-year-old girl strangled after the hood string on her coat became entangled on a fence as she attempted to climb over it. Two strangulations occurred in cribs. In one case, an eighteen-month-old child was found hanging from a corner post of his crib by the tied cord of the hooded sweatshirt he was wearing. Another little girl was hanged by the drawstring of her sweatshirt in her crib the first time she wore the sweatshirt.

Almost one-third of the deaths and non-fatal incidents involved drawstrings at the waist/bottom of children's garments. Most of these involved children whose waist or bottom strings of their jackets got caught on hand rails or in school bus doors, Figure 5-7 (CPSC 1996). In most cases, the drawstrings at the bottom of the jacket snagged in a small space in the hand rail as the child was getting off the bus. Without the child or bus driver realizing that the drawstring was caught on the handrail, the bus doors closed and the bus drove away, dragging the child. Deaths have occurred when children were run over by the bus. Victims of these school bus cases ranged in age from 7 through 14 years old. A 14-year-old boy was killed when the long, trailing drawstring on his jacket got caught in the closed door of a moving school bus and he was eventually pulled beneath the bus and run over.

Figure 5-6 Neck Drawstrings (Courtesy: CPSC)

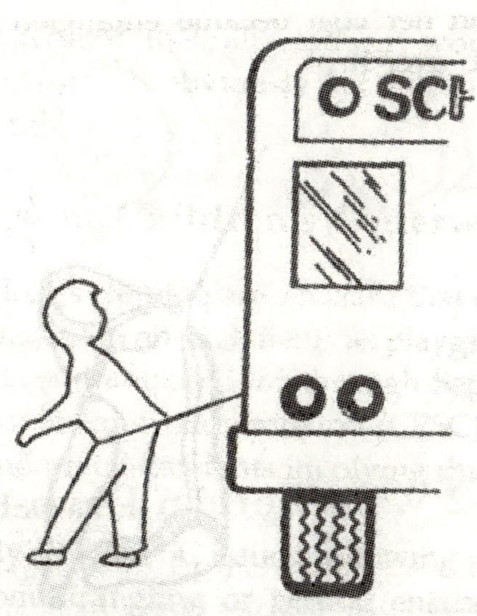

Figure 5-7 Drawstrings caught in a school bus door (Courtesy: CPSC)

Therefore, in early 1996, CPSC issued guidelines to help prevent children from strangling or getting entangled in the neck and waist drawstrings of upper outerwear garments, such as jackets and sweatshirts. (CPSC, 1996).

These guidelines are intended to provide consumers with information to help them prevent hazards with garments now in their possession and make informed purchasing choices in the future. Manufacturers and retailers should also be aware of these hazards, and are encouraged to consider this information in the production and sale of children" garments. CPSC's drawstring guidelines do not represent a standard or mandatory requirement set by the agency.

5-7-1 Hood/Neck Drawstrings

CPSC recommends that parents or caregivers completely remove the hood and neck strings from all children's outerwear, including jackets and sweatshirts, sized 2T to 12. CPSC technical staff has concluded that strings at the neck that are shortened still may present strangulation hazard. Therefore, CPSC recommends the customers purchase children's outerwear that has alternative closures, such as snaps, buttons, velcro, and elastic, Figure 5-8 (CPSC 1996) CPSC also recommends that manufacturers and retailers provide outerwear with these alternative closures, rather than drawstrings at the head/neck area.

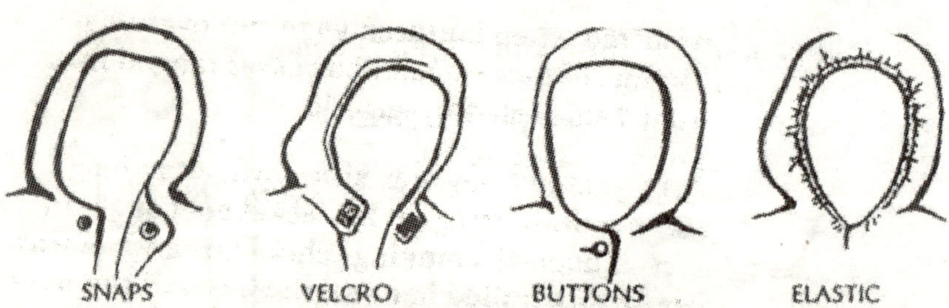

Figure 5-8 Hoods without drawstrings
(Courtesy: CPSC)

5-7-2 Waist/Bottom Drawstrings

For outerwear sized 2T to 16, CPSC recommends to consumers, manufacturers, and retailers that the ends of waist/bottom drawstrings measure no more than 3 inches from where the strings extend out of the garment when it is expanded to its fullest width. Also, the drawstrings should be sewn to the garment at its midpoint so the string can not be pulled out through one side, making it long enough to catch on something. CPSC also recommends eliminating toggles or knots at the ends of all drawstrings. Shortening the length of drawstrings at the waist and bottom of children's outerwear, Figure 5-9 (CPSC 1996) reduces the risk that the strings will become entangled in objects such as school bus doors or other moving objects.

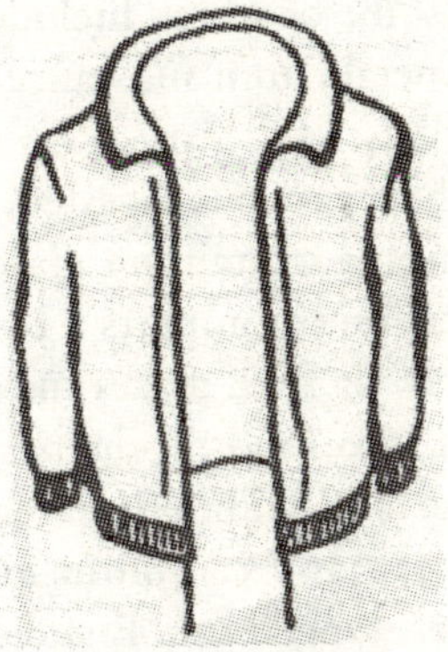

Figure 5-9 Waist/Bottom drawstrings
(Courtesy: CPSC)

Since the beginning of 1996, retailers in the U. S. are not selling any children's garments with drawstrings. Committee F-15 of ASTM on Consumer Products has developed voluntary drawstrings standard, F-1816-97 Standard Safety Specification for Drawstrings on Children's Upper Outerwear.

The United Kingdom recognized this hazard as early as 1976 and banned from sale in the U. K. any children's outerwear with drawstrings.

The German children's clothing industry has issued a voluntary resolution banning drawstrings in the neck and hood areas of children's clothing. This resolution bans drawstrings in neck and hood areas of clothing for children up to 164 centimeters (57.5 inches) in height. The industry is encouraging manufacturers to use hook-and-loop or snap fasteners as alternatives to drawstrings. Decorative cords with a maximum length of 8 centimeters (3.1 inches) can still be used. Finland has issued a voluntary resolution advising against the use of drawstrings in the neck and hood areas of clothing for children less than seven years of age. The French Consumer Safety Commission has advised against the use of drawstrings in children's clothing. The Ireland has laws banning the use of drawstrings in the neck area of children's outer garments for children under four years of age (MTL-ACTS 2002). There is also a draft European standard on drawstrings, EN 14682.

5-8 Heavy Metal Leaching

High levels of certain heavy metals in foods or beverages have always been of concern to the population in general. Heavy metals are those which have a poisoning effect through accumulation in the human body. Once ingested, the body has no way of excreting these metals, some of which include arsenic, antimony, lead and cadmium. Leaching of heavy metals from substance carrying vessels, i.e., dinnerware, punch bowls, wine goblets, etc., can cause serious problems depending upon the amount and type of heavy metals ingested. Ceramic dinnerware may be coated with lead and/or cadmium containing glaze. Lead is used to achieve a shiny, smooth surface, while cadmium imparts a bright coloration to the finish. Improperly formulated, applied, or fired glazes may permit varying amounts of lead and/or cadmium to leach into food products stored in ceramic containers. Even decals used to decorate ceramic dinnerware can be a source of these leach able metals. Ingestion of the lead and cadmium leached from such vessels can cause chronic poisoning with prolonged use. Enamelware (having highly colored interiors), pewter, silver-plated products, brassware, and glassware having painted interiors can present problems associated with release of similar toxic elements.

It is because of this concern that maximum acceptable heavy metal leaching standards have been established by FDA (Food and Drug Administration) as shown in the Table 5-1. Any subsistence carrying vessel sold in the United States must meet these standards.

Products	Maximum Acceptable Limits		Reference
	Lead	Cadmium	
Pottery (ceramics)			
Flatware (average of 6 samples)	3.0 mcg/ml	0.5 mcg/ml	CPG* 7117.07 & .06
Small hollowware (other than cups And mugs) (any one of 6 samples)	2.0 mcg/ml	0.5 mcg/ml	CPG 7117.07 & .06
Cups and mugs (any one of 6 samples)	0.5 mcg/ml	0.5 mcg/ml	CPG 7117.07 & .06
Large hollowware other than Pitchers (any one of 6 samples)	1.0 mcg/ml	0.25 mcg/ml	CPG 7117.07 & .06
Pitchers (any one of 6 samples)	0.5 mcg/ml	0.25 mcg/ml	CPG 7117.07 & .06
Silver plated hollowware			
If product is intended for use by adults (average of 6 samples)	7.0 mcg/ml		CPG 7117.05
If product is intended for use by Infants and children (one or more of 6 samples)	0.5 mcg/ml		CPG 7117.05

* Compliance Policy Guide, FDA

Notes

1. Following test method must be used for determining leach able levels of lead and cadmium:

   ASTM C738-94 (Reapproved in 1999) Standard Test method for Lead and Cadmium Extracted from Glazed Ceramic Surfaces

2. The categories of ceramic ware articles, flatware and hollowware used in preparation, serving or storage of food, are defined as follows:
   a. Flatware: ceramic articles which have an internal depth, as measured from the lowest point to the horizontal plane passing through the upper rim, that does not exceed 25mm.
   b. Hollowware: ceramic articles having an internal depth, as measured from the lowest point to the horizontal plane passing through the upper rim, greater than 25 mm.
   c Small hollowware: a capacity of less than 1.1 liter.
   d. Large hollowware: a capacity of 1.1 liter or more.

Table 5-1 FDA (Food and Drug Administration) heavy metal leaching standards for subsistence carrying vessels

Ornamental or decorative ceramic ware which appears to be suitable for food use is considered to be for food use unless:

a. It bears a conspicuous stick-on label on a surface clearly visible to consumers that states in legible script in letters at least 3.2 millimeters in height one of the following statements:

    (1) Not for Food Use, May Poison Food
    (2) Not for Food Use, Glaze Contains Lead. Food Use May result in Lead Poisoning
    (3) Not for Food Use-Food Consumed from This Vessel May be harmful

    The appropriate place on a plate for the temporary label would be the potential food contact surface, while on a pitcher a temporary label on the exterior of the side would be suitable.
b. The temporary label is in addition to the requirement for a permanent label designed to ensure that decorative ceramic ware would not be used in a manner that is unsafe. Without the temporary labeling there is a significant chance that a consumer will miss the warning on the base of a ceramic ware. A 'conspicuous and legible' permanent statement is to be molded or fired onto the exterior surface of the ceramic ware article or when the ceramic ware is not fired after decoration, permanently painted to the exterior surface of the base of the article. This permanent statement shall be in letters at least 3.2 mm in height, except that if insufficient space exists for the permanent statement in letters of such height, the statement shall be in the largest letters that will allow it to fit on the base of the article, provided that the letters are at least 1.6 mm in height. In addition to one of the three required statements, the permanent label may say "Decorative" or "For Decorative Purposes Only," following the required statement.
c. An optional use of symbol to "be used to advise that a piece of ornamental or decorative ceramic ware is not to be used with food" is acceptable to FDA. The symbol may be used on the temporary label or applied to the base of the article in the same manner as the permanent statement. The symbol, used in the United Kingdom, includes a goblet and a fork enclosed within a circle with a bar running diagonally across the design to indicate that food use is prohibited. The circle of the symbol should be at least 2.54 cm in diameter.

d. An alternative to permanent label statement would be boring a hole through the potential food contact surface of the decorative ceramic ware to make it unsuitable for food use.

e. A hole need not be bored in "antique or secondhand articles of value." Affixing stick-on labels or decals to such articles informing consumers about the risk posed by such articles of questionable safety is acceptable.

There are no standards or maximum limits for heavy metal leaching for pewter ware, brassware, enamelware, etc., however, for these items, generally heavy metal leaching standards for silver plated hollowware are applied.

For crystal ware there are no regulatory standards for heavy metal leaching, however, the International Crystal Federation has voluntary guidelines for lead leaching as follows:

Item	Maximum lead leaching levels
Flatware	3.0 parts per million (ppm)
Small hollowware (capacity of < 600 milliliter)	1.5 ppm
Large hollowware (capacity of > 600 milliliter)	0.75 ppm

Table 5-2 Heavy metal leaching standards for crystal ware

Note: One part per million (ppm) is equal to one microgram per milliliter (mcg/ml)

5-8-1 Proposition 65

All tableware sold in California must be in compliance with California's Safe Drinking Water and Toxic Enforcement Act of 1986 (Proposition 65). Under this proposition the maximum amount of lead and cadmium leaching are as follows:

Products	Maximum Acceptable Limits (mcg/ml) Lead	Cadmium
Pottery (ceramics)		
Flatware (average of 12 samples)	3.164	0.5
Small hollowware (other than cups And mugs) (any one of 12 samples)	0.322	0.5
Cups and mugs (any one of 12 samples)	0.322	0.5
Large hollowware other than Pitchers (any one of 12 samples)	0.084	0.25
Pitchers (any one of 12 samples)	0.322	0.25

Table 5-3 Heavy metal leaching standards—California Proposition 65

Products exceeding the above limits are classified as unsafe for sale in the State of California. Tableware that is classified as unsafe according to Proposition 65, must carry a clear and reasonable warning on or near the item, if it is to be distributed or sold in the State of California.

5-8-2 Checking for Heavy Metals

Under FHSA (Federal Hazardous Substance Act), any firm that purchases a product for resale is responsible for determining whether that product contains heavy metal, if so, whether it is a "hazardous substance."

Considerable volume of daily use ceramic ware is imported into the United States from the People's Republic of China (China). Since all of these ceramic ware cannot be tested upon entry into the United States, the Food and Drug Administration (FDA) has a memorandum of understanding (MOU) with China whereby China has established a certification system that will increase the likelihood that daily use ceramic ware manufactured in China and offered for import into the United States will comply with U. S. law regarding lead and cadmium leaching. Under this MOU, the China Import and Export Commodity Inspection Bureaus (CCIBs) of the State Administration of Entry-Exit Inspection and Quarantine (SAIQ) of China will inspect and analyze factory lots or production lots of daily use ceramic ware to be exported to the United States at a rate commensurate with the compliance history of the CCIB certified factory and sufficient to provide a high degree of confidence that the daily use ceramic ware exported to the U. S. is in compliance with the FDA criteria for lead and cadmium leaching. Each shipping and retail carton of ceramic tableware must have a sticker/logo of CCIB embossed with the unique code number of production facility that produced the ware. The sticker/logo serves as an additional means of identifying a particular consignment as having originated from the SAIQ certified factory (http://vm.cfsan.fda.gov/vlrd/fr990728.html).

A current list of certified factories in China is available on the FDA web site http://www.cfsan.fda.gov/~comm/ceramic.html. This site is updated three to four times a year.

5-8-3 ISO Standards on Heavy Metals

Here are some ISO standards for cutlery, table ware, ceramic ware and glass ware.

ISO 6486-1: 1999	Ceramic ware, glass-ceramic ware and glass dinnerware in contact with food—release of lead and cadmium—Part 1: Test method
ISO 6486-2: 1999	Ceramic ware, glass-ceramic ware and glass dinnerware in contact with food—release of lead and cadmium—Part 2: Permissible limits
ISO 7086-1: 2000	Glass hollowware in contact with food—Release of lead and cadmium—Part 1: Test method
ISO 7086-2: 2000	Glass hollowware in contact with food—Release of lead and cadmium—Part 2: Permissible limits
ISO 8391-1: 1986	Ceramic cookware in contact with food—Release of lead and cadmium—Part 1: Test method
ISO 8391-2: 1986	Ceramic cookware in contact with food—Release of lead and cadmium—Part 2: Permissible limits
ISO 8442-1:1997	Materials and articles in contact with foodstuffs—Cutlery and table holloware—Part 1: Requirements for cutlery for preparation of food
ISO 8442-2:1997	Materials and articles in contact with foodstuffs—Cutlery and table holloware—Part 2: Requirements for stainless steel and silver-plated cutlery
ISO 8442-3:1997	Materials and articles in contact with foodstuffs—Cutlery and table holloware—Part 3: Requirements for silver-plated table and decorative hollowware

ISO 8442-4:1997	Materials and articles in contact with foodstuffs—Cutlery and table holloware—Part 4: Requirements for gold-plated cutlery
ISO 8442-6:1997	Materials and articles in contact with foodstuffs—Cutlery and table holloware—Part 6: Requirements for lightly silver-plated table holloware protected by lacquer
ISO 8442-7:1997	Materials and articles in contact with foodstuffs—Cutlery and table holloware—Part 7: Requirements for table cutlery made of silver, other precious metals and their alloys
ISO 8442-8:1997	Materials and articles in contact with foodstuffs—Cutlery and table holloware—Part 8: Requirements for silver table and decorative holloware

5-9 Lead in Jewelry and Consumer Products

CPSC has issued an advisory urging jewelry manufacturers, importers, distributors and retailers to only produce/sell children's costume jewelry that does not contain lead (CPSC 1998). In cases where substitutes for lead are impractical or unavailable, the agency would like to see children's jewelry carry warning labels alerting consumers that the product is not intended for use by children under six years of age, due to possible lead hazard. CPSC warns that lead can leach from jewelry if the product is mouthed or chewed, especially if the jewelry's plating is broken. While older children are not likely to mouth jewelry, the agency is concerned that children under six or younger could put jewelry in their mouths, exposing them to a possible lead poisoning hazard.

CPSC has also issued guidance on lead in consumer products (Federal Register 1998). CPSC guidance is not a rule. It is intended to highlight certain obligations under an applicable act. Companies should read the applicable act and accompanying regulations.

Under the Federal Hazardous Substances Act (FHSA), 15 U.S.C. 1261 (f)(1), household products that expose children to hazardous quantities of lead under reasonably foreseeable conditions of handling or use are "hazardous substances." A household product that is not intended for children but which creates such risk of injury because it contains lead requires precautionary labeling under this Act 15 U.S. 1261(p).

CPSC has by regulation, banned (1) paint and other similar surface coatings that contain more than 0.06% lead ("lead-containing paint"), (2) toys and other articles intended for use by children bearing lead containing paint, and (3) furniture articles for consumer use that bear lead containing paint.

5-10 Nickel in Consumer Products

European Union (EU) has a directive (94/27/EC) that has established that the metal items intended to come into prolonged contact with the skin would not be allowed to expose consumers to more than 0.5 $mg/cm^2/wk$ of nickel. The EU directive also established following three test methods for the determination of nickel.

EN 1810—Body Piercing Post Assemblies (0.05% nickel limit)
EN 1811—Products Intended to Come into Direct and Prolonged Contact with Skin (0.5$mg/cm^2/wk$)
EN 12472—Coated Items Intended to Come into Direct and Prolonged Contact with Skin (0.5 $mg/cm^2/wk$)

The items that are considered as products intended to come into direct and prolonged contact with skin include earrings, necklaces, eyeglass frames, bracelets/chains, anklets, rings, wristwatch bands, cases and straps, rivets/rivet buttons, zippers along with any major metal component attached to a garment.

5-11 Batteries

The Mercury-Containing and Rechargeable Battery Management Act of May 13, 1996 limits the mercury content in alkaline-manganese button cell batteries to 25 milligrams and prohibits alkaline-manganese batteries manufactured with intentionally introduced mercury, prohibits intentionally introduced mercury in zinc-carbon batteries, and prohibits mercuric-oxide button cell batteries, unless the manufacturer identifies a collection site that meets all federal, state and local recycling and proper disposal requirements (MTL-ACTS 1996).

In Europe, batteries supplied with toys must comply with the EU directive 98/101/EEC. This directive covers marking and controlled disposal of batteries.

5-12 Candles

In the past few years a variety of candles have come into the marketplace and their sales keep increasing. Candles are such that if not used properly with care, they can turn quickly in to a fire hazard. Residential fires in which a candle is the source of heat ignition is one of the few segments of the fire problems that has been increasing in recent years. According to CPSC (2001) in 1998, there were an estimated 12,800 candle fires that resulted in 170 deaths and 1,200 injuries. In an effort to reduce fires caused by candles, CPSC is working with the candle industry through ASTM International to develop safety standards for candles. As a result, ASTM International recently issued a voluntary label standard for candles, ASTM F 2058 Standard specifications for cautionary labeling for candles burned in homes. ASTM International has also issued a provisional candle safety standard, PS 59, Provisional Standard Fire Specification for Candles, which addresses flame height, secondary ignition, end of useful life, and stability.

One retailer has developed its own performance standards for candles as shown in the Chapter 4 on Standards and Specifications.

National Fire Protection Association provides excellent safety tips on candles in one of their fact sheets (NFPA Facts Sheets).

Aside from candles being a fire hazard, there is some controversy about those candles with lead cored wick posing health hazard. Lead-cored wicks are candle wicks with a metal wire in the center made of lead or lead alloy. As a lead-cored wick burns, some of the lead may vaporize and be released into air. Some of the lead may be inhaled or deposited on floors or furniture where children may be exposed to it. Therefore, effective October 2003, there is a ban on manufacturing, importing, or selling candles with lead wicks (CPSC Press Release 2003).

5-13 Art Materials

On November 18, 1988, the President signed into law the Labeling of Hazardous Art Materials Act (Public Law 100-695). This law requires that all art materials be reviewed to determine the potential for causing a chronic hazard and that appropriate warning labels be put on those art materials found to pose a chronic hazard. The term "art materials" includes "any substance marketed or represented by the producer or repackager as suitable for use in any phase of the creation of any work of visual or graphic art of any medium." [15 U.S.C. 1277(b)(1)]. The law applies to many children's toy products such as crayons, chalk, paint sets, modeling clay, coloring books, pencils, and any other products used by children to produce a work of visual or graphic art.

The "Labeling of Hazardous Art materials Act" (LHAMA) amended the Federal Hazardous Substances Act (FHSA) by adding Section 23 and designating the ASTM Standard Practice for Labeling Art Materials for Chronic Health Hazards (ASTM D-4236-88) as a regulation under Section 3(b) of the FHSA. The requirements of the LHAMA became effective on November 18, 1990. These requirements apply to art materials that are intended for use in the household or by children, which are initially introduced into interstate commerce on and after November 18, 1990.

The LHAMA (Labeling of Hazardous Art Materials Act) stipulates that art materials, intended for use in households, schools, or for use by children, must be reviewed by a Board Certified Toxicologist to determine if they have the potential to produce chronic, long term health hazard. According to the regulations, 16 CFR 1500.14(b)(8)(i)(C)(6), "The producer or repackager shall have a toxicologist review as necessary, but at least every 5 years, art material product formulation(s) and associated label(s) based upon the then current, generally accepted, well established scientific knowledge." Companies which distribute art materials within the United States are required by law to have supporting documentation stating that their products are in compliance with the LHAMA. Additionally, the LHAMA labeling requirements include placing either a conformance statement or cautionary label on the product's package or container, in accordance with the specifications called out in the LHAMA regulations.

Since 1940, the Art & Creative Materials Institute, Inc. (ACMI), www.acminet.org has sponsored a certification program for children's art materials, certifying that these products are non-toxic and meet voluntary standards of quality and performance. In 1982, ACMI began evaluating adult artist materials and certifies that these are non-toxic or properly labeled with cautionary language and safe use information. The ACMI uses two seals shown in the Figures 5-10 and 5-11.

The new AP (Approved Product) Seal, Figure 5-10, with or without Performance Certification, identifies art materials that are safe and that are certified in a toxicological evaluation by a medical expert to contain no materials in sufficient quantities to be toxic or injurious to humans, including children, or to cause acute or chronic health problems. This seal is currently replacing the previous non-toxic seals: CP (Certified Product), AP (Approved Product), and HL Health Label (Non-Toxic) over a 10-year phase-in period. Such products are certified by ACMI to be labeled in accordance with the chronic hazard labeling standard, ASTM D 4236, and the U. S. Labeling of Hazardous Art Materials Act (LHAMA). Additionally, products bearing the AP Seal with Performance Certification or the CP Seal are certified to meet specific requirements of material, workmanship, working qualities, and color developed by ACMI and others through recognized standards organizations, such as the American National Standards Institute (ANSI) and the American Society for Testing and Materials International (ASTM Intl). Some products cannot attain this performance certification because no quality standard currently exists for certain types of products.

The CL Seal, Figure 5-11, identifies products that are certified to be properly labeled in a program of toxicological evaluation by a medical expert for any known health risks and with information on the safe and proper use of these materials. This seal is currently replacing the HL Health Label (Cautions Required) Seal over a 5-year phase-in period. These products are also certified by ACMI to be labeled in accordance with the chronic hazard labeling standard, ASTM D 4236, and the U. S. Labeling of Hazardous Art Materials Act (LHAMA).

Figure 5-10 AP Seal

Figure 5-11 CL Seal

Reproduced with the permission of the Art & Creative Materials Institute

Most retailers have a policy of accepting only those art materials certified by ACMI. ACMI periodically publishes a list of certified products.

5-14 Flammability

Clothing and textile products must meet certain flammability standards. These standards are federal regulations and come under the purview of the U. S. Consumer Product Safety Commission (CPSC). Also, the flammability issue is very important from a product liability point of view (PSLR 1980).

5-14-1 Flammability of Clothing Textiles

All fabrics of natural and regenerated cellulose, as well as certain types of finished and unfinished fabrics made from other natural or synthetic fibers, are combustible. Some combustible fabrics, when used for clothing, are potentially dangerous to the wearer because of the speed and intensity of flame with which those fabrics burn and their ease of ignition, and because of the design of the garment. Two of these factors, the ease of ignition and the speed of flame spread can be measured and relied upon to decide whether a fabric tested is dangerous or not.

The flammability of clothing textiles is governed by Title 16 CFR (Code of Federal Regulations)1610 (Federal Register 1984). It excludes interlining fabrics and certain hats, gloves, and footwear. This regulation requires that a piece of fabric, which is placed in a holder at a 45^0 angle and exposed to a flame for 1 second, not ignite and spread flame up the length of the sample in less than 3.5 seconds for smooth fabrics or 4.0 seconds for napped fabrics. This requirement eliminated easy-to-ignite brushed fabrics and prohibited the introduction of equally hazardous textile material. Today, most fabrics in general apparel use meet the requirements of this regulation.

It is interesting to note that since this law went into effect in 1954 there were no reports of violation of this law till August '94, however, between August '94 and June '97 CPSC issued 18 recalls under this act. The products recalled were skirts, sweaters, scarves, shirts, sweatshirts, jackets, and bathrobes. The recalled products were made from chiffon, fleece, and terry cloth fabric and fiber content was 100 % rayon, 88 % rayon & 12 % nylon, polyester & cotton, and 100 % silk. The country of origin of these recalled products were China, Hong Kong, India, Korea, Pakistan, Taiwan, Turkey, and USA.

This standard does not apply to hats, gloves, footwear, and interlining fabrics. Interlining fabrics are not considered dangerously flammable when used as interlinings. When used for other purposes they should be tested and rated the same as any other fabrics.

This regulation exempts following fabrics from meeting requirements of this regulation:

a. Plain surface fabrics, regardless of fabric content, weighing 2.6 ounces per square yard or more.

b. All fabrics, both plain and raised fiber surface, regardless of weight, made entirely from any of the following fibers or entirely from combinations of the following fibers: acrylic, modacrylic, nylon, olefin, polyester, and wool.

For evaluating compliance with this regulation, a test method called 45^0 flammability test is used.

5-14-2 Flammability of Children's Sleepwear

The standards for flammability of children's sleepwear were issued to protect young children from death and serious burn injuries associated with ignition of sleepwear garments, such as nightgowns and pajamas, by small open flame sources. These standards cover two size ranges of children's sleepwear. One standard covers sizes 0 through 6X and the other standard covers sizes 7 through 14.

The safety requirements of the two standards are nearly identical. They prescribe a test which requires that specimens of fabrics, seams, and trim of children's sleepwear garments must self-extinguish after exposure to a small open flame. Both standards require manufacturers of children's sleepwear subject to their provisions to test prototypes of sleepwear garments with acceptable results before beginning production. Both standards also require manufacturers to sample and test garments from regular production. Failure to comply with the sampling and testing requirements of the standards is a violation of the law. The standards do not require or prohibit the use of any particular type of fabric or garment design as long as the manufacturer successfully completes the prescribed prototype and production testing.

5-14-2-1 Sizes 0 through 6X

The flammability of children's sleepwear, sizes 0 to 6X is covered by the Federal Regulation (Title 16 CFR 1615), also known as FF 3-71. This includes any product of wearing apparel up to and including size 6X, such as nightgowns, pajamas, or similar related items such as robes intended to be worn primarily for sleeping or activities related to sleeping. Fabrics or related materials intended or promoted for use in children's sleepwear must also meet this standard. This regulation excludes:

(a) Diapers and underwear
(b) Garments sized for a child nine months of age or younger that:
  (1) If one-piece garment, does not exceed 64.8 centimeters (25.75 inches) in length.
  (2) If a two-piece garment, has no piece exceeding 40 centimeters (15.75 inches) in length.
  (3) Complies with all applicable requirements of the Standard for the Flammability of Clothing Textiles (16 CFR Part 1610) and the Standard for the Flammability of Vinyl Plastic Film (16 CFR Part 1611).
  (4) Bears a label stating the size of the garment, expressed in terms of months of age. For example, "0 to 3 mos." or "9 mos." If the label is not visible to the consumer when the garment is offered for sale at retail, the same information must appear legibly on the package of the garment.
(c) Tight fitting garments sized from 9 months to 6X. Tight fitting garment means a garment that does not exceed maximum dimension for the chest, waist, seat, upper arm, thigh, wrist, or ankle for the labeled size as specified by the CPSC. These dimensions are included in the 16 CFR Part 1615, Flammable Fabrics Act: Children's Sleepwear (Sizes 0-6X) Flammability Standards, and available from CPSC.

5-14-2-2 Sizes 7 through 14

The flammability of children's sleepwear, sizes 7 to 14, is covered by Federal Regulation (Title 16 CFR 1616), also known as FF 5-74. It covers any product of wearing apparel from size 7 to 14 such as nightgowns, pajamas, or similar or related items such as robes intended to be worn primarily for sleeping or activities related to sleeping. This regulation excludes underwear. Fabrics or related material intended or promoted for use in children's sleepwear must also meet this standard. This regulation excludes:

(a) Diapers and underwear
(b) Tight fitting garments. Tight fitting garment means a garment that does not exceed maximum dimension for the chest, waist, seat, upper arm, thigh, wrist, or ankle for the labeled size as specified by the CPSC. These dimensions are included in the 16 CFR Part 1616, Flammable Fabrics Act:

Children's Sleepwear (Sizes 7-14) Flammability Standards, and available from CPSC.

(c) Complies with all applicable requirements of the Standard for the Flammability of Clothing Textiles (16 CFR Part 1610) and the Standard for the Flammability of Vinyl Plastic Film (16 CFR Part 1611).

(d) Bears a label stating the size of the garment; for example "size 7." If the label is not visible to the consumer when the garment is offered for sale at retail, the same information must appear legibly on the package of the garment.

The technical and flammability requirements of this regulation are the same as those for sizes 0 to 6X, except that in the case of sizes 7 to 14 reduced sampling is available.

Occasionally, it is difficult to decide what is and what is not children's sleepwear. To help concerned parties answer this question, the Consumer Product Safety Commission (CPSC) staff has provided a fact sheet providing factors that should be considered when determining whether or not a particular garment is an item of children's sleepwear. Also, for illustrative purposes the CPSC staff has prepared drawings of those styles that have posed the most ambiguity or confusion over the past several years. This fact sheet and a booklet entitled "Garment Diagrams and Assessments" can be obtained from the CPSC.

The flammability of children's sleepwear sizes 0 to 6X and 7 to 14 is evaluated by the vertical flammability test. Both the titles, 16 CFR 1615 and 1616 describe testing in detail along with accept/reject criteria.

For children's sleepwear larger than size 9 months, effective June 28, 2000, CPSC requires hangtags and permanent labels on snug fitting children's sleepwear, made of cotton or cotton blends, to remind consumers that because the garment is not flame resistant, it must fit snugly for safety. The yellow hangtag for snug fitting garments must say: "For child's safety, garment should fit snugly. This garment is not flame resistant. Loose fitting garment is more likely to catch fire." The permanent label should say: "Wear snug-fitting. Not flame resistant," and should be sewn into the neck of the garment. (www.cpsc.gov/cpscpub/pubs/5125.html).

5-14-3 Flammability of Mattress

Flammability of mattress is covered by a Federal regulation,Title 16 CFR 1632, also known as FF 4-72). It includes ticking filled with a resilient material intended or promoted for sleeping upon, including mattress pads. It excludes pillows, box springs, sleeping bags, and upholstered furniture.

In testing a mattress or a mattress pad for flammability, a minimum of 9 cigarettes are allowed to burn on smooth, tape edge, and quilted or tufted locations of a bare mattress. The char length on the mattress surface must not be more than 2 inches in any direction from any cigarette. Tests are also conducted with 9 cigarettes placed between two sheets on the mattress surface described above.

The Directorate of Compliance and Administrative Litigation, Consumer Product Safety Commission considers thin, flexible mattresses, sometimes called "futons," to fall within the definition of the term "mattress" as it appears in the Standard for the Flammability of Mattresses and Mattress Pads at 16 CFR 1632.1(a). Consequently, futons must meet all applicable provisions of the mattress flammability standards (PSLR 1984).

The state of California has a regulation covering flammability of mattress/box spring set, Technical Bulletin # 603, "Requirements and Test Procedure for Resistance of a Mattress/Box Spring Set to a Large Open Flame." (www.bhfti.ca.gov)

Flammability of mattresses is also addressed in the standard E 1590 Standard Test Method for Fire Testing of Mattresses, ASTM Volume 04.07.

5-14-4 Flammability of Upholstered Furniture

According to a report in the Product Safety and Liability Reporter (PSLR, 2003) fires involving ignition of upholstered furniture constitute a leading cause of residential fire loses. Furniture fires killed more people in 1998 than did fires involving any other category of consumer products under Consumer Product Safety Commission's jurisdiction. About four fifths of the estimated deaths and about two-thirds of the injuries were from smoldering ignition by smoking materials. About 80 % of upholstered furniture related annual residential fire losses are related to cigarette ignitions.

While there are no mandatory standards for the flammability of upholstered furniture, the Upholstered Furniture Action Council (UFAC) has developed a voluntary test method as a means of measuring cigarette ignition performance. The UFAC voluntary program contains six cigarette ignition performance tests for different upholstered furniture components, as well as Certification and labeling provisions. (www.furninfo.com/ufac/ufac.htm)

Upholstered furniture sold in the state of California must meet the requirements of the Technical Bulletin 117, Requirements, Test Procedure and Apparatus for

Testing the Flame Retardance of Resilient Filling Materials Used in Upholstered Furniture. (www.bhfti.ca.gov/bulletin.htm)

5-14-5 Flammability of Carpets and Rugs

Flammability of carpets and rugs is covered by 16 CFR 1630 Standard for the Surface Flammability of Carpets and Rugs (FF 1-70). "Carpet" means any type of finished product made in whole or in part of fabric or related material and intended for use which may reasonably be expected to be used as a floor covering which is exposed to traffic in homes, offices, or other places of assembly or accommodation, and which may or may not be fastened to the floor by mechanical means such as nails, tacks, barbs, staples, adhesives, and which has one dimension greater than 1.83 meters (6 feet) and a surface area greater than 2.23 square meters (24 square feet). Products such as "carpet squares", with one dimension less than1.83 meters (6 feet) and a surface area less than 2,23 square meters (24 square feet), but intended to be assembled upon installation into assemblies which may have one dimension greater than 1.83 meters (6 feet) and a surface area greater than 2.23 square meters (24 square feet) are included in this definition. Mats, hides with natural or synthetic fibers, and other similar products in the above defined dimensions are included in this definition, but resilient floor coverings such as linoleum, asphalt tile and vinyl tile are not. "Rug" means the same as carpet and shall be accepted as interchangeable with carpet.

Testing under this regulation involves the exposure of each of eight conditioned, replicate specimens of a given carpet or rug to a standard ignition source in a draft protected environment, and measurement of the proximity of the charred portion to the edge of the hole in the prescribed flattening frame. A specimen passes the test if the charred portion does not extend to within 1 inch of the edge of the hole in the flattening frame at any point. At least seven of the eight specimens shall meet the test criterion in order to conform with this standard.

For complete details of the test method and acceptance criteria refer to this flammability standard (16 CFR 1630).

5-14-5-1 Flammability of Small Carpets and Rugs

Flammability of small carpets and rugs is covered by 16 CFR 1631 Standard for the Surface Flammability of Small Carpets and Rugs (FF 2-70). "Small Carpet" means any type of finished product made in whole or in part of fabric or related material and intended for use which may reasonably be expected to be used as a floor covering which is exposed to traffic in homes, offices, or other places of assembly or accommodation, and which may or may not be fastened to the floor by mechanical means such as nails, tacks, barbs, staples, adhesives, and which has no dimension greater than 1.83 meters (6 feet) and an area not greater than 2.23 square meters (24 square feet). Products such as "carpet squares", with dimensions smaller than these but intended to be assembled upon installation into assemblies which may have dimensions greater than 1.83 meters (6 feet) and a surface area greater than 2.23 square meters (24 square feet) than these, are excluded from this definition. They are, however, included in the Standard for the surface flammability of carpets and rugs (FF 1-70). Mats, hides with natural or synthetic fibers, and other similar products in the above defined dimensions are included in this definition, but resilient floor coverings such as linoleum, asphalt tile and vinyl tile are not. "Rug" means the same as carpet and shall be accepted as interchangeable with carpet.

Testing under this regulation involves the exposure of each of eight conditioned, replicate specimens of a given carpet or rug to a standard ignition source in a draft protected environment, and measurement of the proximity of the charred portion to the edge of the hole in the prescribed flattening frame. A specimen passes the test if the charred portion does not extend to within 1 inch of the edge of the hole in the flattening frame at any point. At least seven of the eight specimens shall meet the test criterion in order to conform with this standard.

For complete details of the test method and acceptance criteria refer to this flammability standard (16 CFR 1631).

5-14-6 Flammability of Sleeping Bags

ASTM International has a test method F 1955-99, Standard Test Method for Flammability of Sleeping Bags, however, it is based on the test method CAPI-75, A Rate of Burn Standard for Sleeping Bags, developed by the Canvas Products Association International, now called Industrial Fabrics Association International (IFAI). This has been the accepted standard in the sleeping bag industry. When tested according to this test method the average burn rate for a sample unit[1] should not be more than 6.0" per minute and no individual specimen within a sample unit should have a burn rate of more than 8.0" per minute.

1- A sample unit has 10 specimens.

5-15 Material Safety Data Sheet (MSDS)

The material safety data sheet (MSDS) is a detailed information bulletin prepared by the manufacturer or importer of a chemical that describes the physical and chemical properties, physical and health hazards, routes of exposure, precautions for safe handling and use, emergency and first aid procedures, and control measures. Producers and importers of chemical or hazardous materials are required under 29 CFR 1910.1200, Hazardous Communication, to provide the hazard information to business or any one who purchases their products. Information presented in MSDS can assist in the selection of safe products and can help to prepare employers and employees to respond effectively to daily exposure situations as well as to emergency situations. MSDS can also help answer a consumer inquiring about safety of some chemicals.

Material safety data sheets are government mandated documents required to show that companies are following proper safety procedures when it comes to hazardous materials covering the proper handling of hazardous materials in the work place, under the jurisdiction of the Occupational Safety and Health Administration (OSHA); accidental spills, which can also be under the purview of the Environmental Protection Agency (EPA); and shipping from distribution center to stores, which is covered by regulations of the Department of Transportation (DoT).

The retailer can rely on the information received from the suppliers. The retailer has no independent duty to analyze the chemical or evaluate the hazards of it. All businesses, including retailers are required to maintain MSDS on every hazardous material they use or sell. Retailers normally do not think that they sell any hazardous materials, however, paints, stains and thinners; lawn and garden supplies; swimming pool chemicals; pesticides; and household cleaning products would require MSDS. While perfume and fingernail polish remover do not come across as hazardous materials, it would be wise to maintain MSDS on those items also. Some retailers contract out management of MSDS rather than do it themselves.

It would be to a retailer's advantage to appoint or designate a single point of contact within the company, either in QA or in the Safety & Security or Loss Prevention department for any inquiry regarding MSDS from customers or employees.

A blank MSDS form can be seen on OSHA's web site www.osha.gov/Publications/MSDS/msdsform.html to get some idea as to what information is on a MSDS.

5-16 Warning Labels

Warning labels on products and packaging are frequently used to influence the safe use of products. There are two standards for warning labels and signs as follows:

ISO 3864-84 Safety Colors and Safety Signs, and
ANSI Z535.4, 2002 Standard on Product Safety Signs and Labels

The College of Engineering, University of Wisconsin-Madison periodically conducts a course "The Role of Warnings and Instructions." Please see Chapter 10, Resources for the address of the University of Wisconsin.

5-17 Product Safety & Counterfeiting

Counterfeiting is not limited to luxury items. With global markets as well as easy and rapid flow of information no product is immune to counterfeiting. As someone has said "if you can make it they can fake it." Some of the counterfeit consumer products found are batteries, toys, razors, light bulbs, lamps, soaps, shampoos, cosmetics, power tools, etc.

Counterfeit products pose safety risks. Counterfeit toys may break easily and may have small, sharp pieces that pose chocking and laceration hazards, respectively, to children. Additionally, because counterfeiters use inexpensive materials to make knock-off toys, the risk of counterfeits containing lead-based paint is increased. Stuffed counterfeit toys may be stuffed with unsafe materials. Counterfeit sunglasses may shatter easily and fail to provide protection against ultra-violet rays as advertised. Counterfeit safety footwear may offer substandard toe protection and may be deficient in dielectric protection creating a shock hazard. Counterfeit cosmetics may contain residue of industrial solvents and carcinogens, which may cause severe allergic reaction when applied to skin.

Several organizations such as International AntiCounterfeiting Coalition (www.iacc.org) and National Intellectual Property Rights Coordination Center, staffed with personnel from the Federal Bureau of Investigation (FBI) and the U. S. Customs Service, are devoted to combating product counterfeiting and piracy.

Several certification organizations such as the Underwriters Laboratories (UL) and CSA-International provide training programs for retailers to increase their familiarity with CSA and UL marks and cover topics such as what to look for when buying/receiving products covered by UL and CSA marks, detecting and preventing counterfeiting of UL and CSA marks. UL and CSA have also developed training programs for the U. S. and Canadian customs agents, police, and regulatory authorities to alert them to the problem of counterfeit marks and arm them with the latest identification techniques.

The price and location often are easiest ways to identify counterfeit consumer goods. However, according to International AntiCounterfeiting Coalition, watching for the following can help one avoid purchasing counterfeit products.

a. Packaging with blurred lettering, labeling that is not crisp, or ripped labels.
b. Misspelling of words or altered names.
c. Drastic changes in product content, color, smell, or packaging without prior notice from the legitimate manufacturer, or products that are not made by the manufacturer listed.
d. Products or packaging lacking manufacturer's codes, trademarks and/or copyrights, 1-800 consumer information numbers, other marks you normally find on your favorite products.
e. Products with unusual claims and warranties, or conversely, those products that completely lack licensing agreements and guarantees typically found with goods such as software, or designer goods.

5-18 Product Recalls

No company likes to recall one of its products, but when a safety problem makes a product recall necessary to prevent injury and save lives it is to everyone's benefit to move quickly and effectively.

It is not common for a retailer to initiate a recall. Most likely, a recall will be initiated by a manufacturer working with a regulatory agency, such as CPSC, FDA, etc. The retailer's role then is to communicate recall information with its customers. This communication can be done in one or more of the following ways.

a. Putting up a recall notice on the notice board and in the area where the item was sold in each store. For example, one retailer posts recall notices on the notice board in each store that is at the entrance of the store so customers can not miss that.
b. Posting a recall notice on the company's web page. For example, one retailer posts recalls on its web page under "Product Recalls" icon. By clicking on this icon, a customer can look at recalls issued within the past three years.
c. A video release. Some retailers show advertisements in their stores on TV monitors. A video of product recall can be shown on these monitors within the stores every so often, such as once an hour or so.
d. Radio announcement. Most retailers have piped in music in their stores. Recall information can be announced on in-house speaker system every so often, such as every hour or so.
e. Direct notice to consumers known to have the product identified through registration cards, sales records, catalog orders, or other means.
f. Paid notices via television and/or radio.
g. Paid notices in local, regional, and/or national newspapers.
h. Point-of-purchase posters.
i. Notices in marketing materials.

Consumers no longer view product recalls in a negative light. Millions of products have been recalled over the years. Today, consumers believe they enjoy a safer, better product as a result of a recall conducted responsibly by a company. How well a company conducts a timely, reasonable recall of a product can have a strong influence on consumers' attitude about the company. Successful product recalls in the past have rewarded companies with continuing consumer support and demand for the company's products.

Here is a framework of what should be covered in a recall message.

CONTACT: It is useful to provide contact information about at least two individuals, i.e., the buyer of the product recalled and the QA specialist who is handling this recall or alert. That way if any store or a customer needs to talk to some one, there is enough information. Always provide complete names, phone numbers, and e-mail addresses.

DATE: Date the recall is issued.

SCOPE: This tells what geographical area the recall is applicable, i.e., all stores worldwide, nationwide, only stores in certain part of the country, etc.

SUBJECT: The sentence should start out saying whether this is a HAZARDOUS or NON-HAZARDOUS recall. Then include the company name and the product name.

FIRST PARAGRAPH: Here describe the product, state name of the company, describe the condition (or defect) for which the product is being recalled. Also, include how the company came to know about the defective condition. A photo of the item should be included here or should be attached at the end of the recall notice.

SECOND PARAGRAPH: Indicate here if there were any injuries or deaths reported due to use of this product.

THIRD PARAGRAPH: Include here detailed description of the product including model/style/serial numbers affected, where to find model/style/serial number on the product, etc.

FOURTH PARAGRAPH: Include where products were sold, during what time period, affected date codes, and sell price.

FIFTH PARAGRAPH: This paragraph should include information for consumers as to how should they respond to this recall. They should stop using the product and where they should return it for a refund or repair. In case they should return it for repair, there should be address where to return, whether the return will be postage paid or not? There should be manufacturer's toll free number and web site address, and any contact information if appropriate.

Note: Before issuing or releasing a recall notice, always check manufacturer's toll free number by actually calling that number and making sure that it is a working phone number. It would be embarrassing to release a recall notice with a non-working or wrong toll free phone number.

LAST PARAGRAPH: This paragraph should include instructions for stores for posting this notice and what to do when customers return this product for a refund.

CPSC has published a "Recall Handbook." This is a guide for manufacturers, importers, distributors, and retailers on reporting under Sections 15 and 37 of the Consumer Product Safety Act and Section 102 of the Child Safety Protection Act and preparing for, initiating and implementing product safety recalls. This handbook is available from CPSC free of charge to any business.

In order to keep up with developments in the product safety area, it is beneficial to subscribe to "Product Safety & Liability Reporter" a weekly published by the Bureau of National Affairs from Washington, DC. Their web site is www.bna.com

The following web sites post and maintain recall information on a regular basis for their countries.

The U. S. government has an inter-agency website www.Recalls.gov where recalls of consumer products, motor vehicles, boats, food, medicine, cosmetics, and environmental products are posted.

Australia Competition and Consumer Commission http://recalls.consumer.gov.au
A listing of product recalls, including food in Australia.

Australia Department of Mines and Energy
http://www.dme.gld.gov.au/safety/electrical/recalls/index.htm This web site provides notices of electrical product recalls in Australia.

Canadian Standards Association Product Recalls
http://www.csa-international.org/english/about_csa/index_audits.htm This web site lists recalls involving CSA certified products.

New Zealand Consumers Institute http://www.consumer.org.nz/recall/index.html
This service provides information on product recalls and safety warnings for consumer products, including food, within New Zealand.

United Kingdom Trading Standards Direct
http://www.oxon-tss.org.uk/cgi-bin/newslist.cgi?news=safe This page includes a listing of all consumer product safety warnings, including food, in the United Kingdom.

U. S. Consumer Product Safety Commission Recalls
http://www.cpsc.gov/cpscpub/prerel.html
Access this web site to obtain the latest recalls (current month), last month's recalls, recalls categorized by topic (children's products, toys, etc.) or search for

specific products using a search engine. The CPSC is not responsible for food related recalls.

U. S. Food and Drug Administration Automatic Detention List
http://www.fda.gov/ora/fiars/ora_import_alert_list.html This web page provides access to all imported products listed on the detention list by the FDA. Products include cosmetics, foods, and food contact articles.

While the Consumer Product Safety Commission is a regulatory agency and a watch dog for consumers, there are many voluntary organizations dedicated to consumer product safety. The two organizations that deserve to be mentioned here are International Consumer Product Health and Safety Organization (ICPHSO) and European Consumer Safety Association (ECOSA).

5-19 International Consumer Product Safety and Health Organization (ICPHSO) www.icphso.org

Founded in 1993, ICPHSO is an organization dedicated to the health and safety issues related to consumer products manufactured and marketed globally. ICPHSO sponsors both annual and regional workshops. These workshops serve as training programs to inform and educate manufacturers, importers, distributors, retailers, and others of their product safety responsibilities. In addition, the organization provides a forum for the exchange of ideas and sharing of information among government, industry, trade organizations, legal representatives, academia, standards writers, consumer advocates, and interested individuals.

5-20 European Consumer Safety Association (ECOSA) www.ecosa.org

ECOSA was established in 1985 as a non-profit organization to promote consumer safety. The founding members were senior representatives of governmental and non-governmental organizations with expertise in the field of product safety and the promotion of home and leisure safety. At present, the ECOSA consists of 60 members representing governments including consumer protection agencies, medical and research institutes, trade and business representatives and consumer organizations. ECOSA's mission is to provide a forum to discuss and analyze consumer safety matters among a diverse group of interested parties at national and international levels. ECOSA's principle aim is to put consumer safety policy on the primary agenda of national and European authorities, whereby national action programs for consumer safety are implemented in each European country. The ultimate objective of these programs is to reduce the number of injuries and deaths due to home and leisure accidents by 25 % within the next 20 years.

5-21 Safety Information

Providing safety information related to consumer products to customers at the point of sale would be an excellent public service. Such information can be in the form of brochures and short video films.

5-21-1 UL Brochures on Consumer Safety

Underwriters Laboratories (UL) offers a number of brochures and videos on consumer safety (www.ul.com/consumers/index.html) as listed here. These can be reproduced with UL's permission for distribution to consumers. UL will even provide print ready artwork for these brochures.

Consumer Safety Guide—Provides tips to help protect consumers from the risk of fire, electric shock and casualty hazards. Includes information on safe use of appliances and fire extinguishers, as well as proper placement and maintenance of smoke and carbon monoxide detectors.

Appliance Safety Quiz—Answers multiple choice questions designed to test one's "safety smarts" using common household appliances.

Home Safety Inspection Checklist—Takes one through a home safety inspection covering living area, garage, workshop and yard.

Brochures can be made from the information available on the following topics from the UL's web site:

- Watch your step! UL offers tips on ladder safety
- Clean those lint traps: UL promotes clothes dryer safety
- Ground Fault Circuit Interrupters (GFCIs)
- Extension Cords: Not 'One Size Fits All'
- Halogen Torchie Lamp Safety Tips

UL also offers following videos:

- Electrical Safety Tips—Targeted to 7-14 year olds, this video and accompanying activity package teach electrical safety principles and provide safety tips to students.
- Operation Decoration—Also targeted to 7-14 year olds, this video promotes holiday decorating safety.
- Seniors on the Safe Side—This video explains often overlooked problem area and points out how seniors can take steps to make their home as safe as possible.
- UL's Appliance Safety Quiz—What should you do when an appliance falls into the water? What's the first thing you do when you purchase or receive one as a gift? The answers to these questions and others are provided in this video.

5-21-2 Association of Home Appliance Manufacturers

The Association of Home Appliance Manufacturers (www.aham.org) can also provide following two brochures free of charge for distribution to consumers.

- 10 Tips for Use and Care of Your Portable Air Heater
- Recipe for Safer Cooking

5-21-3 UK Department of Trade & Industry

The UK Department of Trade & Industry has a web page on consumer competition and policy and there are a number of brochures on consumer safety. This web page is www.dti.uk/ccp/publications.htm

Key Points

- Safety of consumer products is very important. Therefore, safety must be integral part of quality management.
- QA staff of retailers should monitor purchases against the list of regulated products on a regular basis and make sure that if the products they are selling are covered under CPSC, FDA or some other regulations, then they meet the applicable safety or regulatory requirements.

- Organizations such as CPSC, UL, ICPHSO, etc. are excellent resources when it comes to safety of consumer products.

References

Consumer Product Safety Act. *Product Safety & Liability Reporter*, March 10, 1995. pp.21:0101

CPSC Candle Fire Pilot Study Summary. 2001. September 19. Consumer Product Safety Commission, Washington, DC.

CPSC. 1996. *Guidelines for Drawstrings on Children's Outwear*. February. Consumer Product Safety Commission, Washington, DC.

CPSC, October 23, 1998. *Guidance for Lead in Children's Jewelry*. Consumer Product Safety Commission, Washington, DC.

CPSC Press Realease # 03-105. *CPSC Bans Candles With Leas-Cored Wicks*. April 7, 2003 Consumer Product Safety Commission, Washington, DC.

Federal Register. 1998. CPSC Notice of Approval of Guidance Document on Lead in Consumer Products. Vol. 63, No. 14. Thursday, January 22,

Federal Register. 1984. Flammability of Clothing Textiles. Vol.49, No. 242, pp. 48683-48690. December 14.

Federspiel, Benedicte. 2003. Marks-in the service of consumers? *ISO Bulletin*, August. pp. 29-31

LABTEST NEWS. 2004. Vol. 62, January. Intertek Labtest. www.intertek-labtest.com

MTL-ACTS. 2002. Bulletin # 02B-111. German Clothing Industry Issues Resolution on Drawstrings. June.

NFPA Fact Sheets. Candle Safety. www.nfpa.org/Research/NFPAFactsSheets/CandleSafety/CandleSafety.asp

Public Law 92-573; 86 Stat. 1207, October 27, 1972. Consumer Product Safety Act. Codified at 15 U.S.C. 2051-2084

Public Law 86-613; 74 Stat. 372, July 12, 1960, as amended. Federal Hazardous Substances Act. Codified at 15 U.S.C. 1261-1278.

Public Law 83-88; 67 Stat. 111, June 30, 1953, as amended. Flammable Fabrics Act. Codified at 15 U.S.C. 1191-1204.

Public Law 91-601; 86 Stat. 1670, December 30, 1970, as amended. Poison Prevention Packaging Act. Codified at 15 U.S.C. 1471-1476.

Public Law 84-930; 70 Stat. 953, August 2, 1956. Refrigerator Safety Act. Codified at 15 U.S.C. 1211-1214.

PSLR (*Product Safety and Liability Reporter*). 1980. June 20. Excerpt from Minnesota Supreme Court's decision in Gryc versus Dayton-Hudson Corporation, May 23, 1980.

PSLR (*Product Safety and Liability Reporter*). 2002. Vol. 30, No. 16. April 22. pp 357.

Title 16 CFR 1615, Standard for the Flammability of Children's Sleepwear, Size 0 through 6X (FF 3-71). *Title 16—Commercial Practices, Chapter II* Consumer Product Safety Commission. Flammable Fabrics Act Regulations. Office of the Federal Register, U. S. National Archives and Records Administration, Washington, DC. www.archives.gov

Title 16 CFR 1616, Standard for the Flammability of Children's Sleepwear, Size 7 through 14 (FF 5-74). *Title 16—Commercial Practices, Chapter II* Consumer Product Safety Commission. Flammable Fabrics Act Regulations. Office of the Federal Register, U. S. National Archives and Records Administration, Washington, DC. www.archives.gov

Title 16 CFR 1630, Standard for the Surface Flammability of Carpets and Rugs (FF 1-70). *Title 16—Commercial Practices, Chapter II* Consumer Product Safety Commission. Flammable Fabrics Act Regulations. Office of the Federal Register, U. S. National Archives and Records Administration, Washington, DC. www.archives.gov

Title 16 CFR 1631, Standard for the Surface Flammability of Small Carpets and Rugs (F 2-70). *Title 16—Commercial Practices, Chapter II* Consumer Product Safety Commission. Flammable Fabrics Act Regulations. Office of the Federal Register, U. S. National Archives and Records Administration, Washington, DC. www.archives.gov

Title 16 CFR 1632, Standard for the Flammability of Children's Sleepwear, Size 7 through 14 (FF 4-72). *Title 16—Commercial Practices, Chapter II* Consumer Product Safety Commission. Flammable Fabrics Act Regulations. Office of the Federal Register, U. S. National Archives and Records Administration, Washington, DC. www.archives.gov

Who we are, what we do for you. CPSC Web Site, www.cpsc.gov

Bibliography

Adams, Chris. 2002. Product Recalls Are Rising Amid Concern That Public Ignores Them. *The Wall Street Journal*, Friday, March 22. New York New York.

Brooks, Paul. 2002. The Global Marketplace and CE Marking. *Quality Digest*. July

CE marking
http://www.europa.eu.int/comm/enterprise/newapproach/legislation/guide/legislation.htm

CE Marking Service Guide. Exporting to the European Union. 2000. TUV Rheinland of North America, Inc. www.tuv.com

Gooden, Randall. 2003. Quality's Role in Product Liability Prevention. *Proceedings of the 57th Annual Quality Congress*, pp. 443-447. American Society for Quality, Milwaukee, WI.

Gratz, Manny. 2002. *The Threat of Counterfeit Product Approval Marks Warrants Aggressive Detection and Enforcement Action*. October. A white paper published by CSA International. Toronto, Canada.

Felcher, Marla E. 2000. Children's Products at Risk. *The Atlantic Monthly*. November.

Hillersborg, Aage. 2000, Safe toys for the children of the world. *ISO Bulletin*. March. pp. 4-7.

Hoover, Samantha. 1999. CE Marking: Do I Have To? *Quality Magazine*. January.
http://www.qualitymag.com/articles/1999/jan99/0199f5.html

International Toys & Gifts Buyers' Guide. Intertek Testing Services, January 1999. 5th ed.

ISO/IEC Guide 50 Safety Aspects—Guidelines for child safety, 2nd Edition, 2002

ISO/IEC Guide 51 Safety aspects—Guidelines for their inclusion in standards, 2nd Edition, 1999

Kinzie, Mark A. 2003. Prevention & Quality Control—A Brief Introduction to Product Liability. *Proceedings of the 57th Annual Quality Congress*, pp. 443-447. American Society for Quality, Milwaukee, WI.

Mohan, Devendra. 2003. The parallel economists. *Business India*. August 18-31. pp.56-60.

Osterman, David S. and Donald, J. Wylie. 2002. Analysis and Perspective: CPSC Product Defect Reporting. *Product Safety and Liability Reporter*. 16 December. Pp. 1113-1115

Parker, Keith. 2003. Product liability—who takes the hit and why? *WORLD-FOOTWEAR*. May/June. Volume 17, No. 3, pp. 47-50. World Trades Publishing. Liverpool, England.

Peckham, Geoffrey. 2000. The Product safety label: A Critical Component of Compliance. *Compliance Engineering Annual reference Guide*.

Recall Handbook: A Guide for Manufacturers, Importers, Distributors and Retailers on Reporting Under Sections 15 and 37 of the Consumer Product Safety Act and Section 102 of the Child Safety Protection Act and Preparing for, Initiating and Implementing Product Recalls. Office of Compliance, Consumer Product Safety Commission. May 1999.

Schulz, David P. 2000. Retailers Seek Outside Aid in Completing Hazardous Materials Report. *Stores*, June.

Show the UL Mark. 1997. Underwriters Laboratories, Inc. Northbrook, IL.

Standards Setting in the European Union........ NIST Special Publication 891, February 1997, National Institute of Standards and Technology, U. S. Department of Commerce. www.nist.gov

Steorts, Nancy Harvey. 1999. Safety & You. Syracuse University Press

The Product Recall Planning Guide, 2nd edition. 1999. Product Safety and Liability Prevention Interest Group, American Society for Quality. Quality Press. Milwaukee, WI.

White, Trevor. 2002. Gaining a Competitive Edge By Building Safety Into Your Products. A paper presented at the Safe Circle meeting. 19 June. Chicago, IL.

6

Costs Associated with Quality

While it is obvious to understand that there are costs associated with various business activities, costs associated with quality are not that obvious. Costs associated with quality, generally, called quality costs, can be divided into two parts (1) Cost of poor quality and (2) Cost of the QA function.

6-1 Cost of Poor Quality

These are the costs associated with either a retailer or its customers, or both receiving poor quality merchandise. These are also called failure costs. Failure costs can be divided into two parts as follows.

6-1-1 External Failure Costs

These costs are generated after defective products are sold and reported by the customers. Examples of external failure costs are:

- Cost of returned merchandise
- Cost of replacing defective merchandise
- Cost of handling customer complaints
- Costs associated with product recalls, such as, announcing the recall, administrative expenses in handling recalls, refund or replacement of the recalled product, time spent handling recalled product, etc.
- Lost sales (and therefore, profits) due to a failed shipment not reaching stores in time. This is very important in case of fashion merchandise.
- Lost sales as a result of loss of customer confidence in the ability of the retailer to provide quality merchandise. This is hard to

measure, however, it is very real. Customers "spread the word" to others when they have problems with merchandise. Bad news spreads fast via word of mouth and internet.

6-1-2 Internal Failure Costs

Examples of internal failure costs are:

- Cost of re-inspection of a failed shipment, such as, salary and fringe benefit of the inspector performing re-inspection, travel expenses, in case of an in-plant inspector.
- Administrative costs associated with failed shipment, such as, paper work, phone calls, returning a failed shipment when inspection is done at a retailer's DC (distribution center),efforts expanded in scheduling re-inspection of a failed shipment, etc.
- Cost associated with retesting failed samples, such as cost of new samples, time taken to perform tests of failed items, administrative costs associated with writing lab reports, etc.

If some how these costs are quantified and then systematically reduced, they will add to the bottom line, not only by way of reduced expenses but by increased customer satisfaction and increased sales due to increased customer satisfaction.

6-2 Cost of the QA Function

This includes cost of preventing poor quality merchandise reaching customers and cost of appraising quality of merchandise received by a retailer.

6-2-1 Prevention Costs

Just as the name suggests, these are costs associated with those activities that are carried out to prevent defects in products or services and preventing them from reaching customers. Examples of prevention costs are:

- Cost of QA personnel, i.e., pay and fringe benefits.
- Cost of periodic training of QA staff and cost of recertification for some of those staff members who have some sort of professional certification such as CQA (Certified Quality Auditor), CQE

(Certified Quality Engineer), PE (Professional Engineer), CE (Chartered Engineer), etc.
- Cost of periodic transfer of in-plant inspectors
- Cost of day-to-day operation of the QA division, such as office supplies, phone calls, faxes, copying, postage, etc.
- Costs associated with translating customer requirements into standards and specifications
- Developing standards and specifications
- Costs associated with factory evaluations
- Costs associated with supplier quality system audits
- Travel costs associated with visiting suppliers and stores, conferences, training courses, etc.

6-2-2 Appraisal Costs

These are costs associated with measuring, evaluating, or inspection of products to assure conformance with quality standards, purchase and purchase requirements. Examples of appraisal costs are:

- Inspection costs such as travel expense for in-plant inspectors
- Cost of testing such as cost of the sample(s) destroyed in testing, laboratory supplies, etc., shipping expenses associated with samples.
- Cost of maintaining the testing facility, i.e., utilities (heat, electricity, gas, etc.) equipment maintenance and calibration, depreciation allowance for test equipment.
- Cost of using commercial testing laboratory or third party testing
- Cost of third party inspection

Note: Some prefer to consider cost of testing as prevention cost rather than appraisal cost.

It is not hard and fast as to which cost goes under which category. For example, argument can be made that the cost of QA personnel should go under appraisal cost rather than prevention cost because through inspection and testing, QA personnel are appraising quality of merchandise. Regardless of which costs are placed under which category, it is important that costs associated with quality are captured systematically on a regular basis.

Total of the above four elements (external failure costs, internal failure costs, prevention costs, and appraisal costs) is considered total quality cost. Typically, prevention and appraisal costs are considered investments and internal as well as external failure costs are considered expenses.

For more on cost of QA function, please refer to item 2-5, QA budget and item 3-2-6-11, inspection economics.

6-3 Relationship Between Various Quality Costs

There is no standard relationship between prevention costs, appraisal costs, internal failure costs, and external failure costs, however, common sense would suggest that increasing prevention and appraisal costs would result in reduced internal and external failure costs. But by how much? Well, it is anybody's guess. It will vary from retailer to retailer.

Gilmore (1983) has looked at total quality costs and the relationship among prevention, appraisal, and failure costs within the context of different product manufacturers. However, only 17 out of 35 companies responded to the survey and not all 17 respondents provided completely useful data. Therefore, no generalization can be drawn from such limited information.

Conventional wisdom suggests that achieving higher relative quality or low relative costs are alternative goals that require different courses of action, resources, and skills. However, studies (Phillips, Chang, Buzzell, 1983 and Walter, 1983) fail to support the widely held view that a high relative quality position is incompatible with achieving a low relative cost position in an industry.

6-4 Value of Tracking Quality Costs

Just like any business activity, QA activities cost money. Any activity in business must contribute to overall profits; otherwise, it cannot exist, and QA is no exception. Management of QA should remember that senior management understands quality primarily in business terms and not in terms of percent defective, rejection rate, statistical sampling, etc. Therefore, a QA executive should be able to communicate with senior management in terms of costs, profits, investments, returns, etc. when it comes to quality.

It is important to know and keep track of costs associated with quality for the following reasons.

1. Analysis of cost of poor quality can be used to identify areas of opportunity for improving quality and reducing costs.
2. Costs of poor quality will give the QA management something to talk to senior management about in order to prompt not only corrective actions but also some preventive actions. By showing how much poor quality actually costs, senior management commitment can be enlisted in quality improvement efforts.
3. Supplier performance can be judged based on cost of quality related to a supplier.
4. The performance of a QA department can be evaluated in financial terms and it can be determined how much cost is involved in achieving a certain level of quality and whether the QA department is paying its way or not.
5. It will help budget realistically to achicvc a desired quality level.

Aside from the above reasons, since the cost of quality has a direct impact on the profitability of any company, it is natural that senior management would be interested in knowing the cost of quality.

Daniels and Hagen (1999) show how various companies use quality cost as a management tool and in meeting customer needs.

The Director of Quality Assurance of a large well-known upscale children's clothing manufacturer had difficulty getting support and more money for QA efforts from his senior management several years ago. Therefore, over a period of several months, he systematically collected data on the cost of poor quality. i.e., cost of repairs and rework, cost of scrap, etc. for each of their five factories and made a presentation to the senior management. From then on, he had no difficulty getting senior management's attention and all the resources he needed for QA efforts. Not only that, from then on, each month, the operations meeting attended by each of the five factory managers, vice president of operations and the executive vice president of the company opened with his presentation on the state of quality in each of the five factories.

6-5 Reporting Quality Costs

Total quality cost can be reported as a percentage of some base such as labor cost (direct or indirect), cost of manufacturing, cost of raw materials, purchase, sales, or profits. When reporting quality as a percentage of purchase, sales, or profits, one must be careful in evaluating such data. For example, purchase, sales, and profit may vary significantly from year to year but if the quality cost remained fairly steady from year to year, it will give an impression that either the cost of quality went up or down, while that may not be the case at all. Quality cost can also be reported as cost of inspecting and/or testing a sample. This is the most accurate and tangible cost of quality because it gives a true picture of how much it costs to inspect and/or test a sample.

There is no one way of reporting quality costs. It all depends on what your management can understand the best. For example, according to Sullivan (1983)

> "If a quality manager tried to tell the top management of a \$60,000,000 operation that they ought to be concerned about \$40,000 in quality costs, you would probably get them to fall asleep on you, jokes Frank Scanlon, Director of Quality/Education., The Hartford Insurance Group. Rather than reporting that quality costs came to \$40,000 in a year, the quality program identifies that quality costs accounted to two or three staff people. And in an office of 75 people, the idea of two more staff members commands a lot of attention."

There are no industry wide data available on quality costs, because obviously companies would not like to divulge such information. This was quite evident in a survey Gilmore (1983) conducted, where only 17 out of 35 companies responded and not all 17 respondents provided completely useful data. Also, even if such data were available, its usefulness for comparative purposes would not be reliable because of the various ways in which different companies account for cost of quality.

6-6 Return on Investment

Return on investment (ROI) when it comes to quality cost can be calculated as follows

$$\text{ROI} = \frac{\text{\$ amount of defective merchandise prevented from reaching stores}}{\text{Total quality cost}} \times 100$$

Where

$ amount of defective merchandise prevented from reaching stores is the total $ value of all shipments that failed inspection plus total $ value of items that failed testing.

Total quality cost is the total of external failure costs, internal failure costs, prevention costs, and appraisal costs.

QA division of a retailer periodically reports $ amount of defective merchandise prevented from reaching stores. This is one figure that executives can relate to.

For detailed and advanced discussion on quality costs, please refer to Campanella (1999) and the sources listed in the bibliography.

Key Points

- Cost of poor quality and cost of QA function should be measured and reported on a regular basis.
- Senior executives understand dollars and cents more than technical details of quality. Therefore, tracking and reporting quality costs helps the VP of Quality in justifying quality efforts and asking for increased resources, if necessary.
- Quality costs can be used as a tool or vehicle for quality improvement.
- Reduction in the cost of poor quality over a period of time is a true indicator of quality improvement.
- In the long run better quality costs less.

References

Campanella, Jack. Editor. 1999. *Principles of Quality Costs; Principles, Implementation and Use*. 3rd Edition. Quality Press. American Society for Quality. Milwaukee, WI.

Daniels, Susan E. and Hagen, Mark R. 1999. Making the Pitch in the Executive Suite. *Quality Progress*, Vol. 32, No. 4, April, pp. 25-33. American Society for Quality, Milwaukee, WI.

Gilmore, Harold L. 1983. Consumer Product Quality Control Costs Revisited. *Quality Progress*, April. American Society for Quality. Milwaukee, WI

Phillips, Lynn W., Chang Dae R., and Buzzell, Robert D. 1983. Product Quality, Cost Position and Business Performance: A Test of Some Key Hypothesis. *Journal of Marketing*, Vol. 47, Spring '83, pp. 26-43.

Sullivan, Edward. 1983. Quality Costs: Current Applications. *Quality Progress*, April. American Society for Quality. Milwaukee, WI.

Walter, Craig. 1983. Management Commitment to Quality. *Quality Progress*, August. American Society for Quality. Milwaukee, WI.

Bibliography

ASQ Quality Cost Committee. Quality Costs: Ideas and Applications, Complete set of Volumes 1 and 2. Quality Press, Milwaukee, WI.

ASQ Quality Cost Committee and Winchell, William O., Editor. Quality Costs for Continuous Improvement. Quality press, Milwaukee, WI.

Atkinson, Hawley, Hamburg, John, Ittner and Christopher. Linking Quality to Profits: Quality-Based Cost Management. Quality Press, Milwaukee, WI.

Daniel, Susan E. and Hagen, Mark R. 1999. Making the Pitch in the Executive Suite. *Quality Progress*. April. pp. 25-33. American Society for Quality, Milwaukee, WI.

DeFeo, Joseph A. 2001. The Tip of the Iceberg. *Quality Progress*, May. pp. 29-37. American Society for Quality, Milwaukee, WI.

Heinloth, Stefan. 2000. Measuring Quality's Return on Investment. Is Your Quality System Earning It's Keep? *Quality Digest*, February. www.qualitydigest.com/feb00/html/measure.html

Masing, Walter E. 1993. Considerations Concerning Quality Related Cost. *47th Annual Quality Congress Proceedings*. May. pp. 891-892. American Society for Quality, Milwaukee, WI.

Miller, Jon R. and Morris, John S. 2000. Is Quality Free or Profitable? *Quality Progress*, January. pp 50-53. American Society for Quality, Milwaukee, WI

Zimack, Gary. 2000. Cost of Quality (COQ): Which Collection System Should be Used? *54th Annual Quality Congress Proceedings*, Indianapolis, IN, pp. 18-24. May. American Society for Quality, Milwaukee, WI.

7

Customer Returns and Customer Satisfaction

7-1 Customer Returns

Since customer satisfaction, or rather customer delight should be the ultimate goal of retailers, data on customer returns should be a part of quality information system and such data should be reviewed frequently by the senior management. Customers should be encouraged to contact the retailer when customers get defective products or are otherwise not satisfied with the purchase or shopping experience. Instead of viewing a complaining customer as a nuisance, a positive attitude about such complaints should exist and a retailer should believe that a customer is right until proven otherwise. Remember, as somebody has wisely said, there are no "problem customers," only customers who have problems.

If a customer is not satisfied with an item and returns it for either a refund or replacement and has a pleasant experience doing so, chances are that the customer will continue to buy from the same retailer. On the other hand, if a customer does not complain about a defective item or one that did not perform adequately, chances are that he or she will never buy that brand or from that store again. According to a Washington based research organization called Technical Assistance Research Programs (TARP) (1988), on average across all industries 50% of all customers with problems, both individual customers and business customers, never complain to anyone. Another 45% complain to a front-line retail employee who will either handle or mishandle the complaint. Only 5% will complain to the management. Therefore, for every customer complaint reported to corporate headquarters, one can assume that there are at least 19 other similar complaints that simply were not reported or that were handled by the retailer or front line without being recorded. In some instances, this ratio is as high as 1 to 2000! A women's garment manufacturer found, after shipment, that one style of garment would fall apart the first time it was worn due to a defect. However, this manufacturer received only one complaint or return for every 2000 garments shipped! If customers remain unsatisfied, the cost to business in lost sales, directly and through word of mouth, can be substantial. Goodman (1988) provides an excellent discussion on how to quantify losses due to customer complaints.

According to Hallen and Latino (2003), the costs associated with customer complaints can be significant. These costs manifest themselves in a number of ways: lost business, investigative costs, time spent responding to complaints, and claims or credits paid. The Eastman Chemical Co. realized in 1997 that the level of customer complaint had not shown significant reduction in the previous few years despite the company's history of continually improving performance in its processes. A team at Eastman discovered that most complaint investigations were not getting to the root causes and that most investigations stopped after it was discovered who had caused the problem. Eastman turned to the Reliability Center Inc. to help them develop a root cause analysis (RCA) training course for its employees. Training covered three key concepts: use of a structured logic tree process to determine what went wrong; going beyond the human cause of the problem and identifying organizational causes; and digging deeper than the first root cause found to identify and eliminate multiple causes. By 2000, Eastman had almost halved its level of customer complaints. Benefits to the company included improved customer satisfaction, increased sales, reduced waste, and lower costs.

Sometimes it is very difficult for customer return information to filter down to the appropriate level, but the advantages of such information and the analysis of returned garments are tremendous. For example, Latture (1978-79) noted,

> Our analysis of returns over the years has led to improved design and color manufacturing controls. A few examples are:
>
> a. Increased tensile strength in medium weight denim
> b. Use of more appropriate thread sizes and types on major stress seams and seams shown to be abrasion prone
> c. Better enforcement of job quality standards at pressing to avoid damage to zipper sliders
> d. Improved finishes on hardware to better resist rust and corrosion

e. Use of stronger zippers in certain product lines
f. Better enforcement of quality standards on jobs susceptible to latent defects
g. Additional inspection at key jobs on a temporary basis
h. Occasional pattern and method changes.

He further stated,

> Other benefits from a return program that are at least equally as important are:
>
> a. We have a chance to see the latent defects-those that could not be seen at final inspection-shrinkage, raw edges from seams improperly fed into folders, bleeding of dyes, seam slippage, etc.
> b. Improved standards, additional standards and even new test methods have resulted from problems encountered by our customers, many of them latent type of defects.
> c. Vendors can learn a great deal about the performance of their products that should lead to more appropriate standards or stricter conformance to existing standards by them. Lines of communication between buyer and seller are shortened. A vendor's QC program is usually strengthened by his customer's concern. Looking at actual field failures is much convincing than statistics alone. Returns can help to persuade those who design and who purchase materials as well as those who enforce standards in apparel plants.

Some customers told a well-known men's and boys' underwear manufacturer in the United States that the waistbands on their men's underwear sagged after a washing or two and that there was too much shrinkage in their undershirts. The company took these complaints to heart and spent several million dollars on snappier elastic and preshrunk cotton fabric.

It is the experience of this author that sometimes even a single customer complaint reveals a significant problem. Also, there have been cases in which apparel manufacturers were greatly thankful and appreciative of the customer return information they received from retailers because such information helped them improve quality of their products and, of course, the image of those products with it.

Chichester (2003) reports how quick Wal-Mart responded to his complaint. When he called the Bentonville, Ark., headquarters of Wal-Mart to complain about its store in La Plata, Argentina, the switchboard immediately rang the vice president of international operations, who picked up his own phone. He thanked Chichester for calling, asked detailed questions about his dissatisfaction, and inquired whether he was willing to repeat his story for his Latin American VP. He transferred Chichester straight away, and even more detailed conversation followed. Then he was asked if he would be willing to talk with the Argentine store manager if he called Chichester. Ten minutes later Chichester's phone in Connecticut rang. On Chichester's next trip to Argentina, a year later, the store had been transformed! No wonder Wal-Mart is the world's largest retailer!

Some times, poor quality may not be the reason for customer complaints. Goodman, Ward and Broetzmann (2002) report that quality managers respond to customer complaints with the assumption that the problem is product or service failure. Often, however, the cause isn't the fault of the product itself but is due to incorrect use or unreasonable expectation by the customer or misleading marketing claims for the product. Customers use products improperly when they fail to read directions on proper use or assembly of the product. They also have problems when expectations set by advertising material are not met. These problems can result in damage to customer loyalty because customers feel misled.

With the electronic communication that is available today, it is easy to set up a standard form such as the one shown in the Figure 7-1 on e-mail system that a store can fill out every time there is a quality related customer complaint or store suspects an item is defective as they put items on the shelves and send that form to QA. Appropriate QA specialist should receive such e-mail from stores and decide if there is a widespread problem or not. If it is a widespread problem, then QA along with the buyer for that product should decide how best to address the situation. Stores should be encouraged to send feedback even if there is only one customer complaint, because, if there are four or five stores each with one customer complaint on the same product, and they do not report it thinking it is only one complaint, a defective condition will go unaddressed. By getting such feedback, QA will have an overall idea about quality levels at the store level.

One retailer has a 20 minute video on how to report quality related customer complaints to QA. Viewing of this video is a part of mandatory training for all customer service employees in all stores.

7-2 Customer Satisfaction

For the long term success of any business, repeat customers are very important. However, customers will return to buy from the same company only if they remain satisfied customers. Customer satisfaction can be assured by meeting or, even better, exceeding customer expectations through better-quality products and services. Better quality products and services can be provided by:

1. Explicit corporate policy that the customer is number one and that satisfied customers drive the business.
2. Making managers accountable for product quality and customer satisfaction.
3. Constantly upgrading customer-complaint-handling efforts and constantly encouraging customer feedback and acting upon such feedback.

While there are many ways of measuring customer satisfaction, several large retailers in the U.S.A. are having their customer satisfaction measured by the CFI Group and have it rolled into the American Customer Satisfaction Index (ACSI). The ACSI is an economic indicator that measures customer satisfaction. It is based on modeling of customer evaluations of the quality of goods and services that are purchased in the United States and produced by both domestic and foreign firms that have substantial U. S. market share. ACSI was developed by the National Quality Research Center at the University of Michigan Business School. To create ACSI, the National Quality Research Center at the University of Michigan, in partnership with the American Society for Quality and the CFI Group of Ann Arbor, Mich., conducts telephone surveys with about 16,000 customers of the companies surveyed that quarter. Each year, that amounts to 65,000 customers of products from about 190 companies and 70 government agencies. Companies are scored on a scale of 0 to 100. Customers are quizzed about their expectations and their perceptions of value and quality in the services and products they have purchased. Quality is broken down into measures of the product and the service accompanying the product. These are translated through computer models into overall customer satisfaction scores, which are used to predict customer loyalty.

Currently, the U. S. retailers having their customer satisfaction measured by the CFI Group are:

Army & Air Force Exchange Service (AAFES)
Costco Wholesale Corporation
Dillard's Inc.
Federated Department Stores, Inc.
The Home Depot, Inc.
J. C. Penney company, Inc.
Kmart Corporation

Lowe's Companies, Inc.
The May Department Stores Company
Nordstrom, Inc.
Sears, Roebuck & Co.
Target Corporation—Discount
Target Corporation—Department
Wal-Mart Stores, Inc.
Wal-Mart Stores (Sam's Club)

Measuring and tracking customer satisfaction over a time is important because customer satisfaction ultimately affects customer retention and, therefore, profitability.

Companies can use the data from the ACSI to assess customer loyalty, identify potential barriers to entry within markets, predict return on investments, and pinpoint areas in which customer expectations are not being satisfied. ACSI modeling and analysis software is available for sponsoring companies to study how their performance measures up to that of the rest of their industry and the bottom line impact of increasing customer satisfaction.

According to Claes Fornell, director of the University of Michigan Business School's National Quality Research Center, which compiles and analyzes the ACSI data, the satisfied customer is more likely to come back for more, buy more frequently and be less sensitive to price (Quality Digest 2003).

For more information on ACSI and customer satisfaction scores of the retailers mentioned above visit ACSI's web site www.theacsi.org

7-3 Consumer Protection

The U. S. Federal Trade Commission (FTC) has a number of regulations in place to protect consumers from fraudulent and deceptive business practices. The FTC enforces a variety of federal antitrust and consumer protection laws. In general, the Commission's efforts are diverted toward stopping actions that threaten consumers' opportunity to exercise informed choice. Generally, QA is called upon to check whether a particular product complies with the applicable law(s) or regulation(s). Therefore, it helps to have knowledge of such regulations. Titles of some of the regulations and informative material that may be of interest to the retailers are as follows:

7-3-1 Consumer Information

- All That Glitters...How to Buy Jewelry
- Beloved...Bejeweled...Be careful: What to Know Before You Buy Jewelry
- Buying a Washing Machine? It's a Load-ed Question
- Buying Cashmere? Avoid Pulled Wool
- Buying Gold and Gemstone jewelry: The Heart of the Matter
- Caring for Your Clothes
- Clothing Care Symbol Guide
- FTC Explains 'Made in USA' Standard
- Sun-Protective Clothing: Wear It Well
- Sunscreens and Sun-Protective Clothing

7-3-2 Business Information

- A Businessperson's Guide to Federal Warranty Law
- The Cachet of Cashmere: Complying with the Wool Products Labeling Act
- Calling It Cotton: Labeling & Advertising Cotton Products
- Clothes Captioning: Complying with the Care Labeling Rule
- Complying with the FTC's Appliance Labeling Rule
- Complying with the Made in USA Standard
- Down...But Not Out: Advertising & Labeling of Feather and Dawn Products
- In-FUR-mation—How to Comply with the Fur Products Labeling Act
- In The Loupe: Advertising Diamonds, Gemstones and Pearls
- Selling 'American-Made' Products? What Businesses Need to Know About Marketing Made in USA Claims
- Threading Your Way Through Labeling Requirements Under the Textile and Wool Acts

Quality Feedback Report

Date:__________

Log # _______ (QA) E/T # ________ (QA)

Supplier:______________________________________

Item Description: ____

UPC # __________ Quantity Involved: __________

Model/Style # ____________ Sell Price : $ ____ Sub. Dept. ___________

Describe nature of the problem in the following space:

Put an (x) beside the source of this feedback:

Customer return/Complaint ___
Defective Merchandise Found on the Sales Floor _____

Supply Source if Known:

Our DC ______ Direct from Supplier _____

Store Location: ________________________________

Your name: __________________________ Job Title: _____________________

Phone No: __________________________ Fax No: _____________________

Figure 7-1 Store Level Feedback

Key Points

- Customer returns and customer complaints can be a good source of information on quality of merchandise sold by the retailers.
- It pays to encourage customers to complain and return merchandise if they are not satisfied rather than have them silently walk away to your competitor.
- There is a direct correlation between customer satisfaction and profitability.

References

Chichester, Gerald C. 2003. A Letter to the Editor. *FORTUNE*, March 31.

Goodman, John A.; Ward, Dianne; and Broetzmann, Scott. 2002. It Might Not Be Your Product. *Quality Progress*, Vol. 35, No. 4, March, pp. 73-8. American Society for Quality, Milwaukee, WI.

Goodman, John A. 1988. The Nature of Customer Satisfaction. Presented at 1988 National Quality Forum, New York.

Hallen, Gary and Latino, Robert J. 2003. Eastman Chemical's Success Story. *Quality Progress*, Vol. 36, No. 6, June, pp. 50-54. American Society for Quality, Milwaukee, WI.

Latture, William E. 1978-79. Improved Quality through the Analysis of Returned Garments. *ASQC Textile and Needle Trades Division Transactions*, Vol. 6. American Society for Quality. Milwaukee, WI.

Quality Digest. 2003. Customer Satisfaction Could Lead to More Consumer Spending. July, pp.10.

Bibliography

Demers, Mark. 2002. Warranty Data and Claims Management: Administrative Headache or Secret Weapon for Better Product Quality? *Competitive Advantage*, Vol. 11, No. 1, Summer. A Newsletter of the Service Quality Division of the American Society for Quality, Milwaukee, WI.

Hampshire, Stephen. 2003. Satisfaction Is What You Need. *Quality World*. May. Pp. 10-13. Institute of Quality Assurance. London, England.

Hinds, Michael deCourcy. 1988. Seeking Profits in Consumer Complaints. *The New York Times*, Saturday, March 26.

Marr, Jeffrey W. 1986. Letting the Customer Be the Judge of Quality. *Quality Progress*. October. American Society for Quality, Milwaukee, WI.

Marrra, Ted. 2003. Creating Customer Focus. *Quality World*. May. Pp. 14-17. Institute of Quality Assurance. London, England.

Powley, David. 2003. Complaints? What Complaints?. *Quality World*. May. Pp. 18-20. Institute of Quality Assurance. London, England.

Westcott, Russ. 1998. Safeguard Your Customer base. *The Quality Management Forum*. Vol. 24, # 2. Summer. A Newsletter of the Quality Management Division of the American Society for Quality, Milwaukee, WI.

8

Supplier Quality and Relationship

Since everything sold by a retailer comes from other companies, i.e. suppliers (manufacturers, traders, and importers), quality of what is sold by retailers depends on what is bought and supplied by the suppliers or vendors. Therefore, supplier selection is very important. In a KPMG study (KPMG 1999) on best practices in global supply chain, product quality was ranked as the most important factor affecting supplier selection by 55% respondents. An additional 28 % ranked it as second most important. Cost and responsiveness were second and third most important factors, respectively, in supplier selection. Value added service was the fourth most important factor. Interestingly, process quality was the fifth most important factor in supplier selection. Recognizing process quality as one of the important factors in supplier selection makes sense because processes have a strong influence on a supplier's ability to deliver good quality and value-added service at low cost.

Note: The terms "supplier" and "vendor" generally mean the same, however, the term "vendor" has a connotation of arms length relationship and a relationship where the purchasing decision is strictly driven by the price. The term "supplier" has a connotation of a long term relationship, a relationship where there is exchange of information and price is not the only factor driving purchasing decisions. Throughout this book the term "supplier" is used. The term supplier also means either a manufacturer who is supplying directly to the retailer or an agent, distributor, importer, or any company supplying to the retailer.

8-1 Supplier Responsibility

The best way to make sure you receive quality merchandise from your suppliers is to (a) communicate your quality expectations to your suppliers and (b) insist that they must have a quality system in place and they must control quality of items they receive from their suppliers, sub-contractors, etc. Make this a part of requirements for doing business with you. Appendix IV shows an example of quality guidelines and expectations of a retailer and Appendix V shows terms and conditions of doing business with a retailer as they relate to quality of merchandise. Typically, supplier base of a retailer includes small, medium, and large companies. Regardless of the size of the supplier company, at a minimum, their quality system must have one or more of the following elements.

1. Receiving inspection and/or testing
2. In-process inspection and/or testing
3. End item inspection and/or testing

In case of suppliers who are manufacturers, all of the above three elements should be in place. For those suppliers who are importers or traders, receiving inspection and/or testing should be in place.

8-1-1 Receiving Inspection and/or Testing

The supplier should have procedures in place that clearly spell out the following for it's QA/QC staff to follow:

Which shipments to inspect
Frequency of inspection
Statistical sampling plans to be used
Acceptance/rejection criteria
Maintenance of inspection results
Which items to test and for what characteristics
Frequency of testing
How many samples to test
What test method(s) to use
Where to send samples for testing
Acceptance/rejection criteria
Maintenance of test results
Where to send inspection/test results

In lieu of performing it's own receiving testing, some companies rely on a Certificate of Compliance (CoC) from their suppliers. A CoC is a piece of paper where the supplier certifies on it's letterhead that the shipment accompanied by the CoC meets all the requirements of its customer. In some cases, the test results accompany the CoC and in some cases the test results are on file in case the customer wishes to review those results. Usually, the customer specifies which test laboratories the supplier should use in support of the CoC. Some companies also insist on having an inspection report accompany each shipment they receive.

8-1-2 In-process Inspection and/or Testing

Those suppliers who are manufacturers, should have in process inspection and/or testing in place in addition to receiving inspection and /or testing. Elements of in process inspection and testing are as follows:

Identification of points in the entire manufacturing process where inspection and/or testing is needed.
For each inspection and/or testing point the following should be spelled out:
Frequency of inspection
Statistical sampling plans to be used
Acceptance/rejection criteria
Maintenance of inspection results
Which items to test and for what characteristics
Frequency of testing
How many samples to test
What test method(s) to use
Where to send samples for testing
Acceptance/rejection criteria
Maintenance of test results
Where to send inspection/test results

8-1-3 End Item Inspection and/or Testing

Manufacturers should also have end item inspection and/or testing in place to make sure that what is shipped is defect free and in accordance with what a retailer ordered. For end item inspection and/or testing the following should be spelled out:

Which shipments to inspect
Frequency of inspection
Statistical sampling plans to be used
Acceptance/rejection criteria
Maintenance of inspection results
Which items to test and for what characteristics
Frequency of testing

How many samples to test
What test method(s) to use
Where to send samples for testing
Acceptance/rejection criteria
Maintenance of test results
Where to send inspection/test results

Some companies may not have a quality system in place and yet it may be necessary to do business with those companies. In that case the retailer may offer assistance in the quality area even though those companies may be producing quality products. Without any quality system in place there is no guarantee that they will continue to supply quality products. Typically, assisting a supplier in the quality area consists of :

Helping supplier develop quality procedures including statistical sampling plans.
Train supplier personnel in inspection procedures, which includes use of statistical sampling plans, defect scoring criteria, acceptance and rejection criteria; use of appropriate test methods; record keeping; and data collection and analysis.
Inform supplier personnel of applicable standards, regulations, and laws.
Provide supplier a list of resources from where suppliers can buy test equipment and accessories, can have testing done, obtain copies of applicable standards and regulations, and send their personnel for training.

Many companies do not devote necessary resources to help develop suppliers and the result is a huge gap in their cost competitiveness. You cannot optimize your cost performance without having good supplier performance (Sheridan 1998).

Retailers are increasingly looking to their suppliers to ensure that processes down the supply chain effectively provide products that meet customer needs and expectations. Smart retailers do this by offering guidance to suppliers in improving their operations to enhance its own customer satisfaction, thus continuously improving its own competitive position via quality and productivity improvement.

Retailers typically use some method such as supplier survey, supplier quality system audit, factory evaluation, etc. to determine if the supplier can meet their quality requirements in the case of a new supplier and where a supplier can make some improvements in the case of an existing suppliers. Supplier survey, supplier quality system audit and factory evaluation were covered in Chapter 3, Approaches to Quality.

8-2 Supplier Seminars

While supplier quality system audit, supplier certification, factory evaluations, etc. are effective in helping suppliers improve quality, in addition to these efforts, some retailers offer some informational assistance to their current and prospective suppliers in the form of seminars, conferences, briefings, etc. For example, some U. S. retailers hold periodic conferences in Mexico and China for a particular industry such as toys, and explain to suppliers in those countries what U. S. standards and regulations they must meet in order to become suppliers to these retailers. Such seminars can be arranged by a retailer alone or they can be arranged in partnership with some testing and inspection companies and some trade associations as well as regulatory agencies. There is considerable value and benefits to retailers in offering such informational seminars to suppliers.

Here is an actual announcement of such an event published in the September 10, 2003 edition of Plaything EXTRA, the weekly newsletter for toy professionals.

"TIA to hold safety, factory audit events

New York—The Toy Industry Association is sponsoring conferences next month in Shenzhen, China, exploring toy and factory safety, and factory audit preparedness.

The Toy and Toy Safety Conference, Oct. 8-9, will address toy safety, quality assurance and safety testing, and will cover U.S. mandatory and voluntary standards, testing procedures and other product safety related topics. Speakers will include a representative from the U. S. Consumer Product Safety Commission's Office of Compliance and other toy safety experts from the U. S. and Europe. The conference will be TIA's 10th such event held since 1996.

The TIA's first ever Factory Audit Preparedness Seminar, Oct. 13-14, will tackle environmental health and safety (EH&S) practices, and labor conditions such as wage and hour issues, treatment of workers and working conditions. The event will train Chinese factories on the provisions of the ICTI (International Council of Toy Industries) Code of Business practices and ICTI audit process, as well as importance of compliance. The event is designed specifically for those responsible for code of conduct compliance within a factory, including managing directors, quality assurance or human resources managers and EH&S coordinators.

Both events will be held at Shenzhen's Shangri-La Hotel.

For additional information and registration form for either event visit the TIA's Web site <u>www.toy-tia.org</u>"

8-3 Supplier Relations

Since retailers depend on their suppliers to deliver quality merchandise, it is important to develop excellent relationship with suppliers. Some companies use excellent supplier relationships they have with their suppliers as a competitive advantage.

Retailers are increasingly recognizing that in order to be competitive in today's environment they must pay more attention to how and what they are buying. The importance of good suppliers is even more critical to the success of retail organizations because a retailer's ability to satisfy or delight its customers on a continuing basis is based a great deal on the quality and timeliness of goods received from its suppliers.

Juran (1999) defines customer-supplier relations as "the tasks, activities, events, and processes required to facilitate the ongoing interface between suppliers of goods and services and the end users of those goods and services." He defines supply chain as "the tasks, activities, events, processes, and interactions undertaken by all suppliers and all end users in the development, procurement, production, delivery, and consumption of a specific good or service." The coordination, integration, and monitoring of this supply chain are referred to as supply chain management.

It has been well documented in literature that improved customer-supplier relations reduce costs and risks, build revenues, and improve competitive advantage, thereby improving profitability. For example, according to an American Productivity and Quality Center report (APQC 1997) the establishment of strong customer-supplier relationships has allowed Deere & Company to reduce inventory levels by 60 percent, cut cycle time to 14 days, and reduce work-in-progress inventory to eight days. Sheridan (1998) reported that a study by Pittiglio, Rabin, Todd & McGrath, a western Massachusetts based consulting firm, found that 165 blue-chip technology based companies slashed a total of $2 billion from their supply costs in one year by excelling at various facets of supply chain management. The study found that companies that are best at supply chain management hold a 40 to 65 percent advantage in their cash to cash cycle time over average companies. The top companies carry 50 to 80 percent less inventories than their competitors. Leading companies in the automotive and electronics industries have come to realize that competitive advantage is shifting from world-class manufacturing (10 to 20 percent of cost) to world-class suppliers (60 to 70 percent of cost). Once a company's manufacturing operation attains a world class standard, the task is to help suppliers get there as well, and thus dramatically improve the cost base. (Keough 1993)

In order to begin to build or improve existing customer-supplier relationships one must first review procurement practices of a company. This may range from a practice where buying is strictly driven by the price, and therefore, dealing with suppliers is at arms length with no trust. As soon as some other company offers a cheaper price, the current supplier is dropped and buying moved to the company offering the cheaper price. In such a culture it is only a matter of time that the new supplier will be dropped, as some other company will surely come along offering a cheaper price to get its foot in the door. Generally, this happens when retailers buy "off the shelf," meaning the buyers go to various shows and suppliers visit them and show their merchandise, and purchasing is based on what the buyers saw at various shows and/or what was shown to them by the suppliers. Where such procurement practices exist, there is no opportunity to build customer-supplier relationships, as the business is not conducted long enough for the companies to understand each other and learn from each other. This is a lose-lose approach. Then, there are procurement practices where more than price goes into buying decisions, such as delivery, quality, etc. to where there is some trust in dealing with suppliers. Generally, those retailers who buy by their own specifications or have their own labels (private label) usually take this approach. Then, there are procurement practices, though practiced by very few companies, where the customer and supplier companies trust each other to a point where cost structures of both are shared and discussed. This is a win-win approach. Both the customer and supplier companies are working towards satisfying, or perhaps delighting, the ultimate customer. Companies are beginning to realize that, while skillful contract negotiations could extract price discounts of 1 to 5 percent from suppliers, today's cost pressure for 10 to 30 percent price reductions require a totally new set of procurement skills and practices. (Keough 1993)

Bhote (1991) describes four stages of customer-supplier relationships. In stage 1, the customer-supplier relationship is adversarial. There is a total absence of mutual trust. In stage 2, the adversarial relationship gives way to cautious suspicion and beginning of trust. The large, unmanageable supplier base is reduced to preferred suppliers. The supplier base is further reduced to a few partner suppliers in stage 3, where there are less than 10 suppliers for an entire commodity. In stage 4, the partner supplier becomes a virtual extension of the customer's company, except for ownership. The customer's company, in this stage, is actively helping its' suppliers achieve its objectives of best quality, lowest cost and shortest lead time.

Juran and Godfrey (1999) provide an excellent discussion of supplier relations. Kahn (2003) shows how J. C. Penney works with a supplier of its "Stafford" shirts for satisfying the ultimate customer.

"On a Saturday afternoon in August, Carolyn Thurmond walked into a J. C. Penney store in Atlanta's Northlake Mall and bought a white Stafford wrinkle-free dress shirt for her husband, size 17 neck, 34/35 sleeve.

On Monday morning, a computer technician in Hong Kong downloaded a record of the sale. By Wednesday afternoon, a factory worker in Taiwan had packed an identical replacement shirt into a bundle to be shipped back to the Atlanta store.

This speedy process, part of a streamlined supply chain and production system for dress shirts that was years in the making, has put Penney at the forefront of the continuing revolution in U. S. retailing. In an industry where the goal is speedy turnaround of merchandise, Penney stores now hold almost no inventory of house-brand dress shirts. Less than a decade ago, Penney would have had thousands of them warehoused across the U.S, tying up capital and slowly going out of style.

The new process is one from which Penney is conspicuously absent. The entire program is designed and operated by TAL Apparel Ltd., a closely held Hong Kong shirt maker. TAL collects point-of-sale data for Penney's shirts directly from its stores in North America, then runs the numbers through a computer model it designed. The Honk Kong company then decides how many shirts to make, and in what styles, colors and sizes. The manufacturer sends the shirts directly to each Penney stores, bypassing the retailer's-and corporate decision makers."

Key Points

- Most suppliers are willing to meet retailers' quality requirements, however, the key is to spell out your expectations to your suppliers and if necessary, help them understand those expectations.
- While it is better to do business with only those suppliers who have effective quality system in place, it is also worthwhile to help your suppliers develop their quality capability.
- Good supplier relations, including the practice of supplier development, are essential to good quality merchandise.
- Good supplier relations can be a competitive advantage.

References

American Productivity and Quality Center. 1997. *Partnering for Profit: Building and Managing Global Supplier Relationships.* Consortium Benchmarking Study, Best Practices Report.

Bhote, K.R. 1991. *World Class Quality: Using Design of Experiments to Make It Happen*. New York, NY: AMACOM.

Burt, D.N. 1989. Managing Suppliers Up to Speed. *Harvard Business Review,* July-August: 127-135.

Juran, J.M. and Godfrey, B. A. 1999. Section 11, Supplier Relations. *Juran's Quality Handbook*. New York, NY: McGraw-Hill.

Keough, M. 1993. Buying Your Way to the Top. *The McKinsey Quarterly,* Number 3: 41-62.

Khan, Gabriel. 2003. Made to Measure: Invisible Supplier Has Penney's Shirts All Buttoned Up. *The Wall Street Journal,* Thursday, September 11, 2003—Vol. CCXLII No. 51. New York.

KPMG Consulting Consumer Markets Practice. 1999. Global Supply Chain Benchmarking and Best Practices Study Phase II. *Stores,* September. National Retail Federation, New York, NY.

Mehta, Pradip V. 1993. Implementing Supplier Quality Assistance Program. A paper presented at the Annual Conference of the Customer-Supplier Division of the American Society for Quality. November, Dayton, OH. American Society for Quality, Milwaukee, WI.

Sheridan,J.H. 1998. The Supply-Chain Paradox: It Takes More Than Software to Build True Relationships. *Industry Week,* February 2.

Bibliography

Andrade, G.F.; Bossert, J.L., Braun, L.F., Krahula, J., Lawrimore, B., Silver, B. 1990. Customer and Supplier: The Capitalism Connection. *44th Annual Quality Congress Proceedings*. May. San Francisco, CA. pp. 957-967. American Society for Quality, Milwaukee, WI.

Ashkenas, R.N. 1990. A New Paradigm for Customer and Supplier Relationships. *Human Resource Management,* Winter, Vol. 29, (Number 4): 385-396.

Astbury, Mark. 1998. Long-Term Relationships Are Far Better Than One Night Stands. *Quality World,* July. pp. 8-10. Institute of Quality Assurance, London, England.

Asmus, D. and Griffin, J. 1993. Harnessing the Power of Your Suppliers. *The McKinsey Quarterly,* Number 3: 63-78.

Chapman, T.L., Dempsey, J.J., Ramsdell, G., and Reopel, M. R. 1997. Procurement: No Time for Lone Rangers. *The McKinsey Quarterly,* Number 2: 30-40.

Dull, Stephen F.; Mohn, Wilhelm A.; and Noren, Thomas. 1995. Partners. *The McKinsey Quarterly,* Number 4, pp. 63-72.

Dutta, Devangshu. 2001. Supply Base Consolidation—A Step Too Far? *News from the Textile Institute,* Issue 7. The Textile Institute, Manchester, England.

Gordon, Niall. 1990. Supplier Quality Partnership Program. *44th Annual Quality Congress Proceedings.* May. San Francisco, CA. pp. 39-49. American Society for Quality, Milwaukee, WI.

Hacker, Stephen K.; Israel, Jeff T.; Couturier, Laurent. 1999. *Building Trust in Key Customer-Supplier Relationships.* A Performance Center Paper. The Performance Center. The Oregon University. Beaverton, OR.

Heinle, Philip R. 1998. Supplier With an Inside Seat—What a Revolution! *52nd Annual Quality Congress Proceedings.* May 4-6. Philadelphia, PA. pp. 432-435. American Society for Quality, Milwaukee, WI.

Hillman, G. Peter. 1994. Partnering in Practice. *48th Annual Quality Congress Proceedings.* May. Las Vegas, NV. Pp. 471-478. American Society for Quality, Milwaukee, WI.

Kepner, Joseph L. and Aft, Lawrence S. 1993. *47th Annual Quality Congress Proceedings.* May. Boston, MA. pp. 688-694.

Kumar, N. 1996. The Power of Trust in Manufacturer-Retailer Relationships. *Harvard Business Review,* November-December: 92-106.

Landry, J.T. 1998. Supply Chain Management: The Value of Trust. *Harvard Business Review,* January-February: 18-19.

Martin, John A. 1991. Survival with Supplier Management. *45th Annual Quality Congress Proceedings.* May. Milwaukee, WI. pp. 902-907. American Society for Quality, Milwaukee, WI.

Sloan, David and Weiss, Scott. 1987. *Supplier Improvement Process Handbook.* American Society for Quality, Milwaukee, WI.

Sparks, D. 1999. Partners. A Special Report. *Business Week,* October 25: 106-112.

Wolff, Rodger R. 1999. Productive Manufacturing Supplier Management: Simple, Minimal, Common and Motivational. A paper presented at the annual conference of the Customer-Supplier Division of the American Society for Quality.

9

Corporate Social Responsibility and Social Audits

9-1 Introduction

In trying to be socially responsible, typically, the QA organization of retailers is called upon to monitor suppliers to make sure that the merchandise retailers buy from these suppliers is not made in sweatshops. Sweatshops are those factories which have long working hours, poor working conditions, employ child labor, do not pay fair wages, etc.

9-2 Corporate Social Responsibility

The topic of corporate social responsibility (CSR) is in vogue. One comes across an article or a news item on corporate social responsibility, social accountability, or corporate citizenship quite often. However, what exactly does it mean? Well, just like quality, corporate social responsibility means different things to different people. Corporate social responsibility refers to anything from corporate governance to factory working conditions to environment to drug interdiction! There is no universal definition of corporate social responsibility. European Union (EU) defines corporate social responsibility as "the concept that an enterprise is accountable for its impact on all relevant stakeholders. It is the continuing commitment by business to behave fairly and responsibly and contribute to economic development while improving the quality of life of the work force and their families as well as of the local community and society at large."
(www.europa.eu.int./comm/employment_social/soc-dial/csr/csr_whatiscsr.htm)

A common sense definition of corporate social responsibility is simply "managing a company in a way that balances interests of all the stakeholders, i.e., customers, employees, investors, suppliers, society, government, and environment."

The driving forces behind corporate social responsibility are consumers, investors, non-governmental organizations (NGOs), such as trade unions, human rights organizations, religious organizations, etc. Another driving force, to some extent, is companies' concern about their image as many companies' brands, such as Nike, Gap, Polo, etc., are very valuable. Since information travels with great speed across continents, companies cannot afford adverse publicity about working conditions in factories where their merchandise is made. In 2001, Environs International (www.environicsinternational.com) released information concerning a survey on CSR completed in November 2000. According to consumers across the world, a majority of factors, which contribute to corporate reputation, are rooted in the principles of corporate social responsibility. In fact, a company's demonstrated responsibility to the broader society, its labor practices and business ethics, and environmental impacts are having a dominating influence on corporate reputation in 11 of the 20 countries surveyed, particularly in the Americas and Europe. (Corporate Social Responsibility and Standards Online Forum).

9-2-1 Codes of Conduct

In order to fulfill social responsibility, there needs to be some guidelines or procedures. Within the past several years, hundreds of such guidelines or procedures, called codes of conduct, have come into existence. According to an article (Gereffi, Garcia-Johnson, Sasser, 2001), a recent inventory by the Organization for Economic Cooperation and Development (OECD) listed 264 codes of corporate conduct! Because of this proliferation of codes of conduct, ISO council, at its meeting on April 30-May 1, 2001, passed a resolution underlining the importance of emerging issues in relation to social accountability and asked its Consumer Policy Committee (COPOLCO) to consider the viability of International Standards in this area, taking into account the draft Israel Standard (SI) 10000, Social Responsibility and Community Involvement. COPOLCO, at its May 15-16, 2001 meeting in Oslo, Norway, acknowledged the Council's proposal and agreed to explore the feasibility and desirability of developing ISO standards to benchmark corporate social responsibility, accountability, and governance practices.

With this as a backdrop, many retailers have developed their own codes of conduct, which generally comprise of the following elements:

Child Labor	Forced Labor
Working Hours	Compensation and Benefits
Disciplinary Practice	Discrimination
Safe and Healthy Workplace	Freedom of Association & Right to Collective Bargaining
Harassment and Abuse	

For an example of a retailer's code of conduct, visit the web site www.aafes.com/pa/selling/social.htm

Then there are three codes of conducts developed by Worldwide Responsible Apparel Production (WRAP), www.wrapapparel.org, Social Accountability International (formerly known as the Council on Economic Priorities) and known for SA 8000 (Social Accountability 8000), www.sa-intl.org, and Fair Labor Association, www.fairlabor.org, also seem to be of most interest to retailers.

Table 9-1 shows general comparison of elements of codes of conduct developed by these three organizations.

Elements	WRAP	SA 8000	FLA
Compliance with local laws and workplace regulations	x		
Forced labor	x	x	x
Child labor	x	x	x
Harassment or abuse	x	x	x
Compensation and benefits	x	x	x
Hours of work	x	x	x
Discrimination	x	x	x
Health and safety	x	x	x
Freedom of association (unionization)	x	x	x
Environment	x		
Customs compliance	x		
Drug interdiction	x		
Management system		x	
Control of suppliers		x	x

Table 9-1 Elements of Code of Conduct

9-2-2 Monitoring

Normally, retailers do send their suppliers a document outlining what is expected of them in terms of the elements of social accountability such as child labor, minimum wage, etc. Generally, a questionnaire or checklist would be sent out to these suppliers who in turn, fill them out for each factory, either their own and/or their subcontractors' and return them to the retailer. The information from the returned checklist is then used as a basis or a starting point by the retailer to audit how well a factory is fulfilling its social responsibility or to evaluate effectiveness of a factory's social accountability practices. This process is called a social audit. An example of a social audit checklist is shown here. Some retailers also provide a guidance document to their suppliers, which helps them fill out the checklist properly. An example of such a guidance document is also shown here.

Different retailers approach social audits differently. The responsibility for managing a social audit program usually rests with the quality assurance department of a retailer, because quality assurance inspectors routinely visit factories to perform quality inspections where merchandise is made for the retailer. In addition, quality assurance inspectors are well versed in conducting quality audits and, therefore, the same skill sets can be used to build or develop skills for social auditing. Some retailers use their own staff, generally, quality assurance staff, who are trained in conducting social audits, while some retailers use companies specializing in conducting social audits. Some retailers use both.

While it is relatively easy to develop a code of conduct and communicate it to all the suppliers and clearly spell out what is expected of them in terms of social responsibility, it is extremely difficult to monitor hundreds of factories on a continuous basis. An audit of a factory once a year is simply not an adequate monitoring coverage. Therefore, those companies who specialize in social audits or those retailers who conduct their own social audits develop, cultivate and maintain constant liaison with NGOs, such as human rights groups, church groups, trade unions, etc., in respective countries. They rely on these organizations to be their eyes and ears so far as factories' social accountability practices are concerned. Information received from such organizations on a continuous basis and regular social audits of factories would provide adequate information to decide how effective a factory's social accountability practices are or whether a factory is meeting a retailer's expectations in terms of social responsibilities. Some well-known multi-national shoe and clothing companies also rely on independent monitoring of their efforts of managing social accountability of their supplier base.

9-2-3 Social Responsibility Checklist

FACTORY SOCIAL RESPONSIBILITY
CHECK LIST

Supplier ____ Date________________

Production Facility Name ____
Country ___________________________

Address of Production Facility ____
____

Are you a principal or part owner of this production facility? _____
Are you a subcontractor? ________

Name of the Official completing this checklist ____________________________

Title ____

Contact Info:

Phone No ________________

E-mail ____________________

Mailing Address ____

____

1. Has the production facility signed a "Code of Conduct" with any other customers?

   Yes____ No_____
   If "yes", then please list those customers with whom such an agreement has been signed.

   ___________________________________ ______________________________
   ___________________________________ ______________________________
   ___________________________________ ______________________________

2. Is the production facility currently certified by:

   BS 8800, Occupational Health & Safety? Yes____ No_____

   SA 8000, Social Accountability? Yes____ No_____

   WRAP (Worldwide Responsible Apparel Production) Yes_____ No_____

   FLA (Fair Labor Association) Guidelines? Yes____ No_____

   CCC (Clean Clothes Campaign)? Yes____ No_____

   Name the certifying organization(s) ______________________________

3. Is the production facility in compliance with child labor laws of the country? Yes____ No_____

4. Does production facility obtain documentation for proof of age and eligibility for employment from all potential workers prior to hiring? Yes____ No_____

5. Is the production facility in compliance with forced labor laws of the country? Yes____ No_____

6. Does production facility prohibit convict and/or involuntary labor? Yes____ No_____

7. Are all employees hired without regard to race, ethnicity, age, national origin, gender, religion, or disability? Yes____ No____

8. Does production facility prohibit all types of harassment and physical or verbal abuse? Yes____ No_____

9. Is there a union? Yes____ No_____
   If yes, name the union(s) ______________________________________

10. Are all production facility employees compensated at the minimum wage or higher for all hours worked? Yes____ No_____

11. Are employees compensated for all overtime work in compliance with the labor laws of the country? Yes____ No_____

12. Does production facility ensure that the workers do not work more hours per day and per week than the legal limits? Yes____ No_____

13. Are all trainee employees compensated at least the minimum wage rate? Yes____ No_____

14. Do employees receive an itemized statement with their pay that shows wages and itemized deductions? Yes____ No_____

15. Are new employees informed of company policies, including policies regarding rates of pay? Yes____ No_____

16. Does production facility prominently post minimum wage rates, allowance information, benefits policy, and regular and overtime wages in the native language(s)? Yes____ No_____

17. Is there adequate heat and/or ventilation or air conditioning in the production facility? Yes____ No_____

18. Are there sufficient emergency exits? Yes____ No_____

19. Is there adequate fire safety equipment on site? Yes____ No_____

20. Are entrances and exits (doorways) open and/or unlocked during work hours? Yes____ No_____

21. Are there adequate functioning bathroom facilities? Yes____ No_____

22. Is fresh drinking water readily available? Yes____ No_____

23. Are there dining facilities on the premises? Yes____ No_____

    If yes, are they neat and clean? Yes____ No_____

24. Is there a medical facility on site? Yes____ No_____

25. Is there a doctor and/or nurse on site? Yes____ No_____

26. Is first aid available on premises? Yes____ No_____

27. Is there sufficient work space for each worker to perform their duties in a safe manner without interference from other workers, machinery or equipment, and raw materials used in production? Yes____ No_____

28. Does production facility obtain current information on local and national laws and regulations, and incorporate this information in its business practices? Yes____ No_____

Notes/Remarks:

____

____

____

____

____

____

____

____

____

____

____

____

____

____

9-2-4 Guidance Document for Social Responsibility Checklist

This guidance will assist you in completing the Factory Social Responsibility checklist. A "no" response is to be fully explained in the "Notes/Remarks" section of the checklist. If required, attach any additional supporting documentation or remarks. The XYZ Corporation reserves the right to verify the accuracy and validity of "yes" responses. Any false or unsubstantiated responses may result in termination of contract(s) for goods originating from the non-compliant factory.

Please note that a checklist shall be completed for each factory. When you change a factory, you shall immediately notify the XYZ Corporation in writing and complete another checklist for that factory.

Question 1. Has the factory signed a "Code of Conduct" with any other customers?

There are a number of codes of conduct in the Social Responsibility area. Having signed one or more of such codes of conduct is an indication that the factory is aware of its social responsibility and is willingly fulfilling the requirements of same.

Question 2. Is the factory currently certified by BS 8800, SA 8000, WRAP, FLA, CCC?

Certification to one or more of these standards/guidelines is a clear demonstration that the factory not only supports the principles of Social Responsibility and Labor Standards but also practices them. If the factory had an audit or assessment with regards to any of these requirements pending certification, please do mention that in response to this question.

Question 3. Is the factory in compliance with child labor laws of the country?

Refer to discussion below question # 4.

Question 4. Does factory obtain documentation for proof of age and eligibility for employment from all potential workers prior to hiring?

It is the responsibility of the factory management to ensure that all workers hired are of legal age and meet the eligibility requirements of the country where the factory is located. The factory shall have a procedure to screen all workers prior to hiring, to ensure that they meet all applicable age and eligibility requirements.

Copies of all applicable proofs shall be kept on file for all workers. The factory should have a procedure that articulates age and eligibility requirements to all applicants for position applied for.

Question 5. Is the factory in compliance with forced labor laws of the country?

Forcing anyone to work against their will is considered involuntary or forced labor. Workers shall never be forced to work by contract or any other means. Workers should never be forced to work to pay off a debt for himself or herself, a family member or anyone else by signing a contract. Security guards employed by the factory, or security agencies contracted for their services, must not engage in practices that might cause workers to stay in the factory and work against their will. Security guards should be limited to normal security functions such as protecting the factory and products manufactured and the security of the workers and other factory personnel. The factory shall not retain the worker's original identification card, birth certificate, work permit, or any other form of identification.

Question 6. Does factory prohibit convict and/or involuntary labor?

The factory is prohibited from employing or hiring convicted criminals currently in prison for committing a crime. Even though there are conditions where it is permitted to employ criminals under local or national law, it is expressly prohibited to import any product into the United States under United States customs laws, if that product was produced by convict labor.

Question 7. Are all employees hired without regard to race, ethnicity, age, national origin, gender, religion, or disability?

The factory shall not have discriminatory hiring practices. The factory must hire workers based on their ability to do the job and not on any physical or personal characteristics or beliefs. The factory must have a policy that expressly prohibits all forms of discrimination. The workers must be made aware of this policy.

Question 8. Does factory prohibit all types of harassment and physical and/or verbal abuse?

Workers shall be accorded fair treatment, consistent with laws and customs of the country where the factory is located. The factory shall expressly prohibit all forms of harassment, verbal and/or physical abuse. This includes, but is not limited to: Physical or verbal coercion, sexual abuse, harassment, or abuse in the form of disciplinary action, any harassment or abuse from any person, such as security guards, or any manager, supervisor or worker.

Question 9. Is there a union?

While it is not necessary that a factory be unionized, the presence of one or more unions indicates freedom of association.

Question 10. Are all factory employees compensated at the minimum wage or higher for all hours worked?

The factory shall have a payroll procedure that ensures workers are compensated in accordance with local and national laws.

Question 11. Are employees compensated for all overtime work in compliance with the labor laws of the country?

The factory shall have a procedure that ensures employees who work overtime are compensated in accordance with local and national labor laws. The workers shall be made aware of the rates of work in excess of local/national daily and/or weekly norms.

Question 12. Does the factory ensure that the workers do not work more hours per day and per week than the legal limits?

There are times when it is necessary for a factory to work overtime to meet production and delivery schedules. However, workers who work excessive hours will lose efficiency and production will decrease. In addition, the injury rate will increase.

Workers must not exceed the maximum number of hours allowed by local or national law. In the event that there is no local or national law governing maximum working hours, no worker shall be required to work more than 60 hours per week. If the factory determines that it is necessary to work more hours than allowed by law, they must obtain a waiver from the appropriate governing authority. This waiver must list the period of time covered and the amount of hours to be worked. Workers must be paid for extra overtime according to local or national law.

The department or individual responsible for payroll must perform periodic time card reviews to ensure that hours worked by employees (voluntarily or involuntarily) in a given day, week or month does not exceed legal limits. If official waivers have been issued, the limits of the waiver must not be exceeded.

Question 13. Are all trainee employees compensated at least at the minimum wage rate?

All employees, including trainees, must be paid the minimum wage rate established by the local or national laws of your country.

Question 14. Do employees receive an itemized statement with their pay that shows wages and itemized deductions?

The factory should provide a listing of itemized deductions to all workers each time they are paid wages. These deductions could be social security (medical/unemployment insurance/pension), local and national income tax, repayment of loan, or any other deductions. The factory should have a detailed pay slip that shows all the deductions made and the method of calculation. If workers receive cash payments there should be a master payroll record with each worker's signature indicating that they received their pay.

The workers should be notified in writing of any changes in their actual pay and/or payroll procedures and the reasons for these changes. Any miscalculations or under payment of wages shall be corrected immediately. Any worker's complaints regarding wages must be investigated immediately. If it is determined that the workers were not correctly paid, an adjustment shall be made immediately.

Question 15. Are new employees informed of company policies; including policies regarding rates of pay?

When factory workers are hired they shall receive an explanation of their legal rights concerning the working hours of the factory. They should be told if overtime is required and how many overtime hours they can expect to work daily, weekly and monthly. They shall be given an explanation of the laws concerning overtime.

A written explanation of wage and overtime laws shall be provided to the workers. The worker should sign this explanation and a copy should be kept in the worker's file.

The factory shall periodically review the laws concerning hours worked and wage compensation to ensure they are in compliance with the most current laws. Any areas that are not current shall be corrected. Copies of the latest laws should be kept on file.

Question 16. Does factory prominently post minimum wage rates, allowance information, benefits policy, and regular and overtime wages in the native language(s)?

The factory shall list its policies concerning minimum wage rates, regular working hours, overtime hours and benefits. Any applicable local and national wage laws shall also be listed. These postings shall be located in prominent areas, i.e., the worker entrance, time clock, or cafeteria; so the workers can read them at any time.

All postings shall be in the native language of the factory workers and factory management personnel. In the event that the factory hires workers that speak a language other than the language of the country where the factory is located, these postings shall also be in that language. It is possible that the factory may require postings in more than one language.

Question 17. Is there adequate heat and/or ventilation or air conditioning in the factory?

The factory should have comfortable air temperature and ventilation/air circulation within the factory so that the work environment is not unhealthy or unsafe.

Question 18. Are there sufficient emergency exits?

The building shall have enough emergency exits to allow the workers to leave the building in a fast and orderly manner. Exits should be on opposite sides of the building. If the building is more than one story there should be sufficient stairways to allow the workers to get to the ground floor and exit the building in a fast and orderly manner. A traditional fire escape on the outside of the building is preferred.

All exits shall be clearly marked and accessible. Exits must not be locked or blocked in any way. If building security or theft is a concern, then push bars may be used on the exit doors. This will prevent the door from being opened from the outside, but allows the door to be easily opened from the inside in case of an emergency. For additional security an alarm may be installed on the door to advise security personnel when it is opened.

The factory should conduct periodic fire drills to ensure that all workers know how to leave the building in a fast and orderly manner. The factory should have procedures to train all managers and workers in fire safety. The factory shall develop a fire evacuation plan. This plan shall clearly define the nearest exit path and be prominently posted for the workers. For large buildings, several evacuation plans should be posted at different locations throughout the building.

The factory shall conduct periodic fire safety inspections of the building, machinery and equipment. Any failure of this inspection shall result in immediate corrective action.

Question 19. Is there adequate fire safety equipment on site?

Fire safety is extremely important. The factory shall have procedures in place that will ensure the workers are protected against fire and fire related hazards. This should include worker housing.

The building and/or dormitory shall have fire extinguishers placed in every room. A fire extinguisher shall be placed within 50 feet of each worker, and be of an appropriate size that can be handled by the average worker. The type of fire extinguisher used depends upon the type of fire. For example, an area that uses electrical equipment will need a different type of fire extinguisher than an area where chemicals are used. All workers should be trained in the proper use of fire extinguishers. In addition, selected workers should receive extensive fire training and be organized as a fire-fighting brigade.

Fire extinguishers are intended for spot fires, which are usually small fires. These fires can start by spontaneous combustion, defective or overheating machinery and equipment, careless smoking or other causes. Sprinkler systems, fire hoses or other fire fighting devices are intended for large fires, but are not replacements for fire extinguishers. Fire extinguishers shall be serviced annually. Each fire extinguisher should be tagged indicating the date and type of service.

Question 20. Are entrances and exits (doorways) open and/or unlocked during work hours?

Locked and/or closed entrances and exits can be hazardous during an emergency such as fire.

Question 21. Are there adequate functioning bathroom facilities?

Bathroom facilities shall be clean and properly functioning and must have necessary sanitary items such as soap, paper towels, tissues, etc.

Question 22. Is fresh drinking water readily available?

The factory shall provide easy access to fresh drinking water to all workers.

Question 23. Are there dining facilities on the premises? Are they neat and clean?

The factory should provide a neat and clean dining facility for workers so that workers do not have to eat at their workstations. Eating at their workstations amid machinery and materials is not healthy nor safe.

Question 24. Is there a medical facility on site?

Refer to discussion below question # 25

Question 25. Is there a doctor and/or nurse on site?

The facility shall follow local laws regarding requirement of having a medical facility and a doctor and/or nurse on site. All injuries must be reported to the management and records must be maintained.

Question 26. Is there first aid available on premises?

The factory shall maintain an adequate number of first aid kits at strategic locations throughout the factory to take care of minor emergencies.

Question 27. Is there sufficient workspace for each worker to perform their duties in a safe manner without interference from other workers, machinery or equipment, and raw materials used in production?

The factory should be designed and operated in a manner that shall allow sufficient area for each worker to perform their duties without interference from other workers. This area should include sufficient space for materials, tools and other items that are necessary for manufacturing the product. There shall be sufficient room between workers to allow them to leave their work area in a fast and orderly manner in case of fire or other emergency. Each workstation should have adequate lighting to reduce the risk of eyestrain.

The factory shall perform periodic inspections to ensure that the condition of each workstation is safe and well lit. Any defective areas shall be repaired or replaced as required. Workstation inspection records and a corrective action procedure should be maintained.

Question 28. Does factory obtain current information on local and national laws and regulations, and incorporate this information in its business practices?

The factory shall have a procedure that shall ensure that the labor laws and regulations are being followed. There should be a manager or supervisor responsible for monitoring and updating these laws. Any new laws shall be adopted as required by such laws.

It shall be part of the factory's official company policy that all labor laws shall be obeyed.

The European Commission web site provides a number of useful Internet links on the subject of corporate social responsibility at http://europa.eu.int/comm/employment_social/soc-dial/csr/csr_links.htm

Key Points

- In today's globalized world, it is not only quality of products important to consumers, but also the conditions under which those products were made are equally important.

References

http://europa.eu.int./comm/employment_social/soc-dial/csr/csr_whatiscsr.htm What is Corporate Social Responsibility (CSR)?

Corporate Social Responsibility and Standards Online Forum Survey Consumers Driving CSR? Sunday, October 21, 2001.

Gereffi, Gary, Garcia-Johnson, Ronie, Sasser, Erika. 2001. The NGO-Industrial Complex. *Foreign Policy*, July-August.

Bibliography

Andriof, Jorg and McIntosh, Malcolm. Ed. 2001. *Perspectives on Corporate Citizenship.* Warwick Business School, UK and KPMG, Germany. Published by

Greenleaf Publishing, June.
www.greenleaf-publishing.com/catalogue/corpcit.htm

Ascoly, Nina; Oldenziel, Joris; Zeldenrust, Ineke. 2001. *Overview of Recent Developments on Monitoring and Verification in the Garment and Sportswear Industry in Europe*, May. Center for Research on Multinational Corporations. The Netherlands. Entire report can be downloaded from the web site www.somo.nl

Blood, Sweat & Sheers: Corporate Codes of Conduct. A paper published by Interhemispheric Resource Center.
www.igc.org/trac/feature/sweatshops/codes.html

Freeman, Bennett. 2001. *Corporate Responsibility and Human Rights*. A paper presented at the first Global Dimensions seminar on human rights and corporate social responsibility at the United Nations, New York. 1 June. www.globaldimensions.net/articles/ce/freeman.html

Klein, Naomi. 2002. *No Logo*. Picador. New York, NY.

Krall, Karen M. 2001. Good Deeds Deliver: Social responsibility investing reaps ethical and financial rewards. *Industry Week*. January 15.
www.industryweek.com.

Labour practices in the footwear, leather, textiles and clothing industries. International Labour Office, Geneva, 2000 www.ilo.org

Landsburg, Steven E. The Imperialism of Compassion. 2001. *The Wall Street Journal*. Monday, July 23.

Miller, Mark. 2000. *Assessment and Perspectives in Auditing and Monitoring*. A paper presented at CEPAA Conference in Hong Kong, February 23.

Promoting a European Framework for Corporate Social Responsibility. 2001. Green Paper. Commission of the European Communities. Brussels, July 18. Entire report can be downloaded from the web site
http://europa.eu.int/comm/employment_social/soc-dial/csr/csr_index.htm

Rosen, Ellen Israel. 2002. *Making Sweatshops: The Globalization of the U. S. Apparel Industry*. University of California Press. Los Angeles, CA.

Sajhau, Jean-Paul. 1998. *Business ethics in the textile, clothing and footwear (TCF) industries: Codes of conduct*. Working paper. October. ILO, Geneva. www.ilo.org

The Apparel Industry and Codes of Conduct: A Solution to the International Child Labor Problem? A report of the U. S. Department of Labor, 1996. This report focuses on the use of child labor in the production of apparel for the U. S. market, and reviews the extent to which U. S. apparel importers have established and are implementing codes of conduct or other business guidelines prohibiting the use of child labor in the production of the clothing they sell. Entire report can be downloaded from the web site
www.dol.gov/dol/ilab/public/media/reports/iclp/apparel/main.htm. This report

also provides a link to many retailers' codes of conduct at the web site www.dol.gov/dol/ilab/public/media/reports/iclp/apparel/5c.htm

Van Yoder, Steven. 2001. Beware The Coming Corporate Backlash. 2001. *Industry Week*. April 2. www.industryweek.com

Varley, Pamela and Mathiason, Carolyn. Ed. 1998. *The Sweatshop Quandary: Corporate Responsibility on Global Frontier*. Published by Investor Responsibility Research Center, September. www.irrc.org

10

Resources

10-1 General

www.CE-marking.org
This web site contains good information about CE marking requirements

Department of Engineering Professional Development
College of Engineering
University of Wisconsin-Madison
432 North Lake Street
Madison, WI 53706
Phone: (800)-462-0876

For a course on warning labels

www.europa.eu.int/
This is the web site of European Union

Superintendent of Documents
P. O. Box 371954
Pittsburg, PA 15250-7954

For any U. S. Government document

10-2 Laboratory Equipment/Instruments Suppliers

American Association of Textile Chemists and Colorists (AATCC)
P. O. Box 12215
Research Triangle park, NC 27709
U.S.A.
Phone: (919)-549-8141
www.aatcc.org

Advanced Testing Instruments
316 D Business parkway
Greer, SC 29651
U.S.A.
Phone: (864)-989-0566
www.aticorporation.com

Agilent Technologies
395 Page mill Road
P. O. Box 10395
Palo Alto, CA 94303
U.S.A.
Phone: (650)-752-5000
www.measurement.tm.agilent.com

Atlas Material Testing Technology LLC
4114 N. Ravenswood Avenue
Chicago, IL 60613
U.S.A.
Phone: (773)-327-4520
www.atlas-mts.com

Cole-Palmer Instrument Company
625 east Bunker Court
Vernon Hills, IL 60061
U.S.A.
Phone: (800)-323-4340
www.colepalmer.com

Custom Scientific Instruments Inc.
862 Summer Avenue
Newark, NJ 07104
U.S.A.
Phone: (973)-412-8200
www.csi-instruments.com

Instron Corporation
100 Royall Street
Canton, MA 02021
U.S.A.
Phone: (800)-564-8378
www.instron.com

Omega Engineering, Inc.
One Omega Drive
Stamford, CT 06907-0047
Phone: (203)-359-1660
www.omega.com

SGS
Instrument Marketing services (IMS)
www.ustesting.sgsna.com/instrum.htm

Simpson Electric Company
853 Dundee Avenue
Elgin, IL 60120
U.S.A.
Phone: (847)-697-2260
www.simpsonelectric.com

Testfabrics, Inc.
P. O. Box 26
415 delaware Street
W. Pittston, PA 18643
U.S.A.
Phone: (570)-603-0432

10-3 Professional Societies

American Association of Textile Chemists and Colorists (AATCC)
One Davis Drive
P. O. Box 12215
Research Triangle Park, NC 27709-2215
Phone: (919)-549-8141
www.aatcc.org

American Society for Quality (ASQ)
600 N. Plankinton Avenue
Milwaukee, WI 53203
U.S.A.
Phone: (414)-272-8575
www.asq.org

The Institute of Quality Assurance (IQA)
12 Grosvenor Crescent
London SW1X 7EE
England
Phone: 020 7425 6722
www.iqa.org

10-4 Publishers

Fairchild Publications
7 W. 34th Street
New York, NY 10001-8191
Phone: (800)-289-0273
www.fairchildpub.com

Publishes dailies "DNR" and "WWD" covering retail business, with an emphasis on men's wear and accessories, and women's wear and accessories, respectively.

Lebhar-Friedman, Inc.
425 Park Avenue
New York, NY 10022
Phone: (212)-756-5252
www.lf.com

Publishes a monthly "Chain Store Age Executive" covering merchandising information and industry news. Also, publishes a biweekly "Discount Store News" covering mass merchandise retailing.

Quality Press
American Society for Quality
P. O. Box 3005
Milwaukee, WI 53201-3005
www.qualitypress.asq.org

Racher Press Inc.
220 Fifth Avenue
New York, NY 10022
Phone: (212)-213-6000
www.racherpress.com

Publishes a biweekly "MMR" (Mass Market Retailers) covering drug, discount, and supermarket chains.

10-5 Regulatory Agencies

Consumer Product Safety Commission (CPSC)
4330 East West Highway
Bethesda, MD 20814-2771
U.S.A.
Ph: (800)-638-2772
www.cpsc.gov

Federal Trade Commission (FTC)
Pennsylvania Avenue & 6th Street, N. W.
Washington, DC 20580
U.S.A.
Phone: (202)-326-2222
www.ftc.gov

Food and Drug Administration (FDA)
5600 Fisher Lane
Rockville, MD 20857
U.S.A.

Phone: (301)-443-1544
www.fda.gov

National Highway Traffic Safety Administration (NHTSA)
400 Seventh Street, S. W.
Washington, DC 20590
U.S.A.
www.nhtsa.gov

10-6 Safety Organizations

European Consumer Safety Association (ECOSA)
C/O Consumer Safety Institute
P. O. Box 75169
1070 AD Amsterdam
The Netherlands
www.ecosa.org

International Consumer Product Health and Safety Organization (ICPHSO)
P. O. Box 1785
Germantown, MD 20875-1785
U. S. A.
Phone: (301)-601-3543
www.icphso.org

10-7 Social Audit Organizations

Intertek Testing Services
One Tech. Drive
Andover, MA 01810
U. S. A.
www.itslabtest.com
www.itsglobal.com

Merchandise Testing Laboratories, Inc.
244 Liberty Street
Brockton, MA 02401
www.mtlusa.com

SGS U.S. Testing Company Inc.
1827 Walden Office Square, Suite 320
Schaumburg, IL 60173
www.ustesting.sgsna.com

STR
Specialized Technology Resources, Inc.
10 Water Street
Enfield, CT 06082-4899
U.S.A.
www.strlab.com

10-8 Standards Organizations

American National Standards Institute (ANSI)
25 West 43rd Street
Fourth Floor
New York, NY 10037
U.S.A.
Phone: (212)-642-4900
www.ansi.org

American Society for Testing & Materials, International
100 Bar Harbor drive
West Conshohocken, PA 19428-2959
U.S.A.
Phone: (610)-832-9500
www.astm.org

CSA (Canadian Standards Association) International
178 Rexdale Boulevard
Toranto, ON M9W 1R3
Canada
Phone: (416)-747-4000
www.cas-international.org

International Organization for Standardization (ISO)
1 rue de Varembè
Case postala 56

CH-1211 Genève 20
Switzerland
www.iso.ch

Standards Australia
GPO 5420
Sydney NSW 2001
Australia
www.standards.com.au

10-9 Testing & Inspection Organizations

Acts Testing Labs, Inc.
100 Northpoint Parkway
Buffalo, NY 14228-1884
www.actstesting.com

Gemological Institute of America (GIA)
World headquarters
The Robert Mouawad Campus
5345 Armada drive
Carlsbad, CA 92008
Phone: (760)-603-4000
www.gia.org

Independent Gemological Laboratories (IGL)
21 west 38th Street
New York, NY 10018
Phone: (212)-382-0008
www.dia-lab.com

International Gemological Institute (IGI)
579 Fifth Avenue
New York, NY 10017
Phone: (212)-753-7100
www.igiworldwide.com

Intertek Testing Services
One Tech. Drive
Andover, MA 01810
U. S. A.
www.itslabtest.com
www.itsglobal.com

Merchandise Testing Laboratories, Inc.
244 Liberty Street
Brockton, MA 02401
www.mtlusa.com

SGS U.S. Testing Company Inc.
1827 Walden Office Square, Suite 320
Schaumburg, IL 60173
www.ustesting.sgsna.com

Shuster Laboratories
85 John Road
Canton, MA 02021
www.shusterlabs.com

STR
Specialized Technology Resources, Inc.
10 Water Street
Enfield, CT 06082-4899
U.S.A.
www.strlab.com

Underwriters Laboratories, Inc.
333 Pfingsten Road
Northbrook, IL 60062
www.ul.com

10-10 Trade Organizations

Association of Home Appliance Manufacturers (AHAM)
1111 19th Street, Suite 402
Washington, DC 20036
Phone: (202)-872-5955
www.aham.org

International AntiCounterfeiting Coalition, Inc.
1725 K. Street, N.W., Suite 1101
Washington, DC 20006
Phone: (202)-223-6667
www.iacc.org

International Council of Toy Industries
80 Camberwell Road
London SE5 0GE
England
Phone: 44-207-701-7271
www.toy-icti.org

Industrial Fabrics Association International—IFAI
1801 County Road B West
Roseville, MN 55113-4061
Phone: (651)-222-2508
www.ifai.com

Reatil Industry Leaders Association (RILA)
1700 N. Moore Street
Arlington, VA 22209
Phone: (703)-841-2300
www.retail-leaders.org
This organization represents discount retailers and mass merchandisers.

Juvenile Products Manufacturers Association
17000 Commerce Parkway, Suite C
Mt. Laurel, NJ 08054
www.JPMA.org

National Retail Federation Inc. (NRF)
325 Seventh Street, NW
Washington, DC 20004
Phone: (202)-783-7971
www.nrf.com
This is an organization of department stores. Publishes a monthly magazine "Stores."

Toy Industry Association, Inc.
1115 Broadway, Suite 400
New York, NY 10010
Phone: (212)-675-1141
www.toy-tia.org

11

How to Start Managing Quality

Now that you know a lot about managing quality, how would you go about starting a quality assurance program?

11-1 Inspection

The best way to start is to start gradually. First, start with an end item inspection program.

Hire trained inspectors, if that is not possible, then hire some people and train them in the end item inspection. The skills required by the inspectors and the job descriptions as well as qualification requirements are in Appendix I. Decide on sampling plans to use and some examples of standard inspection procedures are in Appendix III.

In the beginning, to obtain an overall picture of where you stand in terms of quality, perform 100 % inspection of as much merchandise as possible for at least two to three weeks and collect information.

Analyze the data collected from 100 % inspection such as shown in the Table 11-1. This is also an example of how a continuous score of defects can be kept for an easy analysis of data. If a pattern of defects emerges, it makes a solution that much easier because now you know where your problems are. If a pattern does not emerge, it means that you have widespread quality problems.

Defects	1st Week	2nd Week	3rd Week	Total	% of Total
Broken button	卌 卌	卌 卌 卌	卌	30	14.4
Broken snap					
Broken stitcing	|||	||||	卌	12	5.8
Defective snap					
Different shade within the same garment	||	卌	||||	11	5.3
Dropped stitches					
Exposed notches					
Exposed raw edgaes					
Fabric defects	卌 卌 卌	卌 卌	卌 卌 卌 卌	45	21.6
Holes					
Inoperative zipper					
Loose/hanging threads	卌	卌 卌		15	7.2
Misaligned buttons and button holes					
Missing button	卌 卌 卌 卌	卌		25	12
Needle cuts/chews					
Open seams	卌 卌 卌	卌 卌	卌 卌 卌	40	19.2
Pulled/loose yarn					
Stains					
Unfinished buttonholes	卌 卌	卌	卌 卌 卌	30	14.4
Zipper too short					
Total defects	80	64	64	208	100
Number of samples defective	70	60	55	185	
Number of samples inspected	500	500	500	1500	
Percent defective	14	12	11	12.3	

Table 11-1 Final Inspection of Style XYZ

Please note that each mark in the Table 11-1 indicates a defect. A garment can have more than one defect. The data in Table 11-1 indicate that the biggest problem is related to buttons. Broken and missing buttons (30 + 25 = 55) make up 26.4 % (55/208) of the total defects found in the three week period. Someone should therefore look into this matter and try to find the root causes of broken and missing buttons. Perhaps, button quality is such that they break in pressing, may be they are attached so poorly that with the slightest stress they come off. A second area of concern here is fabric defects as they constituted 21.6% (45/208) of total defects. Fabric defects can further be analyzed and grouped into various categories of defects such as non-manufacturing defects (stains), and manufacturing defects (slubs, missing picks, dropped stitches, etc.). A third area of concern should be open seams, which constituted 19.2 % (40/208) of total defects.

This table also helps you analyze the number of defective garments for the three week period.

Let us say, for example, that for one month, every shipment that was received from a supplier ABC was inspected on a random sampling basis. The total number of samples inspected were 915 and 133 samples were found defective, resulting in 14.5 % defective rate, which is very high!

The analysis of these 133 defective samples (Table 11-2) clearly indicates that the fabric quality needs urgent attention. If fabric quality can be improved, significant improvements will result in the overall quality of garments.

Type of defects	No. of defects	%	W[a]	M[b]
Dropped stitches	63	47.4		63
Open seams	28	21.0	28	
Broken yarn	23	17.3		23
Misknit	7	5.3		7
Stains	7	5.3	7	
Discolored yarn	2	1.5		2
Holes	1	0.7	1	
Unfinished buttonholes	1	0.7	1	
Unrelated operation	1	0.7	1	
Total defects	133	100.0	28	95

a- Workmanship defects
b- Material defects
Percent defective due to workmanship = 38/915 = 4.1 %
Percent defective due to material defects = 95/133 = 10.4 %
Proportion of workmanship defects = 38/133 = 28.6 %
Proportion of material defects = 95/133 = 71.4

Table 11-2 Defect Analysis

Passing on such analytical information to your supplier and requesting corrective actions will help your suppliers a great deal in meeting your quality levels.

Having collected and analyzed inspection data on all suppliers, or at least high dollar suppliers will help you make intelligent decisions as to where do you need to deploy your inspection efforts.

If you use an inspection program as merely a failure fixing program or a watchdog to prevent defective merchandise from reaching your customers, then your focus will not be on preventing defects from occurring in the first place and you will not get the maximum return out of an inspection program. The inspection program should not merely be a device to separate good from bad, but it should be an essential first step towards continuous improvement. Therefore, the real value of inspection efforts is in what you do with the information you obtain from inspection efforts.

Once you gain some experience and feel comfortable with end item inspection, then it is easier to expand your efforts in supplier surveys, supplier quality system audits, and factory evaluations.

11-2 Testing

When one mentions testing to a retailer, usually, the retailer envisions a full fledge testing laboratory! However, to start with, one does not need to have a full fledge testing laboratory. An effective testing program can include only a pair of washer and dryer! It is amazing how much information can be gathered for decision making by only washing and drying an item of clothing. With a washer and dryer, one can find out something about shrinkage, and colorfastness in laundering, durable press qualities, durability of seams, durability of fusible interlining, if trimming and accessories will withstand appropriate washing and drying, compatibility of trimmings with the rest of the garment in terms of shrinkage and colorfastness and shrinkage of zipper tape.

Proper analysis and use of the above information will go a long way toward improving the quality of clothing. Also, an agreement can be made with a commercial testing laboratory to suit your testing needs. Even though you may not want to invest in extensive testing facilities, it would be certainly advantageous to have at least one employee from your quality assurance department to attend a short course on testing offered by some of the textile and fashion colleges or textile associations.

Just like end item inspection, once you feel comfortable with limited testing, you can begin to expand your testing efforts, rather than start everything at once and be overwhelmed.

By referring to the chapter on testing in this book, one can decide which items to test and for which properties or characteristics. Job descriptions for Laboratory Technician and Manager, Product Testing are in the Appendix I.

11-3 Data Collection and Analysis

Data collection and analysis are fundamental to quality assurance. Here are several very simple, yet powerful tools that will help you collect data and analyze them effectively. These tools are:

Cause and effect diagram
Check sheet
Control chart
Flow chart
Histogram
Pareto chart

Please note that the explanation provided is very basic and simple. Ishikawa (1986) provides a detailed and excellent discussion of these tools.

11-3-1 Cause and Effect Diagram (Sarazen 1990)

Figure 11-1 shows a simple cause and effect diagram. This diagram is also called a fishbone diagram because it looks like skeleton of a fish. Also, this diagram is called Ishiwaka diagram, named after a Japanese quality expert who came up with this concept. The idea is first to identify and state the problem, which is in essence an effect of something that happened in a process, and think through various causes that may have resulted in an undesired effect. Drawing a cause and effect diagram helps one think systematically and logically. It graphically illustrates the relationship between a given outcome and all the factors that influence this outcome. This technique is very helpful in analyzing what may cause defects.

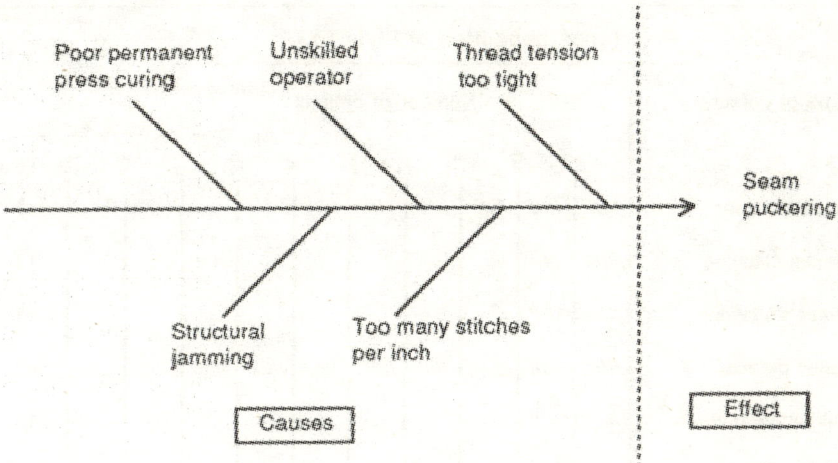

Figure 11-1 Cause and Effect Diagram

11-3-2 Check Sheet (The Juran Institute 1990)

A check sheet is nothing but a form used to collect data in such a way that it makes not only the collection of data easy, but also the analysis of that data automatic. Figure 11-2 is an example of a check sheet. Each mark in the check sheet indicates a defect. The type of defects, number of defects, and their distribution can be seen at a glance, which makes analysis of data very quick and easy. Check sheets provide a logical display of data that are manually derived and yield results from which conclusions can be easily drawn.

Final Inspection of Style XYZ

Type of defects	5	10	15	20	25	30	35	40	45	50	Total
Broken buttons	/////	/////	/////	/////	/////	/////					30
Broken stitching	/////	/////	//								12
Shade variation	/////	/////	/								11
Fabric defects	/////	/////	/////	/////	/////	/////	/////	/////	/////		45
Untrimmed threads	/////	/////	/////								15
Missing buttons	/////	/////	/////	/////	/////						25
Open seams	/////	/////	/////	/////	/////	/////	/////	/////			40
Unfinished buttonholes	/////	/////	/////	/////	/////	/////					30

Sample size = 1500; % defective 208/1500 = 13.9

Figure 11-2 Check Sheet

11-3-3 Control Chart (Shainin 1990)

A control chart is a simple graph or chart with time on the horizontal (X) axis vs. the quality characteristic measured on a vertical (Y) axis, with the control limits for the quality characteristic measured. In other words, a control chart is a continuous graphic indication of the state of a process with respect to a quality characteristic being measured. Let say you are performing the final inspection of garments. You go out on the production floor and just before shipping pull a number of samples, inspect them, and note the number of defects, and calculate percent defective for several days. The results may look something like the following:

No. of samples inspected	No. of samples defective	% defective
392	14	3.6
346	10	2.7
132	2	1.5
141	6	4.2
344	2	0.6
170	7	4.1
164	0	0

The control chart will look like that shown in the figure 11-3.

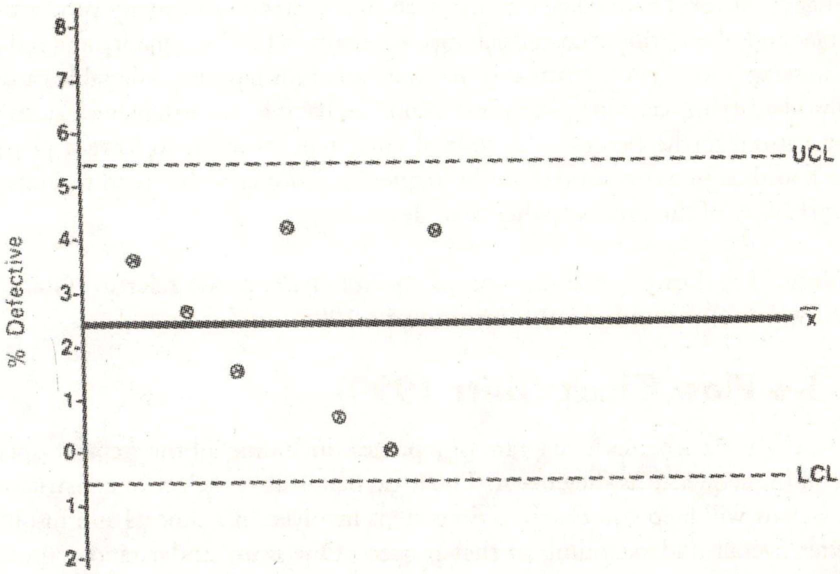

Figure 11-3 Control Chart

Variations or fluctuations in data are generally caused by a large number of small differences in materials, equipment, the surrounding atmospheric conditions, physical and mental reactions of people involved, etc. These small differences cause data to fluctuate or vary in a manner called "normal" or "random" and such variations are termed normal variations. In other words, these are variations normal to the process.

Occasionally, however, there will be a large or unusual difference, much more important than all those small differences put together. For example, material is taken from a different lot, the machine setter makes a new setting, an inexperienced operator takes the place of an experienced operator, etc. These large differences cause changes in a process resulting in variation in the characteristics measured in a manner called "abnormal" and these variations are called abnormal variations. In other words, these are variations that are not normal to the process.

Experience has shown that there are definite detectable differences between "normal" or "natural" variations and "abnormal" or "unnatural" variations. It is possible to detect this difference or to make this distinction using a statistical tool known as the control chart. Abnormal or unnatural variations have identifiable, assignable causes. This makes the diagnosis and correction of many production troubles and often brings substantial improvements in product quality and reduction in scrap and rework. Normal or natural variations have no assignable causes. So by identifying certain quality variations as having no assignable causes or being natural to the process, the control chart tells us when to leave a process alone and thus prevents unnecessarily frequent adjustments that tend to increase the variability of the process rather than decrease it.

For detailed and excellent discussion of control charts please refer to (Grant & Leavenworth 1996) and (AT&T Technologies 1985).

11-3-4 Flow Chart (Burr 1990)

A flow chart is a schematic diagram of a process including all the steps or operations in the sequence as they occur. The logic here is that the act of constructing a flow chart will help you clarify various steps involved in a process and result in a better overall understanding of that process. One must understand a process clearly to be better able to identify and solve its problems. Flow chart can help understand the complete process, identify the critical stages of a process, locate problem areas, and show relationships between different steps in a process. Figure 11-4 is an example of a flow chart. Flow charts are a great help while conducting supplier quality system audit and factory evaluation.

11-3-5 Histogram (The Juran Institute 1990)

A histogram is a bar chart or a bar graph. It is a graphical depiction of a number of occurrences of an event. For example, if you were to draw a histogram of the data contained in Table 11-1, it would look like figure 11-5. A histogram simply shows the distribution of sample data and gives some idea about variability of that data. Histogram is a graphic summary of variation in a set of data, and is a simple but powerful tool for elementary analysis. A histogram can help understand the total variation of a process, and quickly and easily determine the underlying distribution of a process.

11-3-6 Pareto Chart (Burr 1990)

A Pareto chart is nothing but a histogram where a number of occurrences of an event are arranged in descending order. For example, a Pareto chart of the data contained in Table 11-1 will look like the Figure 11-6.

Dr. Joseph M. Juran, the world famous quality management expert, observed in mid-1920s, as a young engineer, that quality defects are unequal in frequency, that is, when a long list of defects is arranged in order of frequency, generally, relatively few of the defects account for the bulk of defectiveness. Dr. Juran named this phenomenon the Pareto principle (Juran 1975). Thus, Pareto chart helps identify those defects that cause most problems, and by addressing those defects, most of the quality problems can be solved and improvement be made. For example, of the 208 defects shown in the Figure 11-6, 45 or 21.6 % are fabric defects. So in this instance, it would be most effective to address fabric quality first because any improvement in fabric quality will significantly improve overall quality of the product. The next defect to address should be open seams, and so forth.

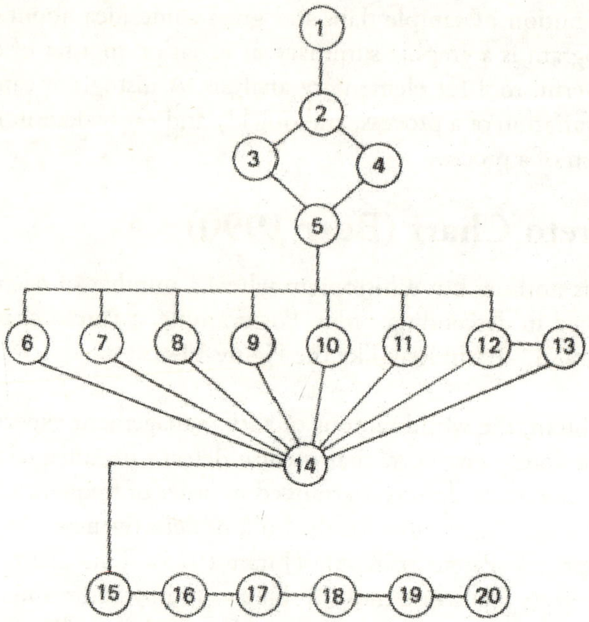

1. Marker lay made according to cutting ticket. Marker lay checked 100 %.
2. Marker and material delivered to spreading operation.
3. Machine knife cut.
4. Die cutting small parts.
5. Cut parts delivered to plant.
6. Collar department: Fuse stays. Run collar tops, trim points. Turn and press (shape), top stitch, trim tops. Hem bands, stitch lining to bands. Band collar. Turn band ends. Top stitch bands. Trim and baste. Quarter mark band. Buttonhole. Button sew.
7. Cuff department: Hem cuff, run cuff. Shape cuff, topstitch. Buttonhole. Button sew.
8. Under fronts: Baste neck. Crease front. Hem button stay. Button sew. Ste pocket. Set flap.
9. Upper fronts: Baste neck. Crease front. Center pleat. Buttonhole. Set pocket. Set flap.
10. Sleeves: Piece binding. Bind sleeve. Tack binding.
11. Backs: Pleat. Backs.
12. Yokes: Label. Sew.
13. Attach yoke backs.
14. Assemble completed bundles of parts, any size, section, ply number and/or shade.
15. Join shoulder seam.
16. Join collar to shirt.
17. Set sleeve, join side and underarm seams (side fell).
18. Cuff attach, hem shirt, trim threads.
19. Button shirt, roll collar, press, fold.
20. Pack.

Figure 11-4 Flow Chart

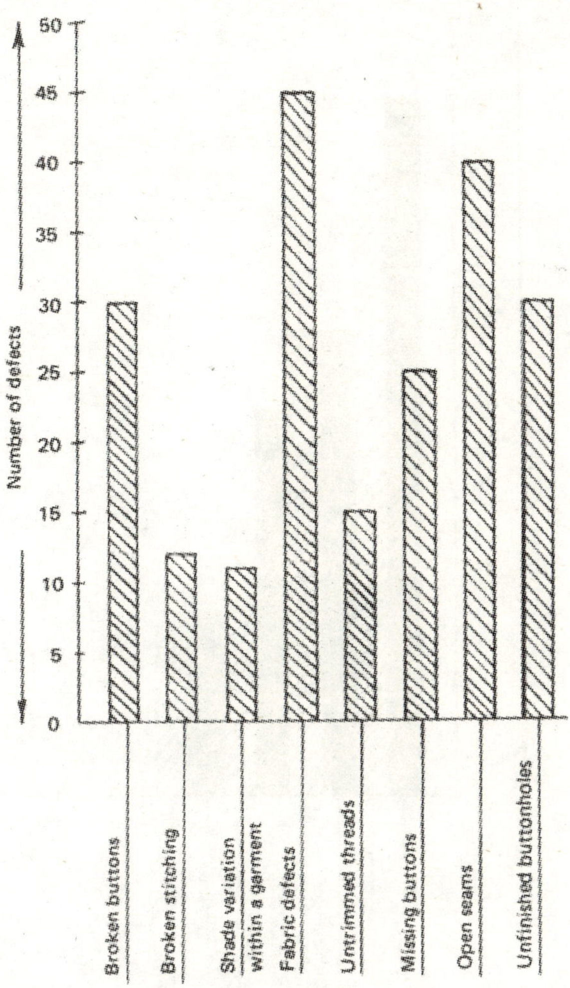

Figure 11-5 Histogram

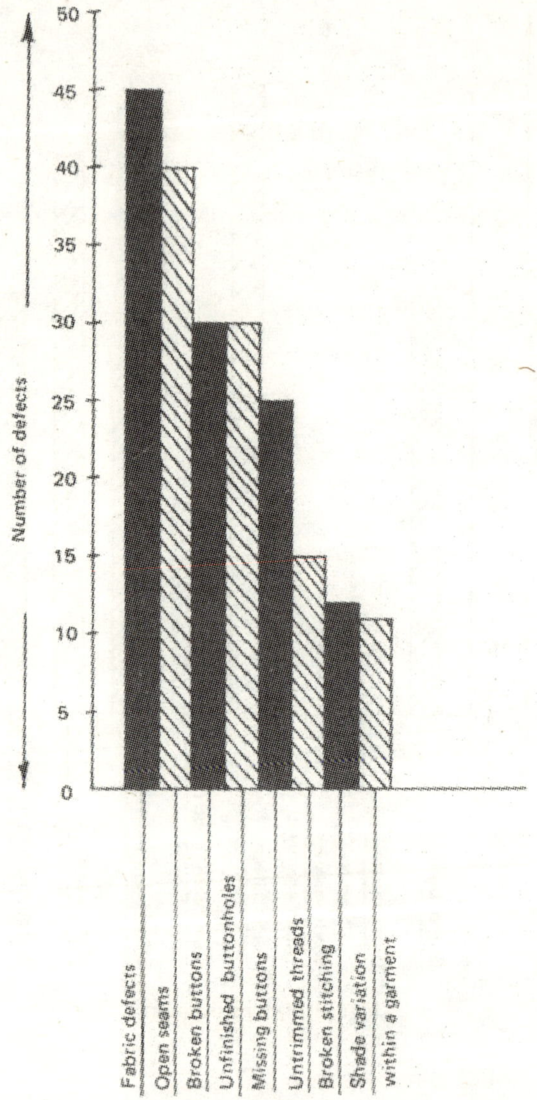

Figure 11-6 Pareto Chart

Key Points

- It is better to start quality assurance program gradually.
- The most effective way to start a quality assurance program is to have a good mix of internal efforts as well as outsourcing some of the inspection and testing activities.
- Quality assurance is information intensive activity. Therefore, effective data collection and analysis are very important to quality management and quality improvement efforts.

References

AT & T Technologies. 1985. *Statistical Quality Control Handbook.*

Burr, John T.1990. The Tools of Quality, Part I: Going With the Flow(chart). *Quality Progress*, June. ASQC, Milwaukee, WI.

Burr, John T. 1990. The Tools of Quality, Part VI: Pareto Charts. *Quality Progress*, November. ASQC, Milwaukee, WI.

Burr, John T. 1990. The Tools of Quality, Part VII: Scatter Diagram. *Quality Progress*, December. ASQC, Milwaukee, WI.

Grant, Eugene L. and Leavenworth, Richard S. 1996. *Statistical Quality Control*, 7th edition. McGraw-Hill, New York, NY.

Ishikawa, Kaoru. 1986. *Guide to Quality Control.* American Society for Quality, Milwaukee, WI.

Juran J. M. 1975. Contributing Editor. Then and Now in Quality Control, the non-Pareto Principle: Mea Culpa. *Quality Progress*, May. ASQC, Milwaukee, WI.

Sarazen, J. Stephen. 1990. The Tools of Quality, Part II: Cause-and-Effect Diagrams. *Quality Progress,* July, ASQC, Milwaukee, WI

Shainin, Peter D.1990. The Tools of Quality, Part III: Control Chart. *Quality Progress*, August. ASQC, Milwaukee, WI.

The Juran Institute. 1990. The Tools of Quality, Part IV: Histograms. *Quality Progress*, September. ASQC, Milwaukee, WI.

The Juran Institute. 1990. The Tools of Quality, Part V: Check Sheets. *Quality Progress*, October. ASQC, Milwaukee, WI.

Appendix I

QA Functional Statement, Job Descriptions and Training Plans

I-1 QA Functional Statement

Quality Assurance

Administers product evaluation program in support of purchasing, merchandising, and store operations. This program includes pre-purchase testing, post-award testing, and acceptance testing as well as testing to verify customer complaints. Testing is accomplished either in-house or outsourced or combination of both. Purchasing and merchandising support includes advise on selection of products, development of product and performance specifications and test methods when necessary, as well as verification of customer complaints. Coordinates test results with the buyers, suppliers, store management, customers and regulatory agencies as appropriate.

Administers end-item inspection program either in-house, outsourced or combination of both. This includes end-item inspections at the distribution centers, and at the suppliers' facilities. Develops appropriate sampling plans, standard inspection procedures and acceptable quality levels.

Conducts supplier performance analysis through inspection and test data as well as customer complaint data.

Administers supplier quality system audits and certification through identification of suppliers requiring quality system audits, performing quality system audits and either assisting suppliers in quality related matters or certifying their quality systems. Conducts training seminars and briefings for supplier development.

Administers product safety program. Conducts investigations of product quality and safety complaints and product recalls when necessary. Coordinates with regulatory agencies and certifying authorities on product safety matters as appropriate.

Monitors suppliers for working conditions and compliance with local labor laws.

I-2 Job Descriptions

Examples of the job descriptions for the following positions are on the next few pages.

Vice President
Director, Testing Branch
Director, Inspection Branch
QA Specialist

Manager, Product Testing
Laboratory Technician

Supervisor, Gemological Testing & Inspection
Gemologist
In-plant Inspector
Supervisor, Inspection Section, Distribution Center
QA Inspector, Distribution Center

I-2-1 Job Description: Vice President

Title: Vice President, Quality Assurance XYZ Corporation

SUMMARY OF RESPONSIBILITIES

Plans, develops, establishes policies and procedures and directs the management and operation of quality assurance program including product safety.

DUTIES AND RESPONSIBILITIES

Plans, develops, establishes policies and procedures, and directs the management and operation of the quality assurance program to include end item inspection, product testing, supplier quality system audits, factory evaluation and monitoring of working conditions in supplier factories. Responsible for deciding the kind and extent of QA programs needed for accomplishing the objectives of the organization and striking optimum balance between product quality and the cost of achieving necessary level and control of quality. Assures that the XYZ corporation complies with applicable product safety regulations system wide. Directs system wide product recalls. Makes decisions and recommendations that are recognized as authoritative and have a far reaching impact on purchasing decisions, quality of products, and safety of XYZ corporation's customers. Develops promising QA associates to take leadership positions within QA career field in the XYZ corporation. Establishes and maintains contacts with industry counterparts to discuss information and issues and keep abreast of developments in quality profession. Demonstrates high degree of creativity, foresight, and mature judgment in planning, organizing, and guiding XYZ corporation's system wide QA activities. Provides overall leadership in any matter related to product quality, safety, and monitoring of working conditions in supplier factories.

QUALIFICATION REQUIREMENTS

Bachelor's degree in industrial engineering, business administration, merchandising or closely related fields is highly desirable. Specialized experience may be substituted for the education requirement at the rate of twelve months of experience for twelve months of study. Three years of progressively responsible experience in quality assurance field plus a minimum of three years specialized experience in assuring quality of consumer goods. Experience must have required the associate to develop, direct, and supervise a subordinate staff. Qualifying college-level education may be substituted for the required experience at the rate of twelve months of study for twelve months of experience. American Society for Quality's Certified Quality Auditor (CQA) certification and ISO 9000 auditor or lead auditor certification is highly desirable. Must possess and be able to apply knowledge of quality assurance/control, methods, principles, and practices, including statistical analysis and sampling; knowledge of statistical sampling plans and a variety of standard test methods such as ASTM, UL, AATCC, etc.; skill in developing, interpreting and applying product specifications, technical data, regulations, policy statements, and other guidelines; excellent oral/verbal and written communication skill. Must have vision correctable to 20/20.

I-2-2 Job Description: Director, Testing Branch

Title: Director, Testing Branch XYZ Corporation

SUMMARY OF RESPONSIBILITIES

Under minimum supervision of the Vice President, Quality Assurance (QA), plans and directs the technical activities of Quality Assurance Division. Approves statistical sampling plans, inspection techniques, test methods, and product acceptance standards. Provides technical training for, and evaluates, inspection and testing staff. Supervises assigned people.

DUTIES AND RESPONSIBILITIES

Independently plans, supervises, and coordinates all testing activities. Directs product testing program. Acts as XYZ Corporation's technical expert. Exercises a high degree of skill, broad experience, initiative, and mastery of QA concepts and principles in constantly adapting the testing program to ever changing industry, product and testing standards, criteria and techniques. Plans and directs implementation of a supplier certification program to insure compliance with XYZ Corporation's requirements. Independently designs, organizes, and carries out special studies and projects related to testing programs' administration resulting in new test methods, policies or organization changes, and in resolving critical problems. Insures compliance with established policies and procedures of the QA program. Maintains close coordination with suppliers' quality control and management representatives. Uses broad experience, diplomacy, and a high degree of skill to arbitrate disputes and to assist XYZ Corporation buyers during disputes or meetings with supplier representatives on QA test techniques, product rejections, or returns of defective merchandise. Provides recommendations to purchasing staff relative to disposition of defective merchandise. Completed work and assignments are seldom reviewed or questioned. May assume the duties of the Vice President, Quality Assurance (QA) during his/her absence.

QUALIFICATION REQUIREMENTS

Bachelor's degree in one of the engineering or science discipline. A Master's Degree in engineering, science, or business management is highly desirable. Specialized experience may be substituted for the education requirement at the rate of twelve months of experience for twelve months of study. Three years of progressively responsible experience in quality assurance field plus a minimum of three years specialized experience in assuring quality of consumer goods. Qualifying college-level education may be substituted for the required experience at the rate of twelve months of study for twelve months of experience. American Society for Quality's Certified Quality Auditor (CQA) certification and ISO 9000 auditor or lead auditor certification, or professional license in engineering is highly desirable. Must possess and be able to apply knowledge of quality assurance/control, methods, principles, and practices, including statistical analysis and sampling; knowledge of statistical sampling plans and a variety of standard test methods such as ASTM, UL, AATCC, etc.; skill in interpreting and applying product specifications, technical data, regulations, policy statements, and other guidelines; excellent oral/verbal and written communication skill. Must have an acceptable score on the Farnsworth-Munsell 100 Hue test and vision correctable to 20/20.

I-2-3 Job Description: Director, Inspection Branch

Title: Director, Inspection Branch XYZ Corporation

SUMMARY OF RESPONSIBILITIES

Under minimum supervision of the Vice President, Quality Assurance Division (QA), plans and directs the inspection operations worldwide. Approves statistical inspection techniques, and product acceptance standards. Provides technical training for, and evaluates, inspection staff. Supervises assigned people.

DUTIES AND RESPONSIBILITIES

Independently plans, supervises, and coordinates all inspection activities. Directs random sampling inspection at suppliers' plants and central inspection points. Evaluates supplier's control systems and production capabilities. Establishes inspection priorities and directs the scheduling of the quality assurance (QA) inspection of all inspectable merchandise procured and sold worldwide. Establishes and controls defect scoring and product acceptance standards for XYZ Corporation. Exercises a high degree of skill, broad experience, initiative, and mastery of QA concepts and principles in constantly adapting the inspection program to ever changing industry, product and inspection standards, criteria, and techniques.

Trains and evaluates inspection staff. Conducts a statistically based Comparability Check Evaluation Program to insure proper and accurate inspection and scoring by inspection staff; takes action to correct and prevent improper or poor inspections.

Visits QA field elements as necessary to train and evaluate QA staff to insure accurate and timely evaluation of, and reporting on, the acceptability of supplier process quality control and inspection systems and quality of merchandise procured and sold. Constantly reviews inspection workload and determines staffing requirements necessary to perform the inspection job in the most efficient and economical way. Independently designs, organizes, and carries out special studies and projects related to inspection program's administration resulting in new inspection methods, policies or organization changes, and in resolving critical problems. Insures compliance with established policies and procedures of the QA program.

Maintains close coordination with suppliers' quality control and management representatives. Uses broad experience, diplomacy, and a high degree of skill to arbitrate disputes and to assist XYZ Corporation buyers during disputes or meetings with supplier representatives on QA inspection techniques, product rejections, or returns of defective merchandise. Provides recommendations to buyers relative to disposition of defective merchandise. May assume the duties of the Vice President, Quality Assurance (QA) during his/her absence.

QUALIFICATION REQUIREMENTS

Bachelor's degree in business. Specialized experience may be substituted for the education requirement at the rate of twelve months of experience for twelve months of study. Three years of progressively responsible experience in quality assurance field plus a minimum of three years specialized experience in assuring quality of consumer goods. Qualifying college-level education may be substituted for the required experience at the rate of twelve months of study for twelve months of experience. American Society for Quality's Certified Quality Auditor (CQA) certification and ISO 9000 auditor or lead auditor certification, or professional license in engineering is highly desirable. Must possess and be able to apply knowledge of quality assurance/control, methods, principles, and practices, including statistical analysis and sampling; knowledge of statistical sampling plans and a variety of standard test methods such as ASTM, UL, AATCC, etc.; skill in interpreting and applying product specifications, technical data, regulations, policy statements, and other guidelines; excellent oral/verbal and written communication skill. Must have an acceptable score on the Farnsworth-Munsell 100 Hue test and vision correctable to 20/20.

I-2-4 Job Description: Quality Assurance Specialist

Title: Quality Assurance Specialist XYZ Corporation

SUMMARY OF RESPONSIBILITIES

Under minimum supervision of the Director, Testing Branch, Quality Assurance Division, provides technical support to the XYZ Corporation elements pertaining to the quality of merchandise.

DUTIES AND RESPONSIBILITIES

Evaluates quality of products by (a) performing visual inspection, (b) conducting research into product standards and specifications, (c) testing and analysis of products within the quality assurance laboratory or by commercial or government laboratories. Writes laboratory reports summarizing the test results and makes decision about acceptability of the product(s) evaluated. Issues product recalls as directed by the Director, Technical Branch, Quality Assurance Division or CPSC (Consumer Product Safety Commission). Prepares quality specifications for products to be purchased and sold by the XYZ Corporation. Reviews specifications and/or purchase descriptions for completeness, appropriateness, and accuracy, and established specific quality assurance provisions, as necessary. Develops acceptable quality standards. Evaluates supplier performance by reviewing inspection, test and other quality data. Recommends corrective action to buyers. Identifies the suppliers for audit visits for either quality improvement or for certification. Initiates audits and conducts audits in the capacity of a Lead Auditor or an Auditor. Visits supplier top management and presents a thorough analysis of findings and provides suggestions for quality improvement. Closely monitors quality performance of those suppliers visited under this program. Develops Standard Inspection Procedures (SIPs) and test methods for use by DC and in-plant inspectors, and/or the laboratory technicians. Completed work products are generally accepted as technically sound. Controversial decisions or findings are reviewed to determine if further action such as additional testing, visiting a supplier, or referring to higher authority, is needed. May assume the duties of the Director, Testing or Inspection Branch in his/her absence. Keeps abreast of quality assurance profession. Performs other duties as assigned.

QUALIFICATION REQUIREMENTS

Bachelor's degree in industrial engineering, business administration, merchandising or closely related fields is highly desirable. Specialized experience may be substituted for the education requirement at the rate of twelve months of experience for twelve months of study. Three years of progressively responsible experience in quality assurance field plus a minimum of three years specialized experience in assuring quality of consumer goods. Qualifying college-level education may be substituted for the required experience at the rate of twelve months of study for twelve months of experience. American Society for Quality's Certified Quality Auditor (CQA) certification and ISO 9000 auditor or lead auditor certification is highly desirable. Must possess and be able to apply knowledge of quality assurance/control, methods, principles, and practices, including statistical analysis and sampling; knowledge of a variety of standard test methods such as ASTM, UL, AATCC, etc.; skill in interpreting and applying product specifications, technical data, regulations, policy statements, and other guidelines; excellent oral/verbal and written communication skill. Must be PC proficient in programs such as Microsoft word, excel, access, outlook, and power point. Must be inquisitive and detail oriented. Must have an acceptable score on the Farnsworth-Munsell 100 Hue test and vision correctable to 20/20. Other requirements may be added as required by the supervisor.

Note: So far as educational requirement, it would make sense for a person to have an appropriate degree. For example, for the position of the soft line specialist, an individual should have a degree in clothing & textiles, fashion design, or textile technology. For the position of a non-electrical hard line specialist, an individual should have a degree in mechanical engineering. For the position of an electrical specialist, an individual should have a degree in electrical engineering.

I-2-5 Job Description: Manager, Product Testing

Title: Manager, Product Testing XYZ Corporation

SUMMARY OF RESPONSIBILITIES

Under minimum supervision of the Director, Testing Branch, Quality Assurance Division, plans, coordinates and administers the XYZ Corporation's testing program to monitor/improve quality of retail merchandise. Manages day-to-day functioning of QA laboratory and supervises assigned personnel and coordinates testing by the commercial and/or government laboratories. Provides QA and technical support to the QA staff, buyers, and XYZ Corporation management in matters related to product testing and analysis.

DUTIES AND RESPONSIBILITIES

Conducts pre-purchase and post-award tests and prepares test reports analyzing test results and defends them when necessary. Verifies customer/store complaints through product testing and analysis. Directs and trains laboratory technicians and plans test projects. Determines items to be sent to commercial or government laboratories for evaluation and interprets their findings. Develops specifications and test methods when necessary or as directed. Functions as a technical authority on testing and analysis of consumer products and represents XYZ Corporation while discussing quality related matters with suppliers. Technical accuracy of work is accepted, however, findings and recommendations are reviewed for compliance with XYZ Corporation's policies and procedures. Keeps abreast of developments/changes in consumer product test methods and regulatory requirements of the same. Maintains liaison with organizations such as CPSC (Consumer Product Safety Commission), UL (Underwriters Laboratories), ANSI (American National Standards Institute), etc. May assume the duties of either Director, Testing or Inspection Branch in his/her absence. Performs other duties as assigned.

QUALIFICATION REQUIREMENTS

A Bachelor's degree in industrial, mechanical, or electrical engineering, physics or chemistry, business administration or closely related field. A Master's degree in either engineering or science is highly desirable. A certification such as CQA (Certified Quality Auditor) from the American Society for Quality, is highly desirable. Three years' specialized experience in the consumer product testing & analysis is required. Must have working knowledge of a variety of standard test methods such as those of ASTM, AATCC, UL, etc. Must be able to analyze test results using various statistical techniques such as t-test, ANOVA, linear regression, etc. Must be able to interpret and apply product specifications and be able to develop those when necessary. Specialized experience may be substituted for the education requirement at the discretion of the Director, Testing Branch. Experience must have required the associate to develop, direct, and supervise a subordinate staff. Must be PC proficient in programs such as Microsoft word, excel, access, outlook, and power point, and have good writing and verbal skills. Must be inquisitive and detail oriented. Must have an acceptable score on the

Farnsworth-Munsell 100 Hue-Test, and vision correctable to 20/20. Other requirements may be added as required by the supervisor.

The following job description for the position of Manager, Product Testing is applicable where product testing is out sourced.

I-2-6 Job Description; Laboratory Technician

Title: Laboratory Technician XYZ Corporation

SUMMARY OF RESPONSIBILITIES

Under minimum supervision of the Manager, Product Testing, conducts product testing. Maintains and calibrates testing equipment, assists in preparing test reports, and performs sample receiving, shipping, and accountability functions.

DUTIES AND RESPONSIBILITIES

Independently plans, coordinates, schedules and completes testing assignments as directed by the Manager, Product Testing and/or Quality Assurance Specialists. Researches appropriate test methods, standards and federal safety regulations prior to testing. Summarizes test results for final review by the Manager, Product Testing, using various Microsoft Office programs. Maintains laboratory test report files. Maintains and calibrates testing equipment. Orders test supplies and/or equipment as appropriate. Assists in maintaining and updating library of test methods, laboratory techniques, and equipment. Performs miscellaneous job-related duties as assigned, such as handling sample accountability, yearly inventory, purchase of test samples, and organizing use tests. Performs other duties as assigned.

QUALIFICATION REQUIREMENTS

Completion of high school or the equivalent. Additional technical education, such as an Associate degree in a related science field, is highly desirable. Three years of progressively responsible general experience (administrative, professional, or technical). Must like working with hands (getting hands dirty). Must be inquisitive, detail oriented and organized. Must be PC proficient in Microsoft programs such as word, excel, access, and outlook, and have good written and verbal skills. Must have an acceptable score on the Farnsworth-Munsell 100-Hue

Test and vision correction to 20/20. Must be physically and mentally able to efficiently perform the essential functions of the position without hazard to themselves or others (e.g., must be able to lift and transport samples weighing up to 50 lbs. and not be allergic to pollutants and chemicals). Other requirements may be added as required by the supervisor.

I-2-7 Job Description: Supervisor, Gemological Testing and Inspection

Title: Supervisor, Gemological Testing & Inspection XYZ Corporation

SUMMARY OF RESPONSIBILITIES

Under minimum supervision of Director, Testing Branch, Quality Assurance, performs inspection and testing of jewelry, and supervises the operation of a gemological laboratory; the grading and inspection of diamonds, colored stones, pearl, and gold jewelry procured and sold throughout XYZ corporation. Provides quality assurance and technical support to XYZ corporation management and buyers regarding fine jewelry, and as required, analyzes customer complaints and recommends actions to be taken. Performs other related duties as assigned. Conducts fine jewelry supplier quality audits.

DUTIES AND RESPONSIBILITIES

Based on the review of the incoming shipments or as directed by the Director, Testing Branch, plans, conducts, and supervises conduct of end-item inspections of jewelry using XYZ Corporation's statistical sampling plans, reviews pass/fail decision about shipments and reviews the inspection results on a daily basis. Coordinates lot failures and causes with XYZ Corporation procurement and DC staff and QA personnel. Trains and supervises assigned personnel. Interviews and selects personnel when necessary for the positions within the Gem Lab. Prepares quality specifications for jewelry to be procured by XYZ Corporation. Reviews specifications and/or purchase descriptions for completeness, appropriateness, and accuracy, and established specific quality assurance provisions, as necessary. Develops acceptable quality standards. Evaluates supplier performance by reviewing inspection and other quality data. Recommends corrective action to the buyers. Identifies the suppliers for audit visits for either quality improvement or for certification. Initiates audits and conducts audits in the capacity of a Lead Auditor or an Auditor. Visits supplier top management and presents a thorough analysis of findings and provides suggestions for quality improvement. Closely monitors quality performance of those suppliers visited under this program. Develops Standard Inspection Procedures (SIPs) for use by the Gem Lab. Functions as a technical authority on quality assurance for fine jewelry and gemology. Completed work products are generally accepted as technically sound. Controversial decisions or findings are reviewed to determine if further action such as additional testing, visiting a supplier, or referring to higher authority, is needed. Work in process is seldom reviewed, however, informal discussions are held to keep the supervisor informed of the rate of progress, difficulties encountered, unusual developments, or particularly unusual or difficult problems. Keeps abreast of jewelry and quality assurance professions. Performs other duties as assigned.

QUALIFICATION REQUIREMENTS

A Bachelor's degree in Fine Arts with a major in jewelry design and manufacturing is highly desirable. Must have a graduate gemologist diploma from the Gemological Institute of America (GIA) or equivalent institution. American Society for Quality's Certified Quality Auditor (CQA) certification is highly desirable. Must possess skill in interpreting and applying product specifications, technical data, regulations, policy statements, and other guidelines. Must have excellent oral/verbal and written communication skill. Must be PC proficient in programs such as Microsoft word, excel, access, outlook, and power point. Three years specialized experience in the inspection of precious jewelry and appraisal of diamond and colored stone jewelry. Experience must have required the associate to develop, direct, and supervise a subordinate staff. Must have an acceptable score on the Farnswell-Munsell 100 Hue-Test, and vision correctable to 20/20. Must pass a color-blindness test such as the Dvorine Pseudo-Isochromatic Plates Test. Other requirements may be added as required by the supervisor.

I-2-8 Job Description: Gemologist

Title: Gemologist XYZ Corporation

SUMMARY OF RESPONSIBILITIES

Under minimum supervision of the Supervisor, gemological Testing & Inspection, performs inspection and testing of jewelry, grading and inspection of diamonds, colored stones, pearl, and gold jewelry procured and sold throughout

XYZ corporation. Provides quality assurance and technical support to XYZ corporation management and buyers regarding fine jewelry, and as required, analyzes customer complaints and recommends actions to be taken. Performs other related duties as assigned. Conducts fine jewelry supplier quality audits.

DUTIES AND RESPONSIBILITIES

Based on the review of the incoming shipments or as directed by the Supervisor, Gemological Testing & Inspection, plans and conducts end-item inspections of jewelry using XYZ Corporation's statistical sampling plans, makes pass/fail decision about shipments and reviews the inspection results on a daily basis. Coordinates lot failures and causes with XYZ Corporation procurement and DC staff and QA personnel. Prepares quality specifications for jewelry to be procured by XYZ Corporation. Reviews specifications and/or purchase descriptions for completeness, appropriateness, and accuracy, and established specific quality assurance provisions, as necessary. Develops acceptable quality standards. Evaluates supplier performance by reviewing inspection and other quality data. Recommends corrective action to the buyers. Identifies the suppliers for audit visits for either quality improvement or for certification. Completed work products are generally accepted as technically sound. Controversial decisions or findings are reviewed to determine if further action such as additional testing, visiting a supplier, or referring to higher authority, is needed. Work in process is seldom reviewed, however, informal discussions are held to keep the supervisor informed of the rate of progress, difficulties encountered, unusual developments, or particularly unusual or difficult problems. Keeps abreast of jewelry and quality assurance professions. May assume the position of the Supervisor, Gemological Testing & Inspection in his/her absence. Performs other duties as assigned.

QUALIFICATION REQUIREMENTS

A Bachelor's degree in Fine Arts with a major in jewelry design and manufacturing is highly desirable. Must have a graduate gemologist diploma from the Gemological Institute of America (GIA) or equivalent institution. Must possess skill in interpreting and applying product specifications, technical data, regulations, policy statements, and other guidelines. Must have excellent oral/verbal and written communication skill. Must be PC proficient in programs such as Microsoft word, excel, access, outlook, and power point. Three years specialized experience in the inspection of precious jewelry and appraisal of diamond and colored stone jewelry. Experience must have required the associate to develop, direct, and supervise a subordinate staff. Must have an acceptable score on the

Farnswell-Munsell 100 Hue-Test, and vision correctable to 20/20. Must pass a color-blindness test such as the Dvorine Pseudo-Isochromatic Plates Test. Other requirements may be added as required by the supervisor.

I-2-9 Job Description: In-plant Inspector

Title: In-plant Inspector XYZ Corporatio

SUMMARY OF RESPONSIBILITIES

Under minimum supervision of the Director, Inspection Branch, Quality Assurance Division, plans and carries out QA inspections at suppliers' facilities and assesses the adequacy of suppliers' inspection and/or quality systems. Informs suppliers of XYZ Corporation's quality requirements and verifies and/or evaluates supplier's quality system. Provides technical advice and assistance to XYZ Corporation elements concerning quality assurance matters. Acts as a representative for the buyer. May supervise lower graded QA inspectors and/or develop instructions and advise on the interpretation of special quality requirements.

DUTIES AND RESPONSIBILITIES

Having received weekly inspection schedule from the HQ-XYZ Corporation, plans and confirms inspection appointments and makes travel arrangements. Performs end item inspections using XYZ Corporation statistical sampling plans, makes pass/fail decision about the shipments and reports the results to XYZ Corporation on a daily basis. When necessary, takes samples from the shipment inspected and forwards them to XYZ Corporation for review and/or testing. Coordinates lot failures and causes with suppliers, XYZ Corporation procurement staff, and QA personnel. Acts as XYZ Corporation's liaison with supplier management, clarifies and interprets QA and other contractual requirements. Evaluates suppliers' inspection/quality assurance system(s) for adequacy and acceptability to XYZ Corporation. Performs pre-award surveys of prospective suppliers to review supplier facilities, production and process controls. Advises supplier management of unacceptable controls and areas needing improvement. Advises suppliers of characteristics needing inspection and testing and criteria for testing. Helps suppliers install an end-item inspection system and trains supplier personnel in statistical sampling. Inputs the daily results of the random sampling inspection into internet based QA inspection report and sends it to HQ, XYZ Corporation. Completed work products are generally accepted as sound.

Controversial decisions or findings are reviewed to determine if further action such as additional inspection and/or testing, or referring to higher authority is necessary. Trains DC (distribution center) inspectors to be in-plant inspectors. Keeps abreast of quality assurance profession. Performs other duties as assigned.

QUALIFICATION REQUIREMENTS

A Bachelors degree in industrial engineering, business administration or other related field is highly desired. Must have excellent oral/verbal and written communication skill. Must be PC proficient in programs such as Microsoft Word, Excel, Access, and Outlook. Three years experience in controlling the quality of merchandise, equipment or supplies is required. Specialized experience may be substituted for the education requirement at the rate of twelve months of experience for twelve months of study. American Society of Quality's (ASQ) Certified Quality Auditor (CQA) certification is highly desirable. Must have an acceptable score on the Farnsworth-Munsell 100-Hue Test and vision correct able to 20/20. Must be physically and mentally able to efficiently perform the essential functions of the position without hazard to themselves or others (i.e., must be able to lift and transport samples weighing up to 50 lbs. and not be allergic to pollutants and chemicals). Must be able to travel to the job by air or automobile. Other requirements may be added as required by the supervisor.

I-2-10 Job Description: Supervisor, Inspection Section, Distribution Center

Title: Supervisor, Inspection Section, Distribution Center XYZ Corporation

SUMMARY OF RESPONSIBILITIES

Under minimum supervision of the Director, Inspection Branch, Quality Assurance Division, manages QA inspections at an XYZ Corporation distribution center.

DUTIES AND RESPONSIBILITIES

Based on the review of the incoming shipments or as directed by the Director, Inspection Branch, plans and supervises conduct of end item inspections using XYZ Corporation statistical sampling plans, and reviews pass/fail decision about the shipments and reviews the inspection results on a daily basis. Coordinates lot failures and causes with XYZ Corporation's procurement and DC staff and QA personnel. Trains and supervises assigned personnel. Interviews and selects personnel when necessary for the DC inspector's position. Work in process is seldom reviewed, however, informal discussions are held to keep the supervisor informed of the rate of progress, difficulties encountered, unusual developments, or particularly unusual or difficult problems. Performs other duties as assigned.

QUALIFICATION REQUIREMENTS

Completion of high school or equivalent. Three years experience in controlling quality of merchandise, equipment or supplies. Must have good verbal and written communication skills. Must be PC proficient in programs such as Microsoft Word, Excel, Access, and Outlook. Other requirements may be added as required by the supervisor. Must have an acceptable score on the Farnsworth-Munsell 100-Hue Test and vision correct able to 20/20. Must be physically and mentally able to efficiently perform the essential functions of the position without hazard to themselves or others (i.e., must be able to lift and transport samples weighing up to 50 lbs. and not be allergic to pollutants and chemicals). Other requirements may be added as required by the supervisor.

I-2-11 Job Description: QA Inspector, Distribution Center

Title: QA Inspector, Distribution Center XYZ Corporation

SUMMARY OF RESPONSIBILITIES

Under direction of the Supervisor, Inspection Section, plans and carries out QA inspections at XYZ Corporation's distribution center.

DUTIES AND RESPONSIBILITIES

Based on the review of the incoming shipments or as directed by the Supervisor, the inspector plans and performs end item inspections using XYZ Corporation's statistical sampling plans, makes pass/fail decision about the shipments and reports the results on a daily basis. Practically all work is closely checked, routine assignments are spot checked for compliance with instructions. Assignment involving new or unfamiliar methods, procedures or products are reviewed closely for adherence to instructions and accuracy and reasonableness of the results produced. Advice and assistance in resolving unusual or unanticipated problems as they occur are available. Performs other duties as assigned.

QUALIFICATION REQUIREMENTS

Completion of high school or equivalent. Must have excellent oral/verbal and written communication skill. Must be PC proficient in programs such as Microsoft word, excel, access, and outlook. Must have an acceptable score on the Farnsworth-Munsell 100-Hue Test and vision correct able to 20/20. Must be physically and mentally able to efficiently perform the essential functions of the position without hazard to themselves or others (i.e., must be able to lift and transport samples weighing up to 50 lbs. and not be allergic to pollutants and chemicals). Other requirements may be added as required by the supervisor.

I-3 Training of QA Staff

The profession of quality assurance in retail is such a niche specialty that it is very difficult to find people with relevant experience and background to fill openings. Therefore, there needs to be some training plans for various jobs within this field. Here are several examples of such training plans. Please bear in mind that these are just examples. Every retailer must tailor it's own training plans for QA staff.

I-3-1 Training Plan for DC Inspector

Week 1

Day 1—Orientation of the job site and related facilities.
Overview of QA function, terminology and inspection methods.
Review of job description and standards of conduct.
Study XYZ Corporation's quality policy and practices.

Day 2-5—Study Standard Operating Procedure for the DC.
Study applicable Standard Inspection Procedures.
Participate in inspection of several products.
Learn to fill out inspection report.

Week 2—Participate in inspections and procedural review.
Study XYZ Corporation's sampling plans.
Study XYZ Corporation's Terms and Conditions related to quality.
Learn severity of defects and non-conformances.
Learn written description of defects and non-confromances.

Week 3—Learn to use different sampling plans
Learn to report workload activity.
Learn to report lot failures and/or non-conformances

Week 4—Continue to work under close supervision by inspecting a variety of products using different sampling plans.

Week 5—As the trainee's progress permits, reduce degree of direct technical supervision.
Receive additional technical/product training in areas needing improvement.

Week 6—Inspect lots independently with trainer's close verification of findings and comparability check.

Weeks 7 & 8—Perform inspections independently with continually reduced supervision, but with frequent verification and comparability checks. Reduce frequency of comparability checks according to the trainee's progress. Continue on the job training and review all previous training.

Total Training Time—minimum expected is 4 weeks and maximum expected is 23 weeks.

Criterion for Determining Completion of Training—The training will be considered complete when the trainee has repeatedly exhibited that he/she can independently and efficiently complete inspections on all types of products going through the DC where this inspector is working, to the satisfaction of the trainer(s).

I-3-2 Training Plan for In-plant Inspector

Prerequisite: Successful completion of DC inspector training and at least 6 months experience as a DC inspector.

Week 1—Learn about the XYZ Corporation, i.e., sales volume, location of DCs, location of stores, etc.
Learn to brief suppliers about XYZ Corporation and the in-plant inspection process.

Learn to review inspection results with the supplier.
Learn to make travel arrangements and appointments with suppliers.
Learn XYZ Corporation's travel expense reimbursement policy and to fill out travel expense voucher and who and when to submit it.

Week 2—Accompany an experienced in-plant inspector. Assist him/her and observe how he/she makes new supplier presentations and reviews inspection results with the suppliers.

Week 3—Repeat the above with another in-plant inspector.

Week 4—Begin to conduct in-plant inspections independently under observation of the supervisor or an experienced in-plant inspector.

Weeks 5 & 6—Repeat the above.

Total training time—Two to six weeks.

Criterion for Determining Completion of Training—The training will be considered complete when the trainee has repeatedly exhibited that he/she can independently and efficiently conduct in-plant inspections to the satisfaction of the trainer(s).

I-3-3 Training Plan for QA Specialist

Week 1

Day 1—Orientation of the job site and related facilities.
Introduction to QA staff and buyers.
Overview of QA function.
Review of job description and standards of conduct.
Study XYZ Corporation's quality policy and practices.

Day 2-5—Study Standard Operating Procedure for the Testing Branch.
Study applicable Standard Inspection Procedures.
Participate in testing of several products.
Learn to write reports.

Week 2—Learn applicable test methods.
Study XYZ Corporation's sampling plans.
Study XYZ Corporation's Terms and Conditions related to quality.
Learn severity of defects and non-conformances.
Learn written description of defects and non-conformances.

Week 3—Continue to write test reports and continue to learn one or more of the same things done during the first two weeks

Week 4 and 5—Continue to work under close supervision on a variety of products.
Learn how to respond to store or complaints about quality of merchandise.
Learn how to conduct product recalls.

Week 7 through 15—As the trainee's progress permits, reduce degree of direct technical supervision. Receive additional technical/product training in areas needing improvement.

Total Training Time—minimum expected is 15 weeks and maximum expected is 52 weeks.

Criterion for Determining Completion of Training—The training will be considered complete when the trainee has repeatedly exhibited that he/she can independently and efficiently perform various duties of a QA specialist.

NOTE: One large retailer in the U. S. which predominantly sells soft line products has made arrangements with a textile company and a garment manufacturer in the U. S. where QA inspectors and specialists from this retailer spend one week each learning how fabrics and garments are made and get a very good overview of various manufacturing processes. Similar arrangements can be made for training QA personnel in other industries.

Appendix II

Standard Operating Procedures (SOPs)

II-1 Standard Operating Procedure for In-plant Inspectors to Conduct In-plant Inspections

The following standard operating procedure is addressed to the in-plant inspectors.

1. Each in-plant inspector will receive his/her inspection schedule on every Thursday afternoon for the following week.
2. Confirm all of your assignments with the respective suppliers before the close of the day on Friday. If you cannot confirm all inspections on Friday, confirm at least, Monday's and Tuesday's inspections. Tell the suppliers your expected time of arrival and the day.
3. As you are confirming inspections with various suppliers, if you can not keep the schedule you were given, inform the in-plant inspection scheduler immediately.
4. Having confirmed your inspections, make travel arrangements.
5. If for any reason you can not keep your appointment, let the supplier know as much in advance as you can as to when can they expect you. Also, let the scheduler know of the change in your plans.
6. Upon arrival at a supplier's facility, brief the supplier if this is the first time the supplier has received an in-plant inspector from XYZ Corporation. Evaluate your work load after you arrive at the supplier's facility. If you feel you can finish the inspection earlier than planned, call the scheduler. The

scheduler will review the schedule for the area you are in to see if any additional inspections are available or if another inspector in your vicinity can use your help. If you feel that you will need more time for this inspection, then call the scheduler. The scheduler will let your next appointment know your estimated time of arrival there.

7. Conduct your inspections in a professional manner. After completion of your inspection, review the results of your inspection with the supplier. Explain assessment of any charges if your inspection results in failure(s). Should a lot fail an inspection and if the supplier disagrees with you about the defects, offer supplier to take defective samples and ship them to XYZ Corporation headquarters for review by QA and the buyer. Ask the supplier if there is additional merchandise ready for inspection besides the purchase orders you were sent to inspect. If so, call the scheduler and make necessary adjustment in your schedule and inform your next appointment.
8. Fill out your inspection results on-line the same evening of your inspection and mail it to QA-HQ.
9. Your personal appearance is important. You must present yourself as a quality assurance professional. High style or casual dress is not in good taste. Remember, you are representing XYZ Corporation to the suppliers you will visit. It is very important that you strictly adhere to the dress code of the XYZ Corporation.
10. Never ask a supplier for personal favors of any kind. Keep your relations with suppliers strictly business.

II-2 Standard Operating Procedure for New Supplier Briefing

The following standard operating procedure is addressed to the in-plant inspectors.

This briefing should be given by the in-plant inspector to the suppliers visited for the first time for in-plant inspection. The purpose behind this briefing is to familiarize the supplier with our business (what we do, our mission and vision), and in-plant inspection procedures.

After introducing yourself, give an overview of our company, the XYZ Corporation. Then explain.

1. The purpose of your visit. The purpose of your visit is to inspect shipment(s) destined for our company in order to make sure that we receive only quality merchandise and what we ordered, i.e., style, sizes, color, quantity, packaging, etc. and that it is labeled and marked right.
2. Our sampling plans, AQLs, and random sampling. Provide a copy of our guidelines to quality. Also, offer to give a copy of our sampling plans and a copy of the standard inspection procedures (SIPs) applicable to the products we buy from them.
3. Our definition of a defect, i.e., anything that affects appearance, serviceability, and/or salability of an item.
4. When the shipment is accepted, supplier should ship as instructed on the purchase order.
5. When the shipment fails, the supplier should hold the shipment until a decision is obtained from the buyer. Explain buyer's options, outlined in the "Quality Terms & Conditions."
6. Procedure for the supplier to follow when the supplier disagrees with your findings and failed shipment or lot failure.
7. Cost assessments in case the shipment(s) fail QA inspection or shipment(s) not ready for QA inspection. Refer supplier to "Quality Terms & Conditions" if necessary.
8. XYZ Corporation's policy on gifts and gratuities. XYZ Corporation's policy prohibits its employees from accepting any gift or gratuity from any person or firm doing, or seeking to do, business with XYZ Corporation. The term "gratuity" includes meal, entertainment, favor (such as special or direct purchase of any item, product, or service through other than a regular business outlet, whether or not payment is rendered). Acceptance of a gift or gratuity subjects XYZ Corporation's employee(s) to disciplinary action to include separation, civil suit for recovery of the value of the gift or gratuity, and criminal prosecution. Any attempt by the supplier to bribe the in-plant inspector will be reported to the QA management of the XYZ Corporation.
9. Ask for a clean, well-lighted area for you to work in and necessary equipment, for example, table, electrical outlets, etc.
10. Ask for assistance, such as, bringing samples to your work area after you have identified samples you need, unpacking and packing samples as you finish inspecting each sample, to speed up your inspection.
11. Tell the supplier that his personnel are welcome to watch you perform inspection and ask questions and learn.

II-3 Standard Inspection Procedure for DC (Distribution Center) Inspections

1. The QA supervisor at each XYZ Corporation DC will review shipment arrivals at the DC every day and decide which shipments will be inspected and farm out inspection work to inspectors each morning.
2. Once a shipment is selected for shipment, put a "HOLD MERCHANDISE SELECTED FOR QA INSPECTION" sign on the shipment and leave it there until inspection is finished.
3. Inspect the shipment and record your results.
4. If the shipment passes inspection, remove the "HOLD" sign and release the shipment to the DC for receiving.
5. If the shipment fails, the DC QA supervisor will review/verify the failure and place a "BUYER DISPOSITION PENDING—HOLD" sign on the shipment.
6. The DC supervisor will relay the buyer's decision concerning the failed shipment to the DC personnel so appropriate action can be taken.
7. Screening (100% inspection of a failed lot) will performed only as directed by the DC supervisor.
8. Fill out the on-line inspection report before the end of the day and mail it to the QA-HQ.

Some retailers require a copy of inspection and or test results from the suppliers with every shipment. This is an assurance to the retailer that the shipment was inspected and or tested. It also gives the retailer an option of skipping receiving inspection and or testing of those shipments accompanied by acceptable inspection and or test results or perform its own inspection and or testing to verify the effectiveness of the supplier's inspection and or testing. The inspection or test report accompanying a shipment is called a "certificate of compliance" or CoC.

II-4 Standard Inspection Procedure for Filling Out an Inspection Report

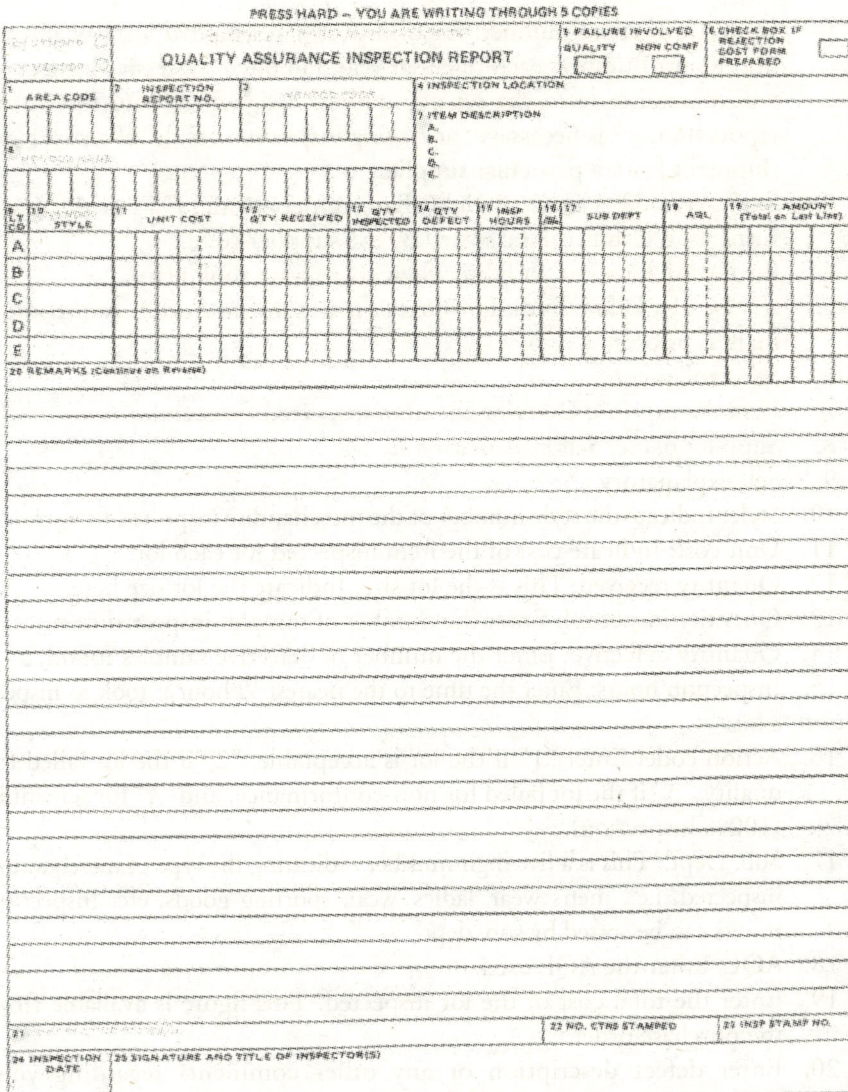

PRESS HARD – YOU ARE WRITING THROUGH 5 COPIES

QUALITY ASSURANCE INSPECTION REPORT

5 FAILURE INVOLVED: QUALITY / NON COMP

6 CHECK BOX IF REJECTION COST FORM PREPARED

1 AREA CODE

2 INSPECTION REPORT NO.

3

4 INSPECTION LOCATION

7 ITEM DESCRIPTION
A.
B.
C.
D.
E.

8

9 LT CD | 10 STYLE | 11 UNIT COST | 12 QTY RECEIVED | 13 QTY INSPECTED | 14 QTY DEFECT | 15 INSP HOURS | 16 | 17 SUB DEPT | 18 ASL | 19 AMOUNT (Total on Last Line)

A
B
C
D
E

20 REMARKS (Continue on Reverse)

21

22 NO. CTNS STAMPED

23 INSP STAMP NO.

24 INSPECTION DATE

25 SIGNATURE AND TITLE OF INSPECTOR(S)

Form 2-1 Inspection Report

Instructions for filling out an inspection report by block number areas follows:

1. Area code: This is a unique five digit alpha code indicating a geographical area. Inspection results can be sorted by area code for a given period of time.
2. Inspection report number: Each inspector is assigned a set of inspection report numbers each calendar year. Fill out a successive inspection report number from the set of numbers assigned to you. Inspection report number is necessary for tracing inspection results of a particular shipment from a particular supplier.
3. Supplier code: This is an eight digit numeric code. Fill out this code. Inspection results can be sorted by the supplier code.
4. Inspection location: Indicate where inspection took place.
5. In case of a failure, indicate whether it was due to quality, non-conformance, or both.
6. Self explanatory.
7. Item description: Describe the item inspected for each lot.
8. Supplier name: Self explanatory.
9. Self explanatory.
10. Style: Indicate the style number of the merchandise inspected for each lot.
11. Unit cost: Indicate cost of the item inspected for each lot.
12. Quantity received: This is the lot size. Indicate the lot size here.
13. Quantity inspected: Enter the number of samples inspected here.
14. Quantity defective: Enter the number of defective samples found.
15. Inspection hours: Enter the time to the nearest ½ hour it took to inspect a lot.
16. Action code: Enter "1" if the lot is acceptable, "2" if the lot failed for quality, "3" if the lot failed for non-conformance, and "4" for screening (100% inspection).
17. Sub. Dept.: This is a five digit number indicating the type of merchandise inspected, i.e., men's wear, ladies' wear, sporting goods, etc. Inspection results can be sorted by sub. dept.
18. AQL; Enter the AQL used.
19. Enter the total cost of the lot inspected. This figure is available from the purchase order.
20. Enter defect description or any other comments regarding your inspection.
21. Enter the buyer name.
22. Enter the number of cartons or samples stamped*.
23. Enter your stamp number.
24. Enter the date this inspection took place.

25. Sign and indicate your title.

* If the lot inspected is accepted, each carton from which inspection sample(s) came is stamped after inspection is finished and the carton is repacked and sealed. These cartons are stamped in such a way that it would be evident if they were tempered with for any reason. In case of hanging merchandise, each sample inspected is stamped on the hangtag.

Information for blocks 3,7,8,10, 11, 12, 17, and 21 can be obtained from a copy of the purchase order.

II-5 Standard Operating Procedure for Conducting Comparability Checks

A comparability check is a statistical test to see if the results of two separate inspections of the same lot are statistically the same. The reasons for comparability checks are to:

- Make sure that the defect scoring criteria are consistent (more or less similar) from inspector to inspector.
- Determine if further training of an inspector is needed.

1. Comparability checks must be conducted at least once a month for each inspector. Also, comparability checks should be done using a variety of merchandise. This will allow for evaluating scoring criteria used by an inspector for a variety of merchandise.
2. The sample size for comparability check must be at least 20.
3. Comparability checks will be done by the immediate supervisors, however, a second or third line supervisor may also perform comparability checks on any one under his/her supervision at any time. QA specialists may also perform comparability checks on behalf of or in coordination with the respective supervisors.
4. Comparability checks will be done at the same place where the original inspection took place. By conducting comparability checks on in-plant inspectors at various DCs some variable are introduced which could have a significant bearing on the outcome of the comparability checks. For example, lighting at a supplier's facility may not be the same as in our DCs; inspection area at a supplier's facility may be cramped, dusty, hot or cold, noisy, etc. while at our DCs there is plenty of room, they are clean and neat, reasonably quiet, and climate controlled. Also, conducting comparability checks on in-plant inspectors at our DCs does

not afford an opportunity to have face to face discussions of the results of the comparability checks.

5. When you decide to do a comparability check on an inspector, do not tell that inspector of your intention till he/she finishes the inspection of a lot. Then, tell the inspector that you are going to conduct a comparability check on him/her, and take your random samples from the same lot that the inspector inspected. After you have finished your inspection, calculate the Z value using the following formula and discuss the results of comparability check with the inspector you just checked.
6. In the case of non-comparability, the supervisor's inspection results will count for making accept/fail decision for the lot involved.
7. Supervisors must record the results of all comparability checks and actions taken and keep it in the respective inspector's file.
8. Comparability check should be viewed as a matter of routine, as a training tool and supervisors must do everything possible to minimize undue stress associated with comparability checks. Comparability checks will not be used, in any circumstances, as a tool to punish or "get after" an inspector. If it is established that a supervisor is using comparability checks to harass an inspector, that supervisor will face severe disciplinary actions.

$$Z = \frac{P_1 - P_2}{\sqrt{[N_1P_1(1-P_1) + N_2P_2(1-P_2)]/N_1N_2}}$$

where

P_1 = % defective found by the supervisor or one inspector
P_2 = % defective found by the inspector or the person being checked
N_1 = sample size of the supervisor or one inspector
N_2 = sample size of the inspector or another person being checked

Comparability Check Formula

If Z = more than 1.96 (regardless of whether it is + or -), there is 95 % probability that comparability between the inspection results of two persons does not exist, or the results are not comparable. If Z = 1.96 or less (regardless of whether it is + or -), there is 95 % probability that comparability between the inspection results of two persons does exist, or the results are comparable.

Appendix III

Standard Inspection Procedures (SIPs)

Here are two examples of standard inspection procedures, produced by the courtesy of the Army & Air Force Exchange Service (AAFES), a large retail and service organization.

A standard inspection procedure outlines step by step how to inspect an item and also lists product deficiencies which are considered defects. Standard inspection procedures help every inspector perform inspection in the same manner as it is important to have consistency and uniformity in inspection between individuals. Standard inspection procedures are good training tools and provide a point of reference in case of a dispute of question about how an item was inspected. Standard inspection procedures should be developed for as many items as possible and they should be periodically reviewed and revised if necessary. SIPs should be readily available to all inspectors regardless whether inspection is done in-house of outsourced. It is also beneficial to make SIPs available to your suppliers so they know how you inspect merchandise and what is acceptable and not acceptable.

Also, listed, by the courtesy of the Army & Air Force Exchange Service (AAFES), are defect characteristic guides for a variety of merchandise.

III-1 Standard Inspection Procedure for Shirts and Blouses

Inspecting SHIRTS and BLOUSES

Step 1

Unfold and place on a flat surface with sleeves out to the side. Inspect for material defects, stains, shaded parts, stitching tension, aligned chest pockets or anything affecting the appear-ance, saleability, or serviceability.

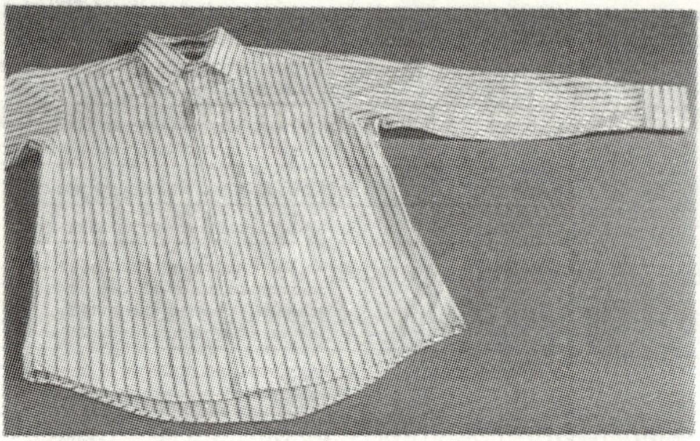

Step 2

Inspect the front of the collar and undercollar on both sides of the garment for tight or loose thread tension, open seams and puckering.

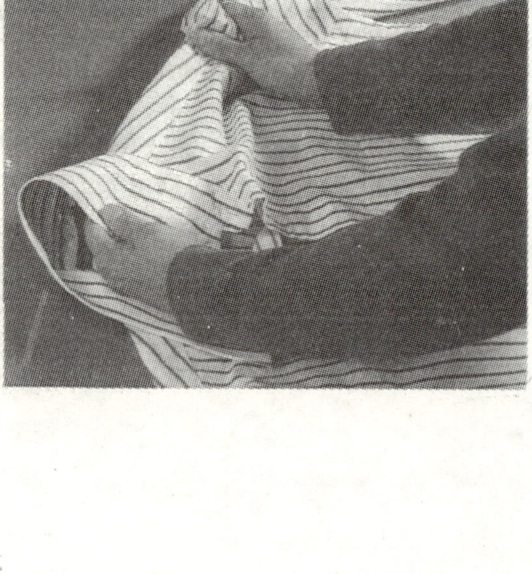

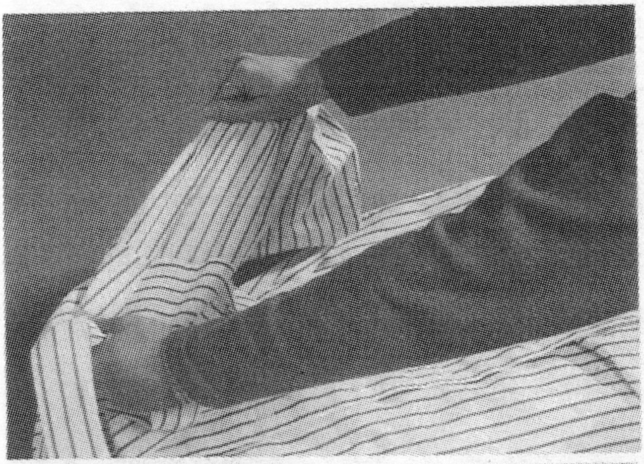

Step 3

Examine the chest pocket, pocket flap, pocket flap button and buttonhole (if applicable), shoulder yoke seam and armhole seam for tension, openings, raw edges, needle chews and skipped stitches.

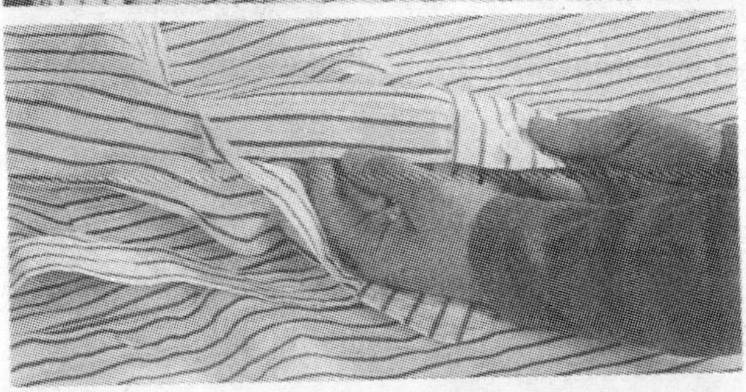

Step 4

Inspect the sleeve placket seams, and examine for secure buttons and finished buttonholes on the cuff.

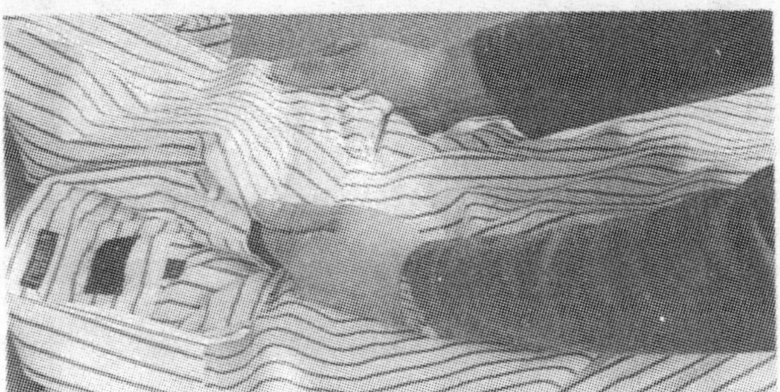

Step 5

Raise the sleeve and inspect the sleeve joining seams as well as the side joining seam for excessive puckering and openings. Repeat on the opposite side.

Step 6 Examine the buttons on the collar points (if applicable) and down the placket. Check for appearance, proper attachment and alignment with the buttonholes, and for complete stitching and loose threads.

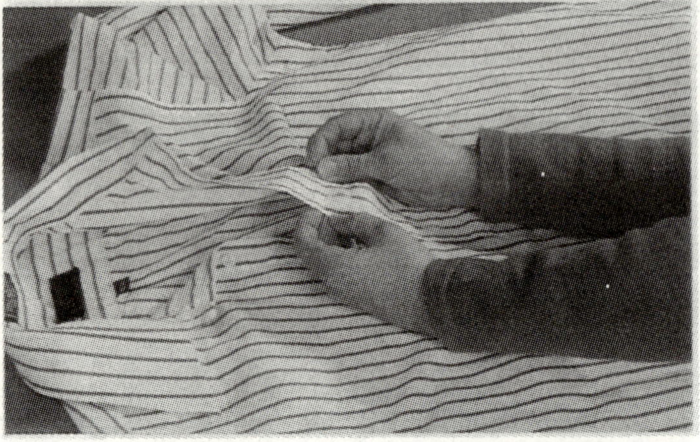

Step 7 Examine the hem for open seams, raw edges, and excess puckering.

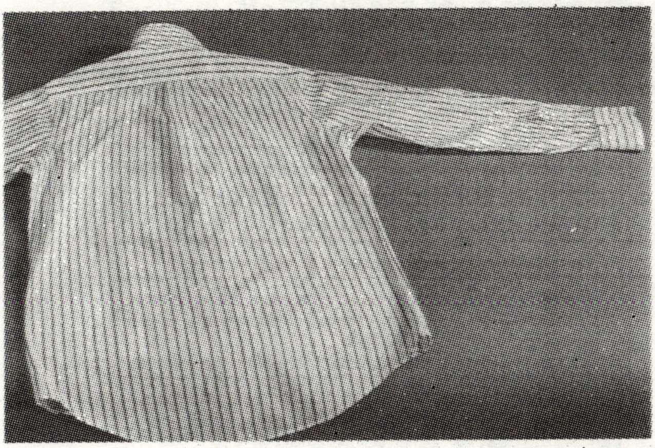

Step 8

Reverse the shirt. Inspect the back collar and under-collar for smoothness and stitching defects. Look for any obvious defects.

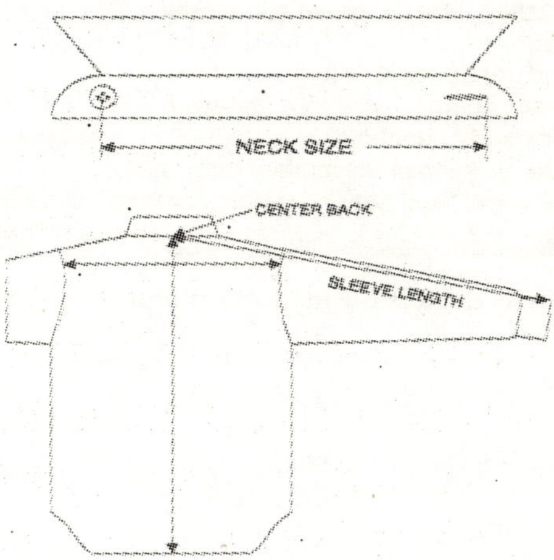

To measure neck size: lay neck band flat; measure from center of button to the far end of buttonhole, as shown.

To measure sleeve length: locate center back as shown. With a sleeve extended, measure in a straight line from center back to top end of sleeve including cuff. For French cuffs, fold back cuff and match buttonholes; measure sleeve to folded edge of cuff.

DEFECT CHARACTERISTICS GUIDE FOR SHIRTS AND BLOUSES

Characteristic	Defect
General	✦ Any condition adversely affecting appearance, serviceability, or saleability.
Marking*	✦ Incorrect, illegible or missing sewn-in care instructions, fiber content, country of origin, size, or brand labels.
Packaging*	✦ Not as specified on the purchase order.
Cleanliness	✦ Any uncleanliness, spots, stains, or objectional odor.
Material	✦ Any fabric defects such as holes, cuts, tears, slubs, jerk-ins, knots, smashes, pulls, runs, dropped stitches, floats, tight or loose picks or ends, and so forth. ✦ Colorfastness: excessive migration of dye from the material.
Workmanship	✦ Any specified component or operation improper or omitted ✦ Seams: twisted, puckered, pleated or open. ✦ Misstitched, broken thread and stitching not caught in other seams. ✦ Thread not compatible to base fabric. ✦ Material caught in unrelated operation. ✦ Buttons and buttonholes mismatched or misaligned. ✦ Frayed, raveling or incomplete buttonholes. ✦ Pockets and flaps not completely covering the pocket. ✦ Any part mismatched, mismated, misaligned or faded.

* Do not score these deficiencies as defects on inspection report. List them in the REMARKS section.

III-2 Standard Inspection Procedure for Men's and Boys' Shoes

Inspecting MEN'S and BOYS' SHOES

Step 1

Remove the shoes from the shoe box. Compare the shoe size marked on the shoes to the size marked on the box. Place shoes on a flat surface and examine for proper mating; that is, one left shoe and one right shoe of the same size.

Step 2

Examine the top, back and sides for balance, alignment of parts, even color, excess cement, open seams, missing components, leather or material defects, and uneven, tight or loose stitching. Check for the proper placement (or seating) and attachment of the heel, if applicable to the style.

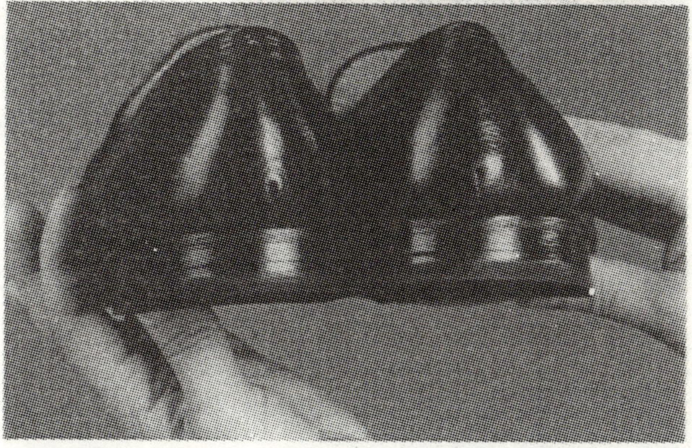

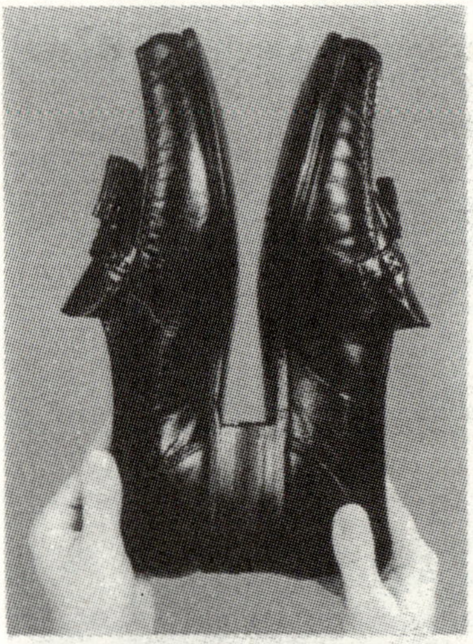

Step 3

Place the heels together, and examine for matching sole and heel width and length.

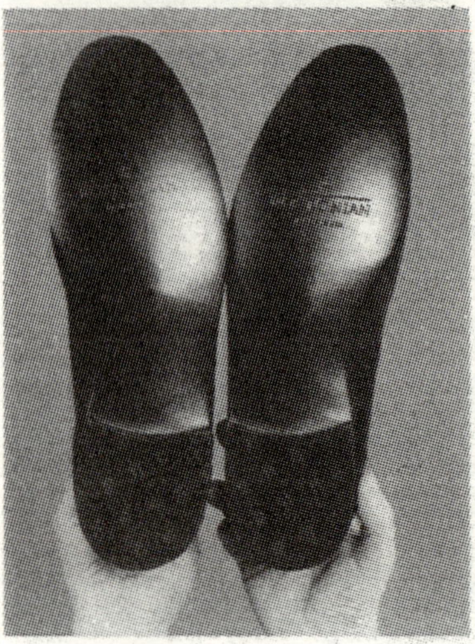

Step 4

Roll shoes outward to check for a smooth and evenly trimmed outsole, proper sole and upper attachment, even stitching (if applicable), and any obvious defects in the leather or material used in the outsole and heel.

Step 5

Examine each shoe separately for workmanship defects, inside and out. When examining the inside of the shoe, look first. Then put your hand inside to feel for any lasting tacks or staples that were not removed. Also, feel for any lumps caused by excess glue, large holes caused by the removal of tacks for staples, short sock linings, rough seams, wrinkled or puckered lining or padding that might cause serious irritation to the wearer.

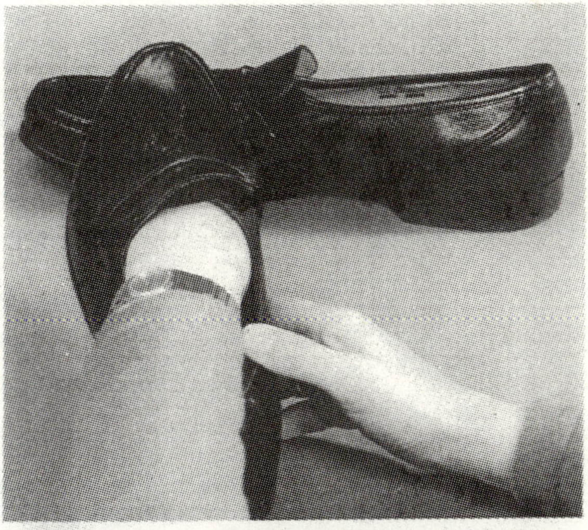

DEFECT CHARACTERISTICS GUIDE FOR SHOES

Characteristic	Defect
General	✦ Any condition adversely affecting appearance, serviceability, or saleability. ✦ Any component part not made of the material specified.
Pairing	✦ Improperly mated, sized or a noticeable variation in color or appearance.
Cleanliness	✦ Spots, stains or foreign matter seriously affected appearance.
Color or Finish	✦ Not specified color, color not uniform, finish streaky, chipped, or flaky.
Construction and Workmanship	✦ Missing components. ✦ Any cut, tear, hole, rip or abrasion seriously affecting serviceability or appearance. ✦ Separation or poor joining of outsole to upper.
Seams and Stitching	✦ Tight tension resulting in puckering or cutting of sole material. ✦ Loose tension resulting in a loosely secured seam. ✦ Needle holes or needle chews.
Counters	✦ Rolled or curled, affecting the comfort of the wearer.
Insole	✦ Any protruding point of a lasting tack/nail or staple remaining in the insole, forward of heel breast line, found in the sample causes rejection of the lot represented. ✦ Any protruding point of a lasting tack/nail or staple in the heel seat area.
Lining	✦ Quarter or vamp lining wrinkles, excessively full or loose, seriously affecting serviceability.

III-3 Defect Characteristics Guides

Here are defect characteristic guides for a variety of items to help you decide what is a defect and what is not. Similar guides should be developed for a full range of merchandise that is inspected by your QA inspectors.

III-3-1 Defect Characteristics Guide for Attaché Cases and Suitcases

Characteristic	Defect
General	Any condition adversely affecting appearance, serviceability, or salability
Marking[1]	Incorrect, illegible, or missing country of origin, size, or brand labels
Cleanliness	Spots, stains, excessive glue on lining or exterior, objectionable odor
Material	Not as specified[1]
	Molded Construction—Streaks, discoloration, pits, scratches, dents, cracks and holes
	Soft side construction—Any fabric defect
	Soft side (Vinyl or imitation leather)—Blistering, cracking, peeling, scuffs, scratches, streaks and discoloration
Hardware	Zippers do not operate smoothly Snap fasteners loose or inoperative or smashed Feet, handles, hinges not properly aligned, damaged or missing Latches or locks not operating properly Keys missing Sharp edges or burrs Rust spots
Workmanship	Any outside parts not properly shaded Seams twisted or puckered Open seams Rivets loose, improperly crimped (smashed) or sharp Lining loose, wrinkled or torn Lining not well glued

Packaging[1]	Not as specified on the purchase order

1- These are non-conformances and not quality defects.

III-3-2 Defect Characteristics Guide for Bicycles

Characteristic	Defect
General	Any condition adversely affecting appearance, serviceability, or salability Manufacturer's warranty, operating instructions missing or not appropriate for the model[1]
Marking[1]	Missing country of origin, brand name
Reflectors	Damaged, missing, incorrect
Frame	Sharp burrs or points, brazing or weld defects, fractures, misalignment, missing hardware, finish seriously scratched, chipped, rough, peeling or runs
Front Fork	Bent, misaligned, too tight
Fender	Misalignment, dented, damaged not anchored properly or securely, finish peeling or chipped, missing hardware
Wheels	Out of alignment, broken, bent, excessively loose or missing spokes
Drive Chain/Sprockets	Drive chain broken or binding, improper size, or cannot be adjusted for uniform tension Sprocket(s) too tight, too loose, wrapped, or obviously out-of-round Too noisy indicating bearing problem
Tires	Material cuts, splits, not mounted on rim properly Incorrect size or type Completely flat and verified as defective

Chain Guard	Missing, damaged, misalignment, inadequate, improperly installed and/or making contact with any part of drive sprocket
Seat (Saddle)	Cuts, tears, splits, open seam/heat seal, broken stitching Incomplete molding, cracks, broken Adjustment clamps broken, inoperable, or missing Missing hardware Design will not prevent seat post penetration through seat upon impact
Pedals	Threads stripped off or lest pedal not reverse threaded Incorrect, cracked, broken, bent
Shifting Mechanism Caliper Brakes	Inoperative, missing, broken, incorrect

1- These are non-conformances and not quality defects.

III-3-3 Defect Characteristics Guide for Cassette Tape Recorders

Characteristic	Defect
General	Any condition adversely affecting appearance, serviceability, or salability Missing third party safety certification such as UL, ETL, CSA, etc. Manufacturer's warranty, operating instructions missing or not appropriate for the model[1]
Marking[1]	Incorrect, illegible, or missing country of origin, or brand labels or markings
Construction	Style, type not as specified[1] Cassette type not as specified[1] Cassette tape cartridge not as specified[1] Switches, knobs, indicators damaged, inoperative Unit case cracked, scratched

	Decals or printing where appropriate, missing, illegible Microphone broken, inoperative
Wire	Cut, spliced, insulation dry and brittle, not completely insulated (exposed)
Plugs	Loose, missing, cracked or deformed Prongs loose, bent or damaged
Electrical	Failure to turn on or unit does not heat Rated more or less than desired voltage, such as 120 volts, 220 volts No electrical rating on the unit[1]
Performance	Unit inoperative, no power Controls do not function Cassette cartridge holder will not seat cartridge Unable to adjust controls (volume, tone) Forward, rewind. Play mechanism inoperative or erratic Batteries, when specified, inoperative, leaking, damaged
Packaging[1]	Not as specified on the purchase order

1- These are non-conformances and not quality defects.

III-3-4 Defect Characteristics Guide for Christmas Lights

Characteristic	Defect
General	Any condition adversely affecting appearance, serviceability, or salability Missing third party safety certification such as UL, ETL, CSA, etc. Any color, size, design (indoor, outdoor or combination indoor/outdoor style) not as specified[1]
Marking[1]	Incorrect, illegible, or missing country of origin, size, or brand labels or markings

Construction	
Wire	Cut, spliced, insulation dry and brittle, not completely insulated (exposed)
Lamp Holders	Cracked, deformed, missing lamp holder or missing tree clips, if specified
Lamps	Broken, missing, or incorrect size Not in assorted colors, if specified Failure to illuminate or twinkle(where twinkle lights are specified)
Plugs	Loose, missing, cracked or deformed Prongs loose, bent or damaged
Electrical	Failure to illuminate Rated more or less than desired voltage, such as 120 volts, 220 volts
Packaging[1]	Not as specified on the purchase order

1- These are non-conformances and not quality defects.

III-3-5 Defect Characteristics Guide for any Clothing Item

Characteristic	Defect
General	Any condition adversely affecting appearance, serviceability, or salability
Marking[1]	Incorrect, illegible, or missing sewn-in care instructions, fiber content, country of origin, size, or brand labels
Cleanliness	Spots, stains, or objectionable odor
Material	Any fabric defect such as holes, tears, cuts, slubs, jerk-ins, knots,

	Smashes, pulls, runs, dropped stitches, floats, tight or loose* picks or ends
Workmanship	Any specified component or operation improper or omitted Seams: twisted, puckered, pleated or open Miss-stitched, broken thread and stitching not caught in other seams Thread not compatible to base fabric Material caught in unrelated operation Buttons and buttonholes mismatched or misaligned Poorly constructed buttonholes Frayed, raveling or incomplete buttonholes Pockets and flaps not completely covering the pocket Lapels and lapel notches mismatched or malformed Lining hanging below shell Zipper not operating smoothly Any part mismatched, misaligned, shaded or faded
Packaging[1]	Not as specified on the purchase order

1- These are non-conformances and not quality defects.

III-3-6 Defect Characteristics Guide for Hair Curling Irons and Hair Dryers

Characteristic	Defect
General	Any condition adversely affecting appearance, serviceability, or salability Missing third party safety certification such as UL, ETL, CSA, etc. Manufacturer's warranty, operating instructions missing or not appropriate for the model[1]
Marking[1]	Incorrect, illegible, or missing country of origin, or brand labels or markings
Construction	Style, type not as specified[1]

	Broken, cracked or missing components Unit case or housing cracked, dented, scratched or other condition adversely affecting appearance Poor adhesion of decals, where applicable Inscribed printing illegible or omitted Decorative embossing poorly defined, unsymmetrical Improper fit or mating of component attachments Poor finish, plated metal surface flaking
Wire	Cut, spliced, insulation dry and brittle, not completely insulated (exposed)
Plugs	Loose, missing, cracked or deformed Prongs loose, bent or damaged
Electrical	Failure to turn on or unit does not heat Rated more or less than desired voltage, such as 120 volts, 220 volts No electrical rating on the unit[1]
Performance	Unit inoperative Unit does not produce steam Unit leaks Cool tip is too hot to touch Controls do not function No discernible change in speeds or exhaust temperature Excessive noise or motor binds Mechanical operation improper Throws sparks, fumes, smokes, overheats or produces hazardous symptoms LED indicators inoperative such as power key One or more operation modes inoperative, unable to program
Packaging[1]	Not as specified on the purchase order

1- These are non-conformances and not quality defects.

III-3-7 Defect Characteristics Guide for Electric Appliances

Characteristic	Defect
General	Any condition adversely affecting appearance, serviceability, or salability Missing third party safety certification such as UL, ETL, CSA, etc. Manufacturer's warranty, operating instructions missing or not appropriate for the model[1]
Marking[1]	Incorrect, illegible, or missing country of origin, or brand labels or markings
Construction	Style, type not as specified[1] Broken, cracked or missing components Unit case or housing cracked, dented, scratched or other condition adversely affecting appearance Poor adhesion of decals, where applicable Inscribed printing illegible or omitted Decorative embossing poorly defined, unsymmetrical Glassware, where applicable, cracked, chipped, broken, crazed Batteries, when specified, leaking, damaged, inoperative Knobs, indicators, switches broken, missing, inoperative Poor welds Improper fit or mating of component attachments Poor finish, plated metal surface flaking
Wire	Cut, spliced, insulation dry and brittle, not completely insulated (exposed)
Plugs	Loose, missing, cracked or deformed Prongs loose, bent or damaged
Electrical	Failure to turn on Rated more or less than desired voltage, such as 120 volts, 220 volts No electrical rating on the unit[1]

Performance	Unit inoperative Functional controls jam, stick or otherwise inoperative Unit leaks Cutting blades bind No discernible change in speeds at different settings Excessive noise, vibrations, intermittent or unstable operation Throws sparks, fumes, smokes, overheats or produces hazardous symptoms LED indicators inoperative such as power key One or more operation modes inoperative, unable to program Safety interlock does not prevent unit from operating
Packaging[1]	Not as specified on the purchase order

1- These are non-conformances and not quality defects.

III-3-8 Defect Characteristics Guide for Electric Blankets

Characteristic	Defect
General	Any condition adversely affecting appearance, serviceability, or salability Missing third party safety certification such as UL, ETL, CSA, etc. Manufacturer's warranty, operating instructions missing or not appropriate for the model[1]
Marking[1]	Incorrect, illegible, or missing country of origin, or brand labels or markings
Cleanliness	Spots, stains or objectionable odor
Material	Any defects, holes, slubs, teats, smashed, thick or thin picks and ends Not colorfast to dry rubbing, shaded top to bottom or side to side

Construction	Style, type not as specified[1]
Workmanship	Twisted, puckering, excessive pleating on edges and binding Unsightly mends Raw edges Stitch margins irregular Dimensions less than specified
Wire	Cut, spliced, insulation dry and brittle, not completely insulated (exposed)
Plugs	Loose, missing, cracked or deformed Prongs loose, bent or damaged
Electrical	Failure to turn on or unit does not heat Rated more or less than desired voltage, such as 120 volts, 220 volts No electrical rating on the unit[1]
Performance	Unit inoperative, no power Controls do not function Night light inoperative Blanket won't heat Only one side heats
Packaging[1]	Not as specified on the purchase order

1- These are non-conformances and not quality defects.

III-3-9 Defect Characteristics Guide for Electric Irons

Characteristic	Defect
General	Any condition adversely affecting appearance, serviceability, or salability Missing third party safety certification such as UL, ETL, CSA, etc. Manufacturer's warranty, operating instructions missing or not appropriate for the model[1]

Marking[1]	Incorrect, illegible, or missing country of origin, or brand labels or markings
Construction	Style, type not as specified[1] Broken, cracked or missing components Unit case or housing cracked, dented, scratched or other condition adversely affecting appearance Poor adhesion of decals, where applicable Inscribed printing illegible or omitted Decorative embossing poorly defined, unsymmetrical Improper fit or mating of component attachments Poor finish, plated metal surface flaking Sole plate pitted, seriously scratched, steam ports clogged or soiled with foreign matter Damaged spray nozzle
Wire	Cut, spliced, insulation dry and brittle, not completely insulated (exposed)
Plugs	Loose, missing, cracked or deformed Prongs loose, bent or damaged
Electrical	Failure to turn on or unit does not heat Rated more or less than desired voltage, such as 120 volts, 220 volts No electrical rating on the unit[1]
Performance	Unit inoperative Unit does not produce steam Unit leaks Cool tip is too hot to touch Controls do not function No discernible change in temperature at different settings Steam spits or sputters in normal ironing position Soiled or rust water emitted with steam or steam spray Throws sparks, fumes, smokes, overheats or produces hazardous symptoms LED indicators inoperative such as power key

Packaging[1]	Not as specified on the purchase order

1- These are non-conformances and not quality defects.

III-3-10 Defect Characteristics Guide for Electric Toasters

Characteristic	Defect
General	Any condition adversely affecting appearance, serviceability, or salability Missing third party safety certification such as UL, ETL, CSA, etc. Manufacturer's warranty, operating instructions missing or not appropriate for the model[1]
Marking[1]	Incorrect, illegible, or missing country of origin, or brand labels or markings
Construction	Style, type not as specified[1] Unit case or housing cracked, dented, scratched or other condition adversely affecting appearance Poor adhesion of decals, where applicable Inscribed printing illegible or omitted Decorative embossing poorly defined, unsymmetrical Improper fit or mating of component attachments Poor finish, plated metal surface flaking Controls, knobs, switches broken, missing, bent
Wire	Cut, spliced, insulation dry and brittle, not completely insulated (exposed)
Plugs	Loose, missing, cracked or deformed Prongs loose, bent or damaged
Electrical	Failure to turn on or unit does not heat Rated more or less than desired voltage, such as 120 volts, 220 volts No electrical rating on the unit[1]

Performance	Unit inoperative, no power Controls do not function Toaster won't heat Toaster rack won't pop up Toaster rack won't stay down
Packaging[1]	Not as specified on the purchase order

1- These are non-conformances and not quality defects.

III-3-11 Defect Characteristics Guide for Portable Electric Typewriters

Characteristic	Defect
General	Any condition adversely affecting appearance, serviceability, or salability Missing third party safety certification such as UL, ETL, CSA, etc. Manufacturer's warranty, operating instructions missing or not appropriate for the model[1]
Marking[1]	Incorrect, illegible, or missing country of origin, or brand labels or markings
Construction	Style, type not as specified[1] Broken, cracked or missing components Display window cracked, broken, fogged
Wire	Cut, spliced, insulation dry and brittle, not completely insulated (exposed)
Plugs	Loose, missing, cracked or deformed Prongs loose, bent or damaged
Electrical	Failure to turn on Rated more or less than desired voltage, such as 120 volts, 220 volts

Performance	Margin sets fail to lock or cannot be released Type of cassette not as specified[1] Typed characters illegible, poorly defined Touch control ineffective, if included Print unit inoperative Improper paper feeding Operating components such as shift or tab keys, margin set, back space carriage return, space adjustment are inoperative or loose Missing ribbon Feed fails Ribbon tape binds, fails to advance Keyboard lettering illegible, smeared, ill defined, poor impressions Keys skip, stick, jam or do not repeat Tab skips past set stops, can not set or clear tab stops LED indicators inoperative such as power key, shift key Characters do not appear in display Cassette tape missing, torn, inappropriately installed One or more operation modes inoperative, unable to program
Packaging[1]	Not as specified on the purchase order

1- These are non-conformances and not quality defects.

III-3-12 Defect Characteristics Guide for Flatware

Characteristic	Defect
General	Any condition adversely affecting appearance, serviceability, or salability
Marking[1]	Missing country of origin, brand name
Construction	Style, type, size not as specified[1] Jagged, sharp edges (burrs), mars, nicks, dents, pits, scratches Metallic irregularity, scorch (hue of metal distinctly differs in any area)

	Very sharp needle tine is potentially hazardous defect Surface abrasions (scratches), unsightly soil or poor luster Imbedded foreign matter and imprinted brand name illegible or poorly defined Poor symmetry of decorative design Peeling or flaking of plating Non-uniformity of length and width of like items Tarnish spots on plated items Partial or complete absence of plating
Packaging[1]	Not as specified on the purchase order

1- These are non-conformances and not quality defects.

III-3-13 Defect Characteristics Guide for Furniture, Knockdown

Characteristic	Defect
General	Any condition adversely affecting appearance, serviceability, or salability
Marking[1]	Missing country of origin, brand name
Cleanliness	Spots, stains or objectionable odor
Construction	Style, type, size not as specified[1] Not assembled to the extent stated Braces or other parts missing, incorrect or not as stated Broken or cracked drill holes Exposed staples or nails Sharp edges or any potential skin pinching, laceration, or cutting condition Open seams, cuts, tears Insufficient metal weld Paint runs, chips Wood cracked, splintered, gouged, smashed Rust, metal finish peeling or flaking

Packaging[1]	Not as specified on the purchase order

1- These are non-conformances and not quality defects.

III-3-14 Defect Characteristics Guide for Furniture, Outdoor

Characteristic	Defect
General	Any condition adversely affecting appearance, serviceability, or salability
Marking[1]	Missing country of origin, brand name
Cleanliness	Spots, stains or objectionable odor
Construction	Style, type, size not as specified[1] Open seams, unsightly splices, patches, needle cuts Cracked drill holes Loose, missing or not properly attached hardware Heat seal inadequacies or burns Serious exposed raw edges
Material	Cuts, holes, tears, cracked through, serious splinters, abrasion marks Not colorfast
Packaging[1]	Not as specified on the purchase order

1- These are non-conformances and not quality defects.

III-3-15 Defect Characteristics Guide for Gloves

Characteristic	Defect
General	Any condition adversely affecting appearance, serviceability, or salability

Marking[1]	Incorrect, illegible, or missing, fiber content, country of origin, size, or brand labels or markings
Cleanliness	Spots, stains, or objectionable odor
Dimensions	Mismatched pair
Finish	Not well shaped, non-uniform in overall appearance Excessive migration of dye from the material
Material (All Types)	Holes or tears
Leather	Pipey leather, excessive wrinkles or cuts and scratches
Woven	Slubs, knots, or broken picks
Knit	Runs or dropped stitches
Workmanship	Broken stitches, runoffs, open seams, skipped stitches resulting in an open seam or skipped for two or more consecutive stitches Exposed raw edge affecting serviceability Seams: twisted, puckered, or pleated Stitching too loose or too tight
Components (buttons, Snaps, fasteners)	Any damaged, omitted or not secured component, seriously affecting the appearance or serviceability
Packaging[1]	Not as specified on the purchase order

1- These are non-conformances and not quality defects.

III-3-16 Defect Characteristics Guide for Grills, Gas and Charcoal

Characteristic	Defect
General	Any condition adversely affecting appearance, serviceability, or salability

	Missing third party safety certification such as UL, ETL, CSA, etc. Manufacturer's warranty, operating instructions missing or not appropriate for the model[1]
Marking[1]	Missing country of origin, brand name
Wheels	Cracked or broken, finish peeling, wrapped or out of round, missing, incorrect size, bent
Legs	Paint chipped or peeling, bent, missing, not adjustable or folded as required, incorrect size
Leg Brace and Shelf	Plating peeling, missing, bent, tines loose from weld, tines missing or broken
Steel Base and Post	Finish peeling, missing, cracked or broken
Ash Catcher and Drawer	Missing, sharp burrs or edges, bent or dented affecting fir, incorrect size
Rotisserie	Any component part missing, inoperable, forks or handle broken Wire: cut, spliced, insulation dry and brittle, not completely insulated (exposed) Plugs: Loose, missing, cracked or deformed, prongs loose, bent or damaged
Electrical	Failure to turn on Rated more or less than desired voltage, such as 120 volts, 220 volts No electrical rating on the unit[1]
Hoods and Bottoms	Finish chipped or peeling, deep gouges or scratches, sharp burrs or edges, vents missing or inoperable, side shelf broken, cracks or missing, heat indicator cracked or missing, crank-up vertical assembly missing or inoperable, handle or hardware broken or missing

Cooking and Charcoal Grates	Plating peeling, missing, cooking grate tine broken or loose from weld, two adjacent welds broken or cracked on charcoal grid, hangers for fire basket missing, step grid missing or damaged, volcanic rock missing or damaged
LP Gas Controls, Burners, Supports and Component Parts	Missing, bent affecting use or assembly, broken or cracked, inoperable, holes on gas burners clogged, missing hardware
Hardware	Missing or not usable
Packaging[1]	Not as specified on the purchase order

1- These are non-conformances and not quality defects.

III-3-17 Defect Characteristics Guide for Microwave Ovens

Characteristic	Defect
General	Any condition adversely affecting appearance, serviceability, or salability Missing third party safety certification such as UL, ETL, CSA, etc. Manufacturer's warranty, operating instructions missing or not appropriate for the model[1]
Marking[1]	Incorrect, illegible, or missing country of origin, or brand labels or markings
Construction	Style, type not as specified[1] Broken, cracked or missing components Unit case or housing cracked, dented, scratched or other condition adversely affecting appearance Poor adhesion of decals, where applicable Inscribed printing illegible or omitted

	Decorative embossing poorly defined, unsymmetrical Improper fit or mating of component attachments Poor finish, plated metal surface flaking Controls, knobs, switches broken, missing, bent Oven tray broken, cracked
Wire	Cut, spliced, insulation dry and brittle, not completely insulated (exposed)
Plugs	Loose, missing, cracked or deformed Prongs loose, bent or damaged
Electrical	Failure to turn on or unit does not heat Rated more or less than desired voltage, such as 120 volts, 220 volts No electrical rating on the unit[1]
Performance	Unit inoperative, no power Controls do not function Timer inoperative Oven fails to heat Tray fails to rotate, if applicable Indicator lights inoperative LED indicators inoperative Oven lamp fails to light, missing, or broken
Packaging[1]	Not as specified on the purchase order

1- These are non-conformances and not quality defects.

III-3-18 Defect Characteristics Guide for Radios

Characteristic	Defect
General	Any condition adversely affecting appearance, serviceability, or salability Missing third party safety certification such as UL, ETL, CSA, etc. Manufacturer's warranty, operating instructions missing or not appropriate for the model[1]

Marking[1]	Incorrect, illegible, or missing country of origin, or brand labels or markings
Construction	Style, type not as specified[1] Scratches, dents, chips, dial not readable Switches, knobs, indicators damaged, inoperative Unit case cracked, scratched Decals or printing where appropriate, missing, illegible
Wire	Cut, spliced, insulation dry and brittle, not completely insulated (exposed)
Plugs	Loose, missing, cracked or deformed Prongs loose, bent or damaged
Electrical	Failure to turn on or unit does not heat Rated more or less than desired voltage, such as 120 volts, 220 volts No electrical rating on the unit[1]
Performance	Unit inoperative, no power Controls do not function Scratchy noises in speakers Unable to adjust controls (volume, tone) Earphone/headphone inoperative, intermittent Meters or light indicators inoperative Batteries, when specified, inoperative, leaking, damaged
Packaging[1]	Not as specified on the purchase order

1- These are non-conformances and not quality defects.

III-3-19 Defect Characteristics Guide for Socks

Characteristic	Defect
General	Any condition adversely affecting appearance, serviceability, or salability

Marking[1]	Incorrect, illegible, or missing, fiber content, country of origin, size, or brand labels or markings
Cleanliness	Spots, stains, or objectionable odor
Material	Any fabric defect such as holes, runs, dropped stitches, thin areas or mends Excessive migration of dye from the material Slubby yarn more than three times the normal yarn diameter Noticeable foreign matter caught in knitting affecting appearance, serviceability or salability Burn or scorch in fabric
Finish	Objectionable odor Not well shaped (not uniform in overall appearance)
Construction	Insufficient stretch (too tight) or loosely knit (slack) Loose ends on outside affecting appearance
Toe Closure	Poor toe closure resulting in lumpy area that could cause discomfort or insufficient closure resulting in a hole
Top	Welt is cut, frayed, raveled, uneven, or not clearly defined Over edge stitching, where applicable, is incorrect, omitted or broken Insufficient stretch
Packaging[1]	Not as specified on the purchase order

1- These are non-conformances and not quality defects.

III-3-20 Defect Characteristics Guide for Sunglasses

Characteristic	Defect
General	Any condition adversely affecting appearance, serviceability, or salability
Marking[1]	Missing country of origin, brand name

Construction

Frames	Jagged, sharp edges (burrs), mars, nicks, dents, pits, scratches, cracks, broken or soiled Poor symmetry of lens holder of frame Ear piece length not uniform Loose or missing screws or rivets on hinges Rust spots or corrosion
Lens	Bubbles, scratches, cracks or broken Objects are distorted through lens Not securely mounted to frame
Packaging[1]	Not as specified on the purchase order

1- These are non-conformances and not quality defects.

III-3-21 Defect Characteristics Guide for Jewelry

Master Sample—A master sample is an item that is inspected against buyer specifications for diamond/ stone quality, color, size, shape, gold weight, stone setting and basic manufacturing quality, and found acceptable. A master sample of an item is kept in QA as the minimum acceptable reference standard for future shipments of that item, thus the term master sample.

Below Clarity of the Master Sample- The master sample sets the minimum acceptable standard for the item. If the diamond/stone clarity does not meet or exceed the quality of the master sample, the item is considered defective and not acceptable.

NOTE: The GIA Diamond Clarity Scale is used to determine the diamond quality.

Below Color of Master Sample—The master sample sets the minimum acceptable standard per item. If the diamond/stone does not meet or exceed the color of the master sample, the item is considered defective not acceptable.

NOTE: The color of diamonds is determined by comparing the stone to a certified GIA Diamond Color Master Sample Set and the use of a Diamond Colorimeter.

Below Weight—Each jewelry item has a contracted karat weight for the metal to assure consistency of the item no matter what karatage. (10kt, 14kt, 18kt, etc.). Any item weighing below required weight is considered defective and not acceptable.

Bent Post—Usually this is used in reference to earring posts, although it can be used for other items of jewelry that make use of posts (pegs) to attach gemstones to the mounting. Bent posts are usually the result of extremely thin posts being used which are not durable and can not withstand normal wear.

Bent Prongs—The prong is the narrow metal support, usually used in groups of four, six, and eight, to hold a gemstone in the mounting. If the prongs are not uniform around the outside of the gemstone, then they are considered bent which causes a durability problem and weakens the security of the setting. This can be a result of poor setting or from impact during a different manufacturing phase.

Broken Links—This refers to a break in a chain or bracelet which is usually the result of poor crystallization or insufficient solder.

Broken Prongs—The prong is broken, usually at the seat or lower, and can be attributed to either poor crystallization or over-cut prongs.

Burnt Facets—This is surface clouding of gemstones, usually diamonds, which is caused by excessive heat generated during the polishing process.

Cavity on Crown—Cavity refers to any opening or indentation on the surface of a polished gemstone. A cavity shall be called when the location is on the crown and is easily visible at 10X magnification or seen with the unaided eye.

Chipped Diamonds/Stones—A chip is a shallow break on a gemstone, which is potentially a durability problem to the future integrity of the stone.

Clasp Won't Hold—Clasps are any device meant to join and hold two parts of a necklace, bracelet, or anklet. If the clasp does not close and hold securely, it does not perform the function it was designed for and is considered a defect.

Cracked Mountings—The mounting is considered the metal part of the piece of jewelry. It can be a ring, bracelet, necklace, pin, etc. The mounting has cracks due to the manufacturing of the item, whether cast or fabricated. These cracks can be actual splits in the metal structure or a series of fine porosity having the appearance of a split in the metal. This affects the durability and life expectancy of an item since the damage is a result of damage to the metal's crystal structure or the bonding of the different alloys together leaving the metal weak and possibly resulting in further damage.

Cracked Prongs—An actual split in the prong, which results in a durability problem. The problem can be a result of improper setting, either over-cutting of a prong, as a result of excessive force in bending the prong resulting in stress damage or fine cracks, or from the metal casting, which could be a result of poor crystallization.

Crown Angles Below 30 Degrees or Above 38 Degrees—This is an acceptable range for crown angles instead of the ideal crown angle of 34 1/2 %.

NOTE: Crown angles along with the table size determine the amount of dispersion a finished diamond displays.

Dangerous Knot—A knot is defined as an included crystal, which reaches the surface of the diamond.

Dangerous Feather—A feather is defined as any break that reaches the surface of the stone/diamond. A dangerous feather is one that could affect the clarity of the stone by extending further causing other durability problems.

Defective Clasp—This pertains to any problem with the clasp other than that the clasp will not hold shut. Examples would be: Clasp will not open; clasp tongue does not fit properly into the box, insufficient solder connecting the clasp to the jewelry, etc.

Diamonds Out of Round—Symmetry plays an important factor in the grading of a gemstone. Any round or brilliant cut diamond that does not have a truly circular girdle outline is considered out of round.

Excessive Glue—Epoxy glues are sometimes used to assist in the setting and securing of a gemstone or pearl into a mounting. The glue should be restricted to the immediate area of the stone or pearl that comes into contact with the mounting. Glue visible on metal or the gemstone or pearl face-up is unacceptable.

Excessive Metal Flashing—Any metal that is not inherent to the design of a piece is considered as excess metal and is usually the result of faulty or insufficient clean-up prior to or after casting. Examples of this would be: little spheres or nodules attached to the mounting caused by poor vulcanization resulting in the attachment of air bubbles to the wax mold prior to burn out or excessive metal flashing caused by wax mold deterioration/ leakage and improper wax clean-up prior to investing the wax mold.

Excessive Tall Prongs—The prongs should never exceed 75% of the height of the stone/diamond and not cover more than 50% of the crown angle. Excessive prongs are those prongs, which are higher than the surface of the stone/diamond face-up. The main problems are that the prongs no longer protect the stone/diamond but actually are a detriment since they catch and snag tending to bend easier and often times resulting in loss of diamond/stone.

Extremely Thick Girdle—An extremely thick girdle is very distracting under 10X magnification as well as to the unaided eye. The extra thickness simply adds unnecessary weight to the finished stone/diamond and can cause setting problems and security issues.

File Marks/Tool Marks—These terms are interchangeable, the first being a bit more specific as to the cause of the defect. These refer to any markings on the surface of the metal, which were not intended per the design, e.g., scratches, nicks, gouges, etc.

Flimsy Earrings Backs—Earring backs must be sufficient for NORMAL use. Earring backs that are too small to hold in your fingers or too thin to bend while trying to place onto the post are not acceptable for normal use.

Glue Failure—Pearls are usually attached to a post on a mounting by applying epoxy cement/glue inside the drill hole of the pearl and attaching to the post. This epoxy cement/glue is formulated by mixing equal amounts of resin and catalyst. Often times the glue loses its bond, whether improperly mixed or having come into contact with a destructive agent, which is noted as glue failure.

Incomplete Casting—This refers to any void, crack, or opening in a finished metal mounting usually a result of the casting process.

Insufficient Prong Coverage/Insufficient Setting—Prongs are used to secure the stone/diamond into the mounting. When improperly set, the stone/ diamond is in danger of coming loose from the mounting and possibly resulting in the loss. When this occurs, we refer to the problem as insufficient prong coverage.

Insufficient Soldier—The area that has been soldered has gaps in the solder flow weakening the solder area/ joint.

Knife Edge Girdle—Defined simply as extremely thin girdle; such a girdle is highly susceptible to future damage. This condition presents a possible and very probable durability problem to the future integrity of the diamond.

Large Extra Facet—An extra facet is defined as any facet in excess of those normally required to complete the faceting pattern of the given cutting style. If there is a large extra facet that detracts from the face-up appearance, at 10X magnification or with the unaided eye, and the symmetry of the diamonds cut, it shall be rejected. If the extra facet is not easily visible face-up or is contained to the girdle area, it could be acceptable.

Large Natural—The definition of a natural is a portion off the original surface or skin, or a rough diamond which is sometimes left on a fashioned stone, usually on the girdle, to indicate the maximum yield has been obtained. As with a large extra facet, an extremely large natural detracts from the face-up appearance as well as the symmetry of the diamond.

Laser Drill Holes—Holes in a diamond's surface produced by a laser. This is an enhancement process used to improve the appearance of a diamond, which contains dark inclusions.

Loose Stones/Diamonds—Merchandise that has been received with insufficient setting of the gemstones resulting in the stones/diamonds moving or spinning in the setting. The stones/diamonds are not secured properly allowing the stones/diamonds to spin causing the prongs to wear quicker than normal and increasing the possibility of loosening the stones/diamonds in the mounting.

Marred Special Finish/Poor Special Finish—Marred defined means to injure or damage so as to make imperfect, less attractive, etc. A special finish is any form of metal treatment that is applied to a mounting other than a polished surface, e.g., matte or sandblasted finish, satin finish directional or non-directional, butler finish, etc.

Mismatched Color—When a piece of jewelry has more than one stone/diamond in the mounting, it should matched in color. This means that all similar colored stones or diamonds in any one item of jewelry should face-up approximately the same color. An example of this would be a diamond cocktail ring with five stones: all diamonds should be approximately the same color. It would not be acceptable for a diamond to be "H" color and the other four diamonds to be an "L" color. The transition in color is too obvious.

Missing Prongs—Stone mountings consist of heads usually with four or six prongs for each stone to be set. If the item has four prongs, then all four prongs should be intact and securing the stone. If one or more prongs are missing, it becomes a durability problem, which is unacceptable.

Nicks On Stones/Diamonds—These are obvious eye-visible abrasions or small chips that detract from the appearance and/or beauty of the stone/diamond. An example would be a huge unpolished or abraded white area on the crown of a polished and faceted deep red ruby.

Nicks On Mounting—Any small cuts, indentations or chips on the surface of a mounting.

Over Cut Prongs -All prongs have seats cut into the prongs to enable stone/diamond placement. The standard for cutting of a seat is the removal of one-third to one-half the prong thickness. The removal of more prong metal than this weakens the prong's durability and the security of the stone/diamond.

Poor Crystallization—This is the result porosity has on the composition of the metal structure during casting. The causes are numerous and can have unlimited combinations from the deviation of routine casting procedures.

> There are two different types of porosity: surface porosity and internal porosity.
>
> Some of the causes could be: faulty spruing, incomplete burnout, air pressure from torch flame, lack of or insufficient flux, excess of old metal, overheating of metal, insufficient metal, trapped gases or improper cooling.

Poor Polish—Polishing is a cutting action where metal is removed using an abrasive compound. Buffing is a combination of a cutting and burnishing action where some metal is removed, although most is burnished to a high, bright finish. This effect produces the glitter and shine that first attracts attention. If steps are deleted or forgotten, the results shall be immediately noticeable as uneven, rough, flat, or scaly areas, which would be detrimental to the sale of the item.

Poor Rhodium Plating -Rhodium plating is the standard practice of plating white metal, gold or silver, with rhodium to make a thin, hard bright white, highly reflective, and oxidation-resistant surface.

There are two common examples of poor rhodium plating:

1. Spotted rhodium, usually eye-visible, is caused by the burning of the plating solution or contamination during the plating process.
2. Matted white rhodium, always eye-visible, is the result of poor metal surface preparation during the polishing phase of production.

Poor Sizing—Finger sizes vary which requires that a method of shrinking or enlarging a ring be developed. This method is referred to as sizing a ring. The process is the removal of metal to make an item smaller and the addition of metal to increase the size. In order to accomplish this, the item is cut and then soldered back together with an alloyed solder. There are established procedures for this process, which, if followed, prevent most problems that are referred to as poor sizing. Poor sizing can be many different things: heavy porosity in the sizing seams, uneven misshapen shank, thin shank, insufficient solder at sizing seam,. file marks, poor polish, etc.

Poor Special Finish/Marred Special Finish—See Marred Special Finish

Porosity—Porosity is the unsoundness in cast metals caused by the presence of small pores, holes or voids in the metal. Also see Poor Crystallization.

Post Thread Damage—Earring posts are often threaded for securing the earring to the back. To achieve this, the metal is threaded using a circular stock or round die holder for making external threads and hand taps are used to make the internal threads in the earring back. As with any thread, the threads can be stripped or damaged easily, especially since jewelry metals are significantly softer than other metals.

Shank Out Of Round—The shank of a ring should be round and symmetrical. Occasionally, the shank is distorted and uneven, which is considered out of round.

Sharp Prongs—Prongs that have not been finished (burred) properly leaving the top or claw sharp. This results in snagging of articles of clothing and possible cuts or scratches to skin.

Shop Wear—When an item of jewelry is manufactured and placed into stock bins waiting for an order to be placed, the item may show signs of slight wear from rubbing, tarnishing or a dullness called shop wear.

Stones/Diamonds Out Of Mounting—Items received for inspection, in which the stones/diamonds have not been secured properly in the setting; stones are separate from the finished piece of jewelry.

Stones/Diamonds Overlapping—This problem is found most prevalently in channel-set and pave-set merchandise. When the setter is placing and securing the stones/diamonds into the mounting, each should be set into the channel mounting without touching or overlapping the other.

Stones/Diamonds Set Crooked—Seats are cut into prongs to assist in securing the stone/diamond in the mounting. Careful precision is necessary to assure that when burring out the seats, that each seat is cut at the same prong depth or the result shall be a tilted or crooked stone/diamond in the head, which is extremely visible to the unaided eye.

Table Off Center—The edge of the table on the left side of the diamond is noticeably closer to the girdle than the table edge on the right. Some diamonds have tables so off center that the reference line bows in on one side and out on the other. The reference line refers to the top bezel facet in the right, the top of the star facet, and the connecting bezel facet top left side.

Table Not Parallel—This occurs when the table is not parallel to the girdle or when the girdle is obviously wavy under either 10X magnification or the unaided eye.

Tarnished Mounting—Tarnishing is the term given to the undesirable dulling, discoloring, luster destroying film that forms on a metal surface during its exposure to atmospheric conditions. Tarnishing develops for other reasons as well. The relative purity of the metal has its effect. Alloyed metal with greater alloy metal content such as copper, tarnish more rapidly and easily in proportion to their alloy metal content. Rough surfaces tarnish more quickly than smooth ones as well as contact with sulfur even in minute concentrations such as storage in cardboard boxes containing sulfur compounds.

Tarnished Solder—See above explanation of tarnishing: usually seen on a piece of jewelry within a seamed area where a lower graded solder was used.

Thin Prongs—A prong is a tapering, pointed, projecting spur that rises from a setting and is bent over a stone to hold it in place. The prong is a very delicate extension of the mounting easily damaged by over-cutting of the stone seat, over-filing or over-polishing. If any of these situations occur, the prong becomes weak and shall not hold the stone securely as its purpose was designed.

Thin Shank—The shank is the area of a ring wrapping around the sides and bottom of the finger. A shank can be over-filed, over-polished or cast thin, which can be a serious detriment to the wear life of a ring.

Twisted Links—This refers to chains. All links should be evenly attached and the chain should lay flat.

Uneven Surface—When an article of jewelry has been finished properly, the metal flows smoothly and evenly. If finishing has been done incorrectly, the surface is uneven and wavy, causing distortion of the item.

Appendix IV

XYZ Corporation's Guidelines to Quality

Here is an example of quality guidelines of a retailer. A copy of these guidelines should be given to the current as well as prospective suppliers so they know what is expected of them. It would be good idea to post these guidelines on your web site also.

While some retailers may rely on customer returns to indicate the quality of merchandise, XYZ Corporation has a quality assurance (QA) system in place to determine quality of merchandise before placing merchandise in our stores. Merchandise may be tested before and after purchase by XYZ Corporation. A substantial amount will be visually inspected at suppliers facilities or XYZ Corp. distribution centers (DCs) using statistical sampling. Our aim is to prevent poor quality merchandise from entering our stores.

Laboratory testing and evaluations are conducted on a wide range of merchandise. Samples are tested, analyzed, and evaluated under varied conditions to determine how well an item will perform under actual use. Such characteristics as colorfastness, shrinkage, elongation, durable press, strength, electrical performance, safety factors, etc, are tested and evaluated.

Our statistical sampling plans are derived from ISO 2859-1:1999 Sampling procedures for inspection by attributes—Part 1: Sampling schemes indexed by acceptance quality limit (AQL) for lot-by-lot inspection, also known as ANSI/ASQ Z 1.4, and formerly known as MIL-STD-105. Acceptable quality levels used by us are 2.5 for hard-line merchandise, and 4.0 and 6.5 for soft-line merchandise. Even a single "critical" defect found in a lot will result in that lot failure.

Our inspection personnel examine shipments of merchandise from a standpoint of a discriminating customer. Each sample is examined for conditions which may adversely affect the appearance, serviceability or salability. Examples of conditions rendering samples defective are:

Soft-line Merchandise

a. Broken, run-off or skipped stitching resulting in open seams.
b. Exposed raw edges of materials at seams.
c. Material damages, such as holes, cuts, tears, mends, burns, abrasions, chews, etc.
d. Clearly noticeable spots or stains.
e. Material defects such as slubs, floats, shades bars, knots, missing or heavy yarns, dropped stitches, etc.
f. Missing, incomplete or misplaced components or operations, such as buttons, snaps, bartacks, buttonholes, belt loops, pocket flaps, etc.
g. Badly shaded parts or components, i.e., noticeable difference in the color or shade of various components of the same garment, or shading difference within a garment.
h. Measurements not as specified.
i. Missing or incomplete care label or care instructions.

Hard-line Merchandise

a. Unsightly dents, scratches, cracks, paint chips, tooling marks, rust spots, badly soiled or poorly finished item
b. Broken, missing, loose, or incorrect parts or components.
c. Inoperative item due to either electrical or mechanical malfunctions, misalignment, mis-adjustment, etc.
d. Hardware loose, missing, or damaged.
e. Paint or plating omitted, pitted, runs.
f. Improper calibration of controls, dials, etc.
g. Distorted audio or video, intermittent operation, mixing of channels, loose electrical connections.
h. Safety related defects, such as sharp edges, ingestible components, poisonous or other hazardous condition
i. Incorrect or missing assembly or operating instructions, warranty card, owner's manual, etc.

Jewelry

Jewelry is inspected by Graduate gemologists to make sure that each item meets XYZ Corporation specifications and Federal Trade Commission requirements for labeling.

Nonconformance

In addition to or aside from quality defects, nonconformance with stated requirements may cause an item or a shipment to be unacceptable. Examples of such nonconformance are missing third party safety certification mark such as Underwriter's Laboratories (UL) mark or its equivalent, size, color, or quantity not as specified, unauthorized substitution, missing caution labels when appropriate, missing country of origin labels, shipping cartons not marked as specified on the purchase order, UPC codes, etc.

XYZ Corporation's statistical sampling plans, standard inspection procedures, and specifications for a variety of merchandise are available from our QA office to current or prospective suppliers of XYZ Corporation.

Supplier liabilities for supplying defective or nonconforming merchandise are spelled out in "Quality Terms & Conditions."

Appendix V

Quality Terms and Conditions

Business is generally conducted based on contracts. Parties involved in business spell out who will do what when and then come to an agreement and all parties sign the contract. Therefore, a contract with a supplier is the proper place for a retailer to spell out expectations of suppliers and actions the retailer will take when those expectations are not met. Here is just an example.

a. The supplier shall maintain an in-process and end-item quality control program to ensure shipments do not include defective or nonconforming items. The XYZ Corporation reserves the right to review and evaluate a supplier's quality control or quality assurance system.

b. Items furnished under this contract are subject to inspection and test at time and place chosen by XYZ Corporation.

c. If items purchased are defective and/or non-conforming, the XYZ Corporation may take any of the following actions:

(1) Prior to acceptance:

- (a) Reject items and return them to the supplier
- (b) Reject items and require the supplier to repair or replace them in a reasonably specified time
- (c) Accept the items at an equitable adjustment in price determined by the XYZ Corporation

(2) After acceptance: The XYZ Corporation may revoke acceptance and proceed under (1) above.

d. If lots or shipments furnished are defective and/or non-conforming, the XYZ Corporation may take any of the following actions:

(1) Prior to acceptance the XYZ Corporation may

(a) Reject and return the lot or shipment to the supplier.
(b) In lieu of rejection, screen the items (inspect every item in the lot or shipment). Items meeting contract requirements will be accepted. Defective and/or non-conforming items will be returned to the supplier
(c) Reject the lot or shipment and require the supplier to screen the items and repair or replace defective and/or non-conforming items in a reasonabl specified time.
(d) Accept the lot or shipment and have the defective items repaired at the supplier's expense.
(e) Accept the lot or shipment at an equitable adjustment in price.

(2) After acceptance the XYZ Corporation may

(a) Revoke acceptance for any reasonable lot (group of items available for inspection) and proceed as in (1) above; or
(b) Revoke acceptance of items and proceed as in "c" above for rejected items.

e. Incidental damages, including expenses reasonably incurred in inspection, receipt, packing, rejection or screening of goods in lieu of rejection, care and custody of goods rightfully rejected, transportation, and any other reasonable expense incident to supplier's failure to fully and timely perform in accordance with the contract provisions will be charged back to the supplier.

f. The items furnished will be merchantable and fit and sufficient for use intended. "Seconds", "imperfects" or "irregulars", as those terms are normally understood in the trade, will be accepted only when specifically required in the contract. This warranty will survive the XYZ Corporation's acceptance of the items and is in addition to other warranties of additional scope given to XYZ Corporation by the supplier. Any warranty given by the supplier will be at least as good as the warranty offered to other companies.

g. Where appropriate, the items furnished under this contract must carry the appropriate third party safety certification or listing mark.

h. Item warranty, packing, packaging, and markings will comply with all contract terms and all laws, rules, and regulations applicable to delivery for domestic resale.

i. No substitution or variation in the quantity of any item called for by this supplier in each order referencing this agreement will be accepted unless authorized by the XYZ corporation.

j. The supplier warrants that any product furnished under this contract that can reasonably be used to carry food or liquid for human consumption and made of a substance prone to heavy metal leaching, such as pewter ware, earthenware, ceramic ware, chinaware, ironware, lacquer ware, bronze ware, brassware, leaded crystal ware, and coated and or plated items with heavy metal base, contains no leachable levels of metals dangerous to users.

k. The XYZ Corporation reserves the right to test supplier's products on an unannounced basis. If a heavy metal leaching failure is found, supplier agrees to reimburse the XYZ Corporation all follow-up costs to sample test the remainder of the items ordered. This provision does not supersede other provisions allowed by the contract. Supplier further warrants that products have been tested by either the U. S. Food and Drug Administration or a nationally recognized independent test laboratory and found to be in compliance with the current U. S. Food and Drug Administration action levels and test methods. Test data will be furnished to XYZ Corporation upon request by the XYZ Corporation.

Appendix VI

Quality of Customer Service

Quality of customer service includes everything other than product quality. This includes

Hours of Store Operations. Everyone today is pressed for time. Therefore, it is important that the store hours are convenient to your customers. In the United States, for example, most stores are open seven days a week. In some countries, stores are closed on Sundays.

Parking Lot. Is your parking lot clean and safe? Remember, it is so basic to want a clean and safe environment. No matter how good your products quality and how great your store interior may be, not having a clean and safe parking lot will turn off your customers.

Staffing. It is important that the store associates (employees on the sales floor) are easily available to customers for questions and assistance. This is not possible unless there are enough store associates. Not only that, they should be knowledgeable in store policies and procedures as they affect customers, in addition to being knowledgeable about the products they are responsible for selling. In order to help customers spot store associates readily, some stores require store associates to wear a uniform or certain color vest and also to wear their name tags. Those store associates who are either bilingual or multilingual should show on their name tag the languages they speak fluently so diverse customer base can approach them in their respective languages. The store associates should be courteous, people oriented, and must enjoy working with people and dress neatly. No one wants store associates who do not enjoy working with people. Remember, every interaction your customers have with your store associates will determine whether your customers will come back to shop in your stores or not. To the customers, store associates represent the store.

Layout. Is your store laid out in an organized manner? Are aisles wide enough and clear all the time? Cluttered aisles can be hazardous as they can result in accidents and injury resulting in financial loss to the company and ill will. Are shelves stacked so high that customers cannot reach without help of a sales associate? Is like merchandise grouped together?

Appearance. Do you keep your store clean and aisles uncluttered? Do you keep merchandise on shelves and displays well organized? Is your store well lighted and the atmosphere pleasant? Do the surroundings or atmosphere in your store make your customers feel like spending more time in your store? Remember it is human nature to like quiet, pleasant, relaxing surroundings.

Stock. Does your stock assortment reflect what your customers want and do you keep products on the shelves? Your customers would be frustrated if you are constantly running out of stock. Consumers today are pressed for time and for them not to find what they came to buy from you is a waste of time. Most likely, those customers will go somewhere else and buy from your competition. Good quality products are of no use unless you can keep them in stock.

Check Out. Do you have enough check out counters and are they open or do your customers have to wait in line forever to pay for what they want to buy? Do you have a policy that as soon as there are more than 3 or 4 persons in line at check out counters, additional check out counters are opened? Are your check out associates friendly and knowledgeable and well trained or do they have to call for help frequently, slowing down transactions? Are your check out associates focused and busy conducting transactions or are they chatting among themselves? There is nothing more annoying than to have to wait in line because check out associates are chatting among themselves and thus slowing down transactions. Are your products marked with correct UPC and price tag so that they scan correctly? Otherwise, it would be waste of time for customers to have to wait while the prices are verified. Even worse, a customer may not buy an item if the scanned price is higher than the labeled price because the purchasing decision may have been based on the price tag on that item. Not only is this frustrating and embarrassing to the customer, you lose a sale!

Customer Service. Are your customer service counters manned by knowledgeable and friendly associates? Is your merchandise refund or return policy clearly written and posted so customers can readily read it? When customers come to return or exchange an item are they treated with respect and courtesy and transactions completed promptly or are they given run around? This is an excellent opportunity to make customers happy, who otherwise are not happy with your products, and in turn get them to come back to your store rather than go to your competition. If you think you have no competition, you are not living in the real world and you won't be in business for too long.

These things are important because they collectively convey a message, an impression, to your customers about their shopping experience in your store.

A study conducted by Indiana University's Kelley School of Business and KPMG, LLP (2000)
found that in retail stores, shoppers want knowledgeable and courteous sales help, competitive prices, fast check out and convenient payment options.

While there is no standard definition of quality customer service, my definition of quality customer service is treating customers the way you like to be treated, or even better, treating customers the way they like to be treated. How do you know how your customers want to be treated? Ask them periodically through customer surveys and focus groups.

Here is, one each, personal example of bad and good customer service.

While in a certain city in a certain country several years ago I bought a pair of earrings for about $ 12 for my daughter from a store in an upscale area. I liked the design so much that after going back to my hotel, I took them out of the package to look at them again before packing them, and noticed some pit marks. Being the quality person that I am, I immediately decided to go back to that store and either exchange them or return them for a refund. When I went to the store at about 11:30 am and walked up to the jewelry counter and told the sales clerk there that I wanted to simply exchange that pair of earrings that I considered defective and showed her my receipt. She asked me to come back about an hour later as she did not work there. She was merely filling in for the clerk who had gone on her lunch break. I told the young lady that I did not have time to hang around the store for an hour and not only I did not have time to come back to the store again but I did not want to spend money for a cab to come back. After some haggling she exchanged that pair of earrings for me. I could not understand why she gave me a run around in the beginning. Had I not been assertive, I would have ended up going back. Needless to say, I will not go back to that store. Not only they were not sorry for selling me a defective product, they did not respect me nor value my time.

Now compare this to the experience I had in my hometown, Dallas, Texas. We bought a 65" Mitsubishi digital/high-definition TV with a decoder for receiving high definition programs and a small stereo system, including delivery and installation, for about $ 5,000 from an upscale home entertainment/home electronics store. After going home, I had second thoughts about this purchase so the next day I called this store and told them that I would like to cancel my purchase of the TV but keep the stereo and if I should stop by the store to do the paper work. The first question they asked me was whether I was canceling it because I found the same item cheaper somewhere else, and the sales person told me if that was the case, they will match the price. I said "no, that was not the case." I had looked around and theirs was the best price. The sales person who had sold me the TV said "you do not need to stop by the store and waste your time. We will send you another invoice crediting all but $ 400 for the stereo, and you will receive that paper work in about two days. All of this took about two minutes on the phone! Now, do you think I will go back to this store when I am ready to buy another piece of home electronics? Absolutely.

For excellent pointers on how to provide great customer service see Leonard (1996) and Sartin (1996).

Based on my personal experiences and of those that I know, consumers evaluate the entire shopping "experience," not just product quality.

References

Indiana University Kelley School of Business and KPMG, LLP. 2000. *Creating the Ideal Shopping Experience: What Consumers Want in the Physical and Virtual Store.* A study.

Leonard, Berry. 1996. Providing Great Service. A paper presented at the Fifth Annual Service Quality Conference in Las Vegas. September 16-17. American Society for Quality.

Sartin, Libby. 1996. The Secret Formula for Great Service. A paper presented at the Fifth Annual Service Quality Conference in Las Vegas. September 16-17. American Society for Quality.

Bibliography

Danaber, Peter J. and Trust, Ronald T. 1996. Indirect Financial Benefit from Service Quality. *Quality Management Journal*, Vol. 3, Issue 2. American Society for Quality, Milwaukee, WI.

Epilogue

Customer expectations are rising everywhere due to information available easily through television, print media and electronic means such as internet and e-mail. Customer expectations are also rising because of the last best experience consumers had, such as my experience I described in the Appendix VI. Therefore, customers are asking today that if one company can do better, how come other companies can not do the same? Thus, raising the bar for all companies. Hopefully, application of the body of knowledge presented in this book will help you meet or exceed expectations of your customers in the product quality arena.

About the Author

Pradip V. Mehta

Pradip V. Mehta, a Fellow of the American Society for Quality, was Director of Quality Assurance, Army & Air Force Exchange Service (AAFES), a multi-billion dollar, multi-national retail and service organization. In that capacity was responsible for managing product quality and safety of consumer goods bought and sold by

AAFES as well as overseeing private label suppliers' compliance to AAFES' code of conduct regarding child labor, minimum wage, work hours, etc. Mr. Mehta has 30 years of experience in quality assurance of consumer goods. He authored a book "An Introduction to Quality Control for the Apparel Industry" published in 1985 and 1992 and has co-authored another book "Managing Quality in the Apparel Industry." Mr. Mehta taught quality assurance at the National Institute of Fashion Technology (NIFT), New Delhi in 1996 under the United Nations Development Program. Mr. Mehta also conducted Certified Quality Auditor (CQA) refresher course for the Dallas section of the American Society for Quality in 2002 and 2003. Mr. Mehta was a Senior Examiner for Texas Quality Award as well as was an Examiner for the U. S. President's Quality Award. He was an ISO 9000 Lead Auditor certified by RAB (U.S.A.) and IRCA (England) for a number of years. Mr. Mehta is on the editorial review board of Quality Progress, a monthly of the American Society for Quality. He was also Chair of the Customer Supplier Division of the American Society for Quality for the year 2000-01.

Mr. Mehta has a Master's degree in Textile Engineering, and an MBA, and is a Professional Engineer.

Pradip V. Mehta, P.E.
310 Breseman Street
Cedar Hill, TX 75104
U. S. A.
PradipMehta@comcast.net

Index

B

C

E

Extension cords, 162, 168, 205

F

G

H

I

J

K

L

M

N

Q

R

S

T

V

W

Z